LAND OF THE
BASQUES

MIRANDA

ARAGON

LAND OF THE
CATALANS

GOS

ZARAGOZA

E B R O

BARCELONA

TILLE

ADRID

VALENCIA

SPAIN

DALQUIVIR

IA

MURCIA

A

MEDITERRANEAN SEA

AFRICA

SAHARA

WITOLD GORDON

VIRGIN SPAIN

SCENES FROM THE SPIRITUAL
DRAMA OF A GREAT PEOPLE

WALDO FRANK

NEW YORK
BONI & LIVERIGHT
1926

To

those brother Americans

whose tongues are Spanish and Portuguese
whose homes are between the Rio Grande
and Tierra del Fuego

but whose America
like mine

stretches from the Arctic to the Horn.

OFTEN, MEDITATING ON THE FERVOR WITH
WHICH SPAIN HAS EVER DEFENDED AND PRO-
CLAIMED THE DOCTRINE OF THE IMMACULATE
CONCEPTION, I HAVE THOUGHT THAT IN THE
DEPTHS OF THIS DOGMA THERE MUST BE A MYS-
TERY AKIN WITH THE MYSTERY OF OUR NATIONAL
SOUL: THAT PERHAPS THIS DOGMA IS A SYMBOL
. . . OF OUR BEING. . . .

ANGEL GANIVET.

ACKNOWLEDGMENTS

¶ The wanderer upon the face of the earth will love these lands whose drama is the burden of my book, if for no other reason for the pure hospitality of their peoples. To move from the Sahara of the Arabs to Biscay of the Basques, is to move from hospitable home to hospitable home: is to be chained forever in the remembrances of kindness. Unto all my friends, whose names are not too numerous to mention but whose grace would feel itself abused by public thanks, my thanks, then.

¶ Acknowledgments more intellectual are more easy. Above others, I am indebted to Federico de Onís, Head of the Department of Spanish Literature at Columbia University. Professor de Onís, whom I was fortunate to find in Spain, carried me to his native Salamanca (whence alas! Unamuno had just been exiled). After my book was written, he took time to read the proofs and to give me the unstinted, generous, invaluable aid of his erudition. I must name also José Ortega y Gasset, the outstanding intellectual master of the younger generation in Spain; Juan Ramón Jiménez, the poet; Luis Araquistáin, the satirist and social critic; Manuel Cossío, the authority on Greco; Azorín and Pío Baroja, Spain's leading novelist; Ramiro de Maeztu and Enrique Díez-Canedo, critical leaders in Spain's cultural renascence; Ramón Carande, the historian, and Pedro Salinas, the poet. All of these eminent men of Spain, in long conversations, helped me with a hospitality truly of their land, to my search for understanding of a people notoriously poor in critical and historical tradition. Nor can I neglect to mention Alfonso Reyes, the Mexican poet and Ambassador to the Argentine Republic, and Baldamiro Sanín Cano, the Colombian essayist, who helped to clarify for me that so urgent aspect of the Spanish spirit which is American. It must, however, be understood that none of these men is to be held responsible for the conception or for any of the ideas of this book.

¶ Much of the materials of my work has appeared in article form in magazines. To the Editors of *The Commonweal, The Dial, The Menorah Journal, The Nation, The New Republic, The North American Review, La Revista de Occidente* (Madrid), *The Saturday Review* and *The Virginia* (University) *Quarterly,* my acknowledgments, also.

¶ Finally, a word by way of explanation. What I have attempted might be called a Symphonic History. Spain is a complex integer: some of the elements which compose it are known commonly under such terms as climate, geography, historical events, literature, manners, custom, laws and art. Since I felt the Personality of Spain to hold all of these *immediately,* as a body holds all its organs, I have essayed, not to discuss them severally, not to relate their passage and chronological order, not primarily to picture or to dissect them. But I have let them come, each in its measure and its turn, upon the scene: and like actors in a play, like themes in a symphony, they have spoken their parts. If I could have my way, the pages of my book would come unto my reader as a drama he sees acted in an evening, or as a work of music he hears performed in an hour. I cannot command this proper and impossible hearing. I can but pray my reader, in some such spirit and attention, to take the book which lies now in his hand. Let him do this for me, and I shall gladly leave to him the judgment of my failure or success.

W. F.

New York, December, 1925.

CONTENTS

CONTENTS

PART TWO: *The Tragedy of Spain*

PART THREE: *Beyond Spain*

PRELUDE
THE SKY OF SPAIN

The sky of Spain is high. It is above earth very high. It is above Spain very high. It is separate from Spain. . . It is a clear white sky. Sunlight is white in it. And the clouds are white. . . It is a still sky. The clouds stand still in a great height and fixed as in a crystal. . . The light of the sun becomes the light of the sky, becomes the light of the clouds, far from the dark red earth of Spain. Spain is her earth and her sky. . . I am within the pasture plains of Extremadura. Behind me lies Badajoz. . .

I have walked at dawn upon an ancient bridge of granite across the summer-shrunken river. The water curls and swerves through gold sand. In little steel-blue pools it lies deep; then it runs off in thinning saffron ribbons. Soldiers sit on black horses who drink the water silkening at their knees. The bridge swings in yellow arches. There is a bastioned gate cut with the conquering arms of Leon and Castile.

In the east, a low sun. Its horizontal hand touches my face. It is hot, striking across cool dawn. Badajoz is houses gray and gold over shut streets around a Gothic church. The sun is outside the cool city. On the Cathedral porch sit two old women. Their day has begun: it is to sit with open claw and to close on coin and to bless the giver of coin.

In my pocket is naught but the moldy paper of Portugal and the silver duros of Spain. I shake my head at the two aged women. "No tengo suelto. Lo siento." I smile. She to my left smiles back. The other frowns and mutters. They are one, save for the difference between a frown and a smile.

Hairy goats clatter, swinging creamy udders. Burros pass with men and women, stolid, on their haunches.

Through the crevice of leaning walls the sun lays a hot finger on my brow. My body is chill.

The bread in the fonda tastes coarse. It is sour and hurts my mouth. The coffee is tasteless . . a sort of gray heat . . good. Now I have a pocket full of coppers. I cross to the Cathedral porch. The two old women . . one, split by a frown and a smile. To the frown, I give five coppers, to the smile I give one. The smile and the frown do not change. I am in Spain!

The shut town is expanding. The sun is still outside; streets twist to avoid it. But the sun works. The city expands. Men and women are a melting on the street. Men and women are motes of life within the melting city. . .

Badajoz is behind. The sun is high, and here the pasture plains. The Guadiana treeless wanders to the south. It is a thirsty river. It is a river homesick for the hills of its youth; moved by a dream of coolness southward, languidly stirred to win this dream in the south. Cities have no sky. Beyond the walls of Pax Augusta which centuries have mellowed from the Roman Camp holding harsh soldiers to this Badajoz . . now the sky of Spain. .

I have never seen a sky so far from my head: I have never seen a world so sharp in my eye. The sky lifts me to a realm of visions. And as I pass into its moveless search, still I stand fixed within this graphic world. . Sheep bleat in a wave of dust. . The dust is dense. Curling, swirling, puffing, streaking down, the dust is clear as glass. The sheep are solid masses of tempestuous wool; each sheep is a writhe about four feet, about stalks of sinewed bone jerking it on. Here's a man. A solid body. Hands crustaceous; face crisp skin drawn on a gaping skull: and over the skin porous as soapstone, bristles of separate hair, sweat, huddles of dust. The smoke from the cigarette cuts rising through the air. Over his shoulder, miles and miles away, a ruined village rests on the hump of a hill. Barbary figs stand at the walls of a splintered chapel. Solid Spain! The earth is clotted, corrugation, furrow. In a red gulch a blackish water drips. And there are flowers, purple like shreds of morning.

Everywhere sky. So far away, and everywhere. Its apartness is a force lifting the broken things of Spain as in a great dance Godward. Dust and sheep-hoof, ash of cigarette, pound of the shepherd's staff on the earth, swish of his chaps, the dog's soft pads against stone . . rise all in this various clarity, as in a dance, to the sky.

I have a vision which has not left me. I shall love this people and this world. For in my vision I have been born as they. . . There is a Funnel. Its walls are the round, white sky. It is thewed together by the rays of the sun. And at the Funnel's mouth is the mouth of God, speaking the words which are the things of earth. Down this Funnel as in birth, we fall. Until we strike upon the land of Spain.

PART ONE

Spain

CHAPTER I

HINTERLAND IN AFRICA

a. Oasis
b. Moghreb
c. Ishmael and Israel

a. Oasis

In the desert, night is reason; the day is magic and madness. This is a law of the desert, and of the desert dwellers.

The light of the sun turns air into an incantation; it is dangerous to man as the sharpest steel or the fire. And the air possessed makes marvels of the land. The sky is opaque like a baking stone. The sterile hills are in perennial motion. They are not hills docile and quiet for the feet of man. They are enactments of geologic drama. By æons they displace not man alone, but the first life that crawled. Each rim of the hills is an age; they gyre in cosmic emotion.

Under a cloudless sky that is too still, earth veers; and under the hills, sand by some magic teems with forms of flesh. The light on a dune turns it into a thigh. Far off the waste becomes a sea, a snow-field. But this exquisite flesh and snow and sea are aloof. Man is contemporary only with the birth and with the death of worlds. And the hushed counterpoise of life, which is his mortal span, is desert.

But with the night the world becomes a world that he can dwell in. The evening star, sending its ray through opalescent dusk, is a sun he can dwell with. The sky grows soft. The hills are shrouded like his body; they are compounded like his soul of silences; they behold a sky that does not sear and an earth he can walk. The moon strides like a master, subduing the caravans of stars. The moon is male, and human.

The world of the day is a world of violence. It has no water and it has no sweetness. It is the world of this life: best spent in marching, passionate-shrewdly, toward dusk. Night is man's kingdom, his dear reality: it is a place of gardens under which flow waters: it is a place of measurable fires: a place of shadows and of meditation: a place of dew and of love.

Wonder therefore not at the triumph of Mohammed, master of lands of desolation, who leads his peoples still across a day of flame to the revealing sleep of his dusk paradise.

. . . .

This magic of the desert day is ironic; at odd places the irony turns smile. Just enough welcoming the smile to tempt man to live on within the toils of the desert. The name of the smile is Oued—whence our word Oasis. The Oued is a spill of water from the breast of a mountain. Hidden springs converge and burst the rusty slope; and there is a tiny river till the sands have drunk it. Where it flows, the desert smiles: smiles date-palms, fig trees, thickets of oleander. So the desert keeps its perennial victims living.

At the bottom of the Oued is the town.

The mountains raise their convolutions in a great struggle, ere they break and die under these southern sands. The heights grow steep. Water falls through rock, pours through curtains of brush that hang upon the gorges. There is verdure: cataracts of stone with silver veins of water, flats of sand where the palms rise seeking the sun above a precipitous gulch, water mills hid in orange-groves, terraced houses with many roofs and every roof a place for looms, for women. The water broadens, is caught into a hundred irrigating ditches. The date-palms thicken and camp like an army; the town huddles with its white walls windowless.

The morning sun comes late to the Oasis, for it must rise above the hills. But dawn dwells already on the desert. It is a subtle radiance of decaying night. Infinitesimal browns and blacks fleck the dim waste: these are the camps of nomads who use the Oasis as a trading center. Their tents are of undyed camel wool, strung low so that they look like camels crouching. The great slow beasts are at anchor by the tent. Dry grass is piled for them; they turn their delicate heads on the arched neck that fronts the body like the prow of a ship. Camel grass burns within. The Arab, swathed in his white burnouse, squats at the mouth of the tent and strikes his brow to the dust, saying his dawn-prayer. Unveiled behind him is his wife over the flame of twisted grass, and cooks and watches her children. On the horizon stand two caravans of twenty camels, bulging with dates. Now the thread of their approach writes upon the desert. It is market day in the Saharan center. There will be many caravans. And the wide scatter of nomads will close in like fragments of iron magnetized; making an irradiant design from the town to the horizons.

The market place is a low square, on the edge of the town away from the Oasis. One side of it is a mosque, a Koran school, a string of Moorish cafés where already merchants huddle with their coffee. The corner breaks into a labyrinth of streets strident with tiny shops. Upon a third side, the desert road cuts into the breast of sand-dunes; far away is the white solitary shell of a Marabout's tomb.

The crowd is the town and the desert: an Arab world, drawn by hunger from far gold slopes, to make this thick and hardy organism. Most of the men wear burnouses of unbleached wool; their heads are covered by the ample hood and the skirt falls low over the inner jacket, over the naked legs, to the feet which are either bare or shod with sandal soles of grass thonged to the ankle. Time has dyed the virgin wool and use has torn it; the shreds and rents are fantasies in dirt. Within the hoods, sun-baked faces stare. The hands are talonous; the legs are like the tendoned legs of some great bird. And yet the dirtiest garment falls to the dust with grace; and the most squalid head is high.

The merchants sit on straw mats: they bake round acorn cakes on brasiers; they sell dates gold-dry, bronze-rich;

they measure thimblefuls of palm oil dripped from reeking goatskins; they cobble sandals; they sell liver of camel
and *couss-couss,* a staple dish of wheat, flaked with vege-
tables or with meat. (Donkeys stand mournful, charged
with juniper from the distant Atlas.) They sell dust and
fragments of silver, potsherds, amulets against devils, hal-
ters, tea; they sell the dry leaf of the favorite henna. The
crowd sways, bartering, laughing. The Arabic is vowel-
less and the burnouse is proud. The Arab is shrewd; his
eyes glint, his fingers snap, his voice pelts. He is the sur-
vivor of countless children who have died.

Children not yet dead weave through the intricate clamor.
The boys wear a burnouse over a naked body; the girls
are bound in a thick wool garment that will announce to
the men when the breasts bud. They beg, they snatch a
date, they nibble. Half of them are blind in an eye. For
Islam makes no answer to the Ophthalmia of Egypt:
is not Allah good to the blind son, giving him fortune as
a beggar, as a ballad singer, as a muedzin to call the
prayer from the mosque tower? Blind eyes, ravaged flesh,
hard voices—most of the children will die. And their
survivors are these hooded men at barter.

Therefore, the men are strong: it is the law that they
eat first and what remains may go to the women and the
brood. Women are here, too. Ancients with foul rags
to bind their bulging udders and their bony legs; ancients
almost bald with hands and faces splotched in the henna.
They sell wool or weave mats from the coarse camel grass
that bunches in the sand dunes like the hair on a mole.
Younger women hold the veil so that a single eye peers
at the ominous world. They buy wood, slices of liver,
oranges from the East. In the weave of laughter, guttural and fleshless, of bray of donkey, of rumble of camels
like the ebbed roar of a furnace, twines the call of children . . the call of begging, the life-call. A hand plashes
a drum, a strain of song rises and binds this chaos.

He sits between a cobbler and a nomad ebon-black with
the drooped tender lip of the Semite. He is the blind

singer. He wears a clean tunic of white and his head is swathed in the turbash. His bare legs gleam like metal. His hands are delicate as prayer within the market clamor. He clasps the shallow drum; and his fingers fall like rain.

He sings the deeds of the warriors of Allah. From Mecca they came, and Al-Medinah; they spread from Araby to Egypt and down to Sudan and east to India. They brought the sword of the Prophet to the hand of the world. Like the sun, they went west; like Gabriel they rose into the Spanish north, bridging the sea with minaret and prayer. . . .

Metal he sings: his song is sparse like shreds of grass on a sand hump. Five notes, naked, timbreless, make this intricate weave. They start like arrows, like catapulted stones, like horse-hoofs on the desert. This music is stripped like war; and like war single-willed.

The blind bard's face is gray beneath the sumptuous swathes of his turbash. His lips twist like cord; his face like an engine discharges the song of Islam—single of key, terrible in singleness. .

. . . .

The sun stands beside the minaret that forms part of the west wall of the town. The eastern mountain is gold and over it lies a pallid crescent moon. There will be moon tonight upon the desert! From the *fondoukhs*, camels are beaten forth. They are prodded to their knees which are then bound so that they cannot rise. And the fragile humps are heaped with the exchange of the mart. Great bags, here, oozed sugar of the date: now there is wheat and wool. Fifteen camels, lashed and hobbled, groan: then sway into the air like an armada moved by the wind of guttural call and staff-blow. Fifteen camels swerve through a narrow gate into the desert.

The town stands behind, low mosqued: the minarets rise from the flat roofs like acrobats. Palms make a misty coronal to the east: thousands of palms, mazed like a camel's hair: and over all the sterile mountain, a chart of ages, working to the sky. Now, from the minarets comes a voice.

Alláh acbar. . Echhed en la ila ella Alláh.
Echhed en Mohammed Rasou Alláh.
Haï ala Elsalat. Haë ala Elfaláh.
Alláh Acbar. . La ila ella Alláh.

It is the call of the muedzin. Invariable his word, his key: invariable the five points of the day . . dawn, noon, mid-afternoon, sunset and dark . . when from all the minarets of town, in all the towns of the land, in all the lands of Islam, the muedzin calls to prayer. The voice is of iron. Myriad muedzin voices, like strokes of some intricate machine, weave together, and bind Islam holy.

> Allah is great. . I affirm there is no God save only Allah.
> I affirm Mohammed is the Prophet of Allah.
> Come ye to prayer. Come ye to adore him.
> Allah is great. . I affirm there is no God, save only Allah.

Belal, first muedzin, crier for Mohammed, spoke these words. They are a redolent poem: ecstasy was in them, and resolve. They have not changed in syllable since Belal received them from his master, a year after the Hegira, the year of our era 623. But they have hardened. They are a terrible horizontal stroke upon a prostrate people. Harder than bells of Christendom they are; harder than the Jewish plaint which Mohammed hated, which Mohammed strove to wipe from the ears of the earth.

The caravan has halted. The camels stand docile, pathetic, shifting their great loads; for it hurts the soft pads of their feet to stand laden, it is easier to walk. The men scatter and squat, each by himself, but each turned from the setting sun toward Mecca. The water of the desert is the sand; and with the sand the men make their ablutions. They place their sandals beside them; all that is unclean in the folds of the burnouse they lay aside. Their mouths mutter fast; their hands perform intricate

gestures. To swerve from the immemorial forms, even
by a finger twitch, is to be in heresy and to be damned.
Their brows touch the sand. . . .

> . . . For man is earth. The brow is his highest
> and his noblest part. Let his brow therefore, five
> times with each day, be lowered to earth. This is
> ISLAM. . . . .

The camels fall into the rhythmic swing which will
not swerve while the moon swings over the sand and the
sand swings under the night, and the silent men round the
ocean of the desert.

.   .   .   .   .   .

From the town, as from a smoldering fire, smoke. There
are no chimneys; Allah takes care of the smoke. After
the bright street, the house is a cavern. The eyes, re-
focused to the dark, observe a long, high chamber, its walls
black with ages of grime, its ceiling stanchioned by wooden
posts that shine like ebony. There is no table, there is
no chair, there is no bed. Dry grass is piled in corners, and
serves for sleeping. Four families live in this lower half
of the house. Four women squat in its several quarters;
about them nurslings, before them a little brasier to which
the children feed chips of wood, shreds of rush. The
women cut turnips, bake wheat for the *couss-couss*. There
is a stair that is scarce a stair: ages of feet have worn it
to an incline. The upper story has more light; there is
a hole in the center of the ceiling which leads to the roof.
If it rains, the water falls through the heart of the house;
but light comes in, smoke rises out. Here, too, there is
no furniture. A chicken pecks in the crumbled floor; an
old woman weaves at a loom. Her hands know an immemorial process of weaving, like the mouth of her husband
praying.

The roof is the domain of the women. The street is
for the men and all that the street leads to. But the
housetop is the street and the playground of women. On
sunny afternoons of the cool season, here is their escape

from the drudge and dark of their homes. This house is high among the houses whose flat roofs move away in waving whiteness. A minaret thrusts up . . there is a gap, a square . . then the packed counterpoint of roof and turning wall and wall again to the green dense at last of palms, to the gorge of the Oued, to the sand-stretch southward where the sun lies in a mist as in a sea of opal.

The white roofs are gay with the color of women. Veils are put aside. Babes suck at ruddy breasts. Red shawls and red babouches touch the color of laughter. Women are carefree. Even the onus of prayer that sits on Islam is not for them. Let them but bear children and hold the good will of their men.[1] One woman, the rich blood clear beneath the bronze of her cheek, presses to her bosom a child who will soon die. Children come and often children go. The way of the child, to manhood or the grave, is in the hand of Allah. A girl, candid and great-eyed with a flinty note upon her luscious flesh, like steel on velvet, holds to her lovely breast which motherhood has not distorted from its apple-rondure, a babe whose eyes are already shut with pus. She will have a blind son—perhaps a muedzin, perhaps a poet: certainly a Seer.

. . . . . .

When the sun is good, many women follow up the Oued, with their brood, for a day's washing. The river is gracious within its precipitous banks. The winter sun, sweet like our sun of June, has yet the reverberant Saharan weight. It strikes the top of the hills, it rolls down over the clay-maze; it strikes the level sand, down once more it bounds into the gorge, over drenched bushes, over hanging rock and fills the Oued. Here, knee-deep, with their thin gowns lashed to the thigh and the rondures of their bodies speaking, stand women: and the sun comes to them. Other women lay the washed clothes on rocks and with bare feet dance on them, mangling and rinsing in song.

[1] The so prevalent notion that in Mohammedanism women have no souls and cannot gain heaven is false.

The sun and the vigil of the hills, and the town distant,
release the spirit of this flesh. Allah is far away, and
the pure violence of Mohammed. Women are pagans
again, and the Oued has gods. Children peal. Girls let
fall their tunics and their breasts dance with their feet.
Old women have eyes hot with memories, as they watch
the crisp bodies of their daughters.

But beyond the Oued, beyond its walled mouth where
the water disappears in sand, and beyond the date-palms,
lies another town. It is more drear than its graveyard.
So far, doubtless, in old days the river ran ere it had
clotted and shortened its way with silt. The town is almost
a ruin. A few children play, but the houses are silent.
No windows break the seared patched blocks of clay. The
graveyard is higher, and it has a wall. Here one can sit
and watch the ruined town and the maze of gardens by the
Oued and the palms, and the present town and the desert
sea. The muedzin has thrust his call to sunset prayer.
The muedzin is gone. The sun is gone. The mountains
are sapphires in a cornelian heaven. The Sahara moves
in copper from the town: grows argent: its dunes are
swathed in mist like women's bodies in irradiant shawls.
The desert fades into a fume of opal under a bronze
horizon.

Intricate designs stir in the graveyard chaos. Between
the head stones and the foot stones the thin earth is raised
so that the body may lightly rise to Heaven. (Jackals and
dogs, as well as souls, find the shallow graves to their taste.)
And now, to meet this subtle stir of dust, comes music.
Common notes, sordid notes, between the sand and the sky.
Drone of men in prayer, sudden motley of boys who sit
in a black room and shout the Koran, girl laughter, donkey
bray, banter—a music secret as this world. It comes with
the night, swift, like any revelation. It fuses with the
graveyard stones, with the world. The labyrinth of walls,
enclosing gardens down to the Oued, is one with it. Fig
tree, palm, volute Barbary cactus, winding path to the
river, muddy river stretch, litter of refuse, excrement,

manure, fuse with the music and the graveyard stones, rhyme in the oneness of Allah.

A late worker jogs past on a burro. A Caïd—Judge—swings with his basket-saddle on a mule. Another worker sticks his rod into the open sore on his burro's haunch. On one side of the glimmering Oued is the town—a wall with many breaks, cobbles on mud, that lead into alleys and that grow into streets. The walls, within, flank out into a square from which turn several streets. The houses here are open to the night, and on the doorsteps before brasiers red with coal, sit women. Allah is one. They wear gay shawls, striped skirts. They wear massive barbarous bracelets, anklets, necklaces. Their faces, in the gloom, are heavy with designs: brow, cheek, chin painted with henna or with kohl. From eye to temple run delicate starry lines. And the hands are henna-splashed. When man approaches they sing the song of invitation. Behind them crouching on their brasiers, freshening their faces, gleams a room with a samovar and a couch. Now, the classic song of lust from their still lips. The crystal and the song of Islam! One note for all prayer, one note for all begging, one note for lust. Allah is one.

The whole town has caught the day's fair fever. A man sits with a metal pipe whose saccade cadence flies . . splinters of steel . . into the night. And women dance. They move in strange reply to the music. For it is violent, swift and lean; it is the clang and charge of martial hoofs. But the women are slow, almost imperceptible their feet; almost moveless their thick bodies. The arms wave languid like branches of the willow. The whole town in the dead day's fever. Dance and laughter and flame blossom in the shadows of the street. A ballad singer sits among the girls: he sings of the chieftain whose head was left upon the field and how the Prophet came and joined it to his body, for the Resurrection. But girls dance in a rising tide of Spring. His hands upon the drum make running of swift steeds, his voice is a javelin: the girls move like their breathing breasts.

Here is a large blank house. The court is high, and all about ring little doors of oak. Below is a hall. Its walls are muffled in rugs, its floor is far under carpets. Before the divans are tables, and the tea is spiced. Men in white squat and play upon pipes, and their black eyes gleam. The music's shrillness shrieks. Now come women. They are four. Unminding loveliness moves within thick brocades and clashing gems. The faces are exquisitely painted. Verdant and nervelessly, they dance. The body is quiet as a tree, the hands are pliant and susurrous like leaves. The male music works. . . A stomach wrench, violent as childbirth, shatters upon the mellifluous woman's body. Above the music comes a cry from her mouth; it is a piercing call made pulsant with the hand clapped periodically to the open lips. It dies; the elemental bodies stir again within the dress and a sleep. But the male music works. The women pause. The musicians turn about, so that they cannot see. With unfeeling hands, the dancers loose the bonds of their thick robes. They step from the splendor fallen to their feet; they are naked. Only the jewels flash and bite upon their musing flesh. They dance. The muscles of their thighs flow upward toward their breasts; the arms twine sleepy. The male music works. The stomach, sudden, as if in unseen violation, wrenches, cascades, in passional response. The shrilling pipes are visited whole upon the naked women. They shriek: their cry, overtoned, fluted, pulsant, marries flesh and iron: blots out the music, and the music falls.

The town is asleep. Swarming reeking streets of the town are gray and are shells. The walls stand white under the sky, and over the depths of brooding human darkness. The crescent moon, with the dark sphere visible within its horns, sends scimitar rays into the sleep of Islam.

b. *Moghreb*

A semi-desert land holds well the squalors and the splendors of its past. This edge of Africa is the western end of the world whence the sun slides down to the sea. The bleak steppes, studded with sage and cactus, rise to sudden mountains; snow fields balance palm groves. It was a harsh place for a great world to grow in. But glories long since dust in Bagdad and Damascus have still their form in the cities of Morocco.

The prehistoric source lives in the prehistoric mountains. The Moor here is Berber. No one knows who is the Berber save that his speech is kin to the speech of Abyssinia and Egypt. His villages are perched on the slopes of the Atlas and in the stony fastness of the Rif, much as the Roman found them—and the Phœnician. Squat rectangular houses with thatch roof form a semicircle on the crest of a divide. Below is a thousand feet of air and a torrent; above are the clouds. The houses are of mud and grapple like goats to the earth. In the low, flat lands between the tiers of mountain, the houses are round. Closer to them than the houses of Europe are the huts of the Congo. They form a full circle within which dwell the cattle at night and sleeps safety.

The archaic world lies whole in the stratified history that is the Moghreb. Ages before Christ the Semite scattered markets on the coast and Carthage grew great. Rome became a mere machine for periodic taxes. Roman order and Vandal havoc left the Berber untouched. He is a hard, dark, leathery man. His head is close-cropped. He is prone to silence. Despite the myth of the Moroccan Sultanate—that feeble creature of the French and Spaniard—he is still unconquered.

Between the coast and the valley of Meknes and Fez he has lived, sullen and declining. The spark in his eye, the curl of his black lip tells that as he has outlived a long parade of empires, he will outlive this French one. In such mood, he dons his woolen tunic broidered red or blue, loads his olives on his donkey's back and goes down to effete Fez or Marrakech for barter. Yesterday he bartered with the Arab, with the Vandal, with the Roman. Earlier, he knew the men of Carthage, the silver lords of Tartessos. *He* is a Berber.

Islam alone has won him. But not until Islam had passed him many times, conquering half the Mediterranean world. The first Arabs converted some Berbers and took them along, not loitering in these mountains. Berber horsemen were soldiers and captains in Spain. But the Berber at home did not stir from his stone somnolence. Córdoba and Toledo kindled fires that warmed the monastic cells of Italy and England. Egypt awoke once more. Mecca and Bagdad grew great. Morocco, halfway between the east and the west, was invaded by new waves of Arabs. Hillalians and Idrissides built fine towns in Algeria and Tunis. Morocco was surrounded by splendors. The mountains remained mountains.

Three hundred years the streams of culture flowed through this frustrate land, from Spain to the east and from the east to Europe. Now came a Berber tribe from the southern desert: the Almoravides with their great chieftain Yusuf. Twenty-two hundred years since the Phœnician had builded in the Moghreb, and now the Moghreb in its own name grew great. Fez, Marrakech, Rbat bloomed and their power spread to Tunis and to Spain. Many ages did this stubborn world take to blossom; many ages has it taken to die. The greatness of the Almoravides, of the Almohades, of the Merinides lives still in Morocco.

Fez is the metropolis of a world that is gone: the head of a missing body. A hundred thousand Moors in Fez-el-Bali live in an age synchronous with the Crusades and

with the Gothic. The modern world is here like a mirage
—or like a curse of Allah.

A river, plenteous in water for Morocco, makes of the
hills a single grove for olive, fig and eucalyptus. The
town lies solid, within them. Most cities are a crust of
houses split into streets and squares. Old Fez is a solid
carapace of roofs, its rise and fall like the articulations
of a body.

Underneath the roofs are the *soukhs*, intricate like the
wrinkles on an old man's face. These are streets of myriad
and tiny shops. In one section there will be only gold-
smiths—hundreds of men squatting before their little bellows and their little gems. In another congregate the sellers
of fish, the vendors of soap and grease, the ironmongers,
the makers of leathern ware. The typical *soukh* is not more
than three paces wide; and each shop is an open box,
slightly above the level of the walk, and large enough for
a single squatting man. Overhead, is a roof of grape-
vine or of rush, joining the two sides of the street together
and letting in mere crevices of light.

Back and forth in this myriad-textured warren move
the Fasi. The rich swathe through on mules; asses laden
with produce are led by uncouth Berbers from the mountains or by black slaves from the south of the Sahara.
The human pigment is bewildering. The city Arab is pale
as a dweller of the northern towns of Europe: the Kabyl
is dark-skinned, blue-eyed: the Ethiop is black as the
shadows in the tiny shops. Burnouse and turbans are
pied. Vendors shout for the passers-by to stop. And from
time to time there is a break in the ceaseless lineage of
bazaars: the carved, closed shutter of a Koran school shields
the incessant coil of adolescent voices, strident, wild, un-
meditative—shouting the words of their Prophet. Along
the bare walls of the mosques and the medersas, beggars
are posted. Their stintless catch-word weaves with the
beat of ass-hoof, with the thresh of human feet, with the
shop-calls, with the chanting of students.

Each beggar has his phrase. It invokes alms with the

patronage and to the glory of a particular saint. It guarantees to the almsgiver a saint's word in Heaven. He sits in the shadow of the holy buildings. The carven door leads through a passage of mosaic to a court, gorgeous with tile and woodwork laid perhaps with mother-of-pearl. The holy students of the medersa live in cells, mounting in honey-comb mass to the minaret.

From the crowded *soukhs*, streets toweringly high and sinisterly narrow twist in all directions. A band of Moorish minstrels moves from dark door to dark door. The voices of drum and pipe give forth a ghost of music. The voices are shrill like the calls of mountain life. Arab music was lean and violent, a gray fusion of thrusts. This song of the true Moor is almost disembodied. It has accent, but no texture. It stands against the intricate mellow noise of the city, enfolded in the liquid sconce of hills, like a savage summons. A door opens, a copper falls in a drum. The leader of the band gives his toned blessing; the slender men move on, weaving with their song a pall on Islam.

On a hill stands the mosque of Bab-Guissa (one of the 785 mosques built in Fez by the Almohades, exclusive of monasteries and medersas). By this mosque is the north gate through which the Berber from the Rif passes with donkey-charge of olive or of grain. Each donkey-load pays duty to the Sultan; and each appraisal calls for threats from the custom officer—degenerate Moors who are truly slaves of France. The Riffian pays his pence in sullen silence. And his non-resistance maddens the Fasi. Nearby is an olive market, *Fondouk el lhoudi.* The olives ripen in winter. Vast rush troughs and baskets hold the black fruit in the open Square, under the sun and the flies, and the sweating men and donkeys. With the barter come blows. A negro catches a bargainer with his teeth and is flung off with a ripped cheek. The crowd buzzes, deeply unmoved. The open baskets of olives, black-gemmed in the air, give an intenser note. . . . . .

On the heights above Bab-Guissa are the ruined tombs

—the *koubbas*—of the Merinides. Their crumbled arabesques look down on the long valley of Oued Fez. A spirit of those ancient rulers could still find his Fez-el-Bali: know this shut and terracing carapace of stone, blue tile, gold ceramic, fumy beneath the sun. The old walls are there, too, although time and cactus have splintered them. And the mosques rise like a thousand claws toward Allah—the hold of the pious town on the One God.[1]

The sun is sinking on the Almohadian wall that forms a corner with the mosque Bab-Guissa. Soon will come from myriad minarets, the call for evening prayer. The mountain donkeys no longer lurch through the Gate; and the slaves of the imprisoned Sultan are gone. This rocky height studded with moldering tombs, this wall and this tower form a natural amphitheater. It is crowded with Moors. They squat on the ground, swathed in burnouses. Water-boys thread silently. All indeed is silent, facing down to a central point within the wall where sits a man.

His beard is white and his voice is gentle: he is a man with exquisite hands and manners of the Court. And he is speaking so quietly, that the massed crowd must hold silent indeed, if it would hear him. He is the Chronicler of Fez—poet, historian, journalist: one of the great sons of the Moghreb. Each day at nightfall, for an hour, he bespeaks in his own verse the glory of Islam. Each of his tales lasts three months: there are four of them to the year. His unemphatic words give to the men of Fez two realities of Islam: the splendor which was, and the splendor which is eternal. He speaks, not without humor; his immobile body radiates peace. He tells of the gardens underneath which

[1] To the west, sprawls another Fez which the old ruler would not know. This is Fez-el-Djidid—Fez the New—a Fez of the sixteenth century. It is a squat, chalk town filled with Bedouin types—Syrians, Arabs, Negroes, Spaniards, Jews: a conglomerate of squalid shops and *louche* cafés. It is like Tangiers, the invaded and corrupted Moorland. Farther west, there is a third Fez—still stranger. Here are a railroad station, a wireless tower, and a *garnison* for "Frankish" troops. Since 1911—this visitation of the wrath of Allah.

flows water—the Garden whither Islam somnolently moves through this demonic hour of wireless, guns and railways. . .

. . . .

The capital of the Sultanate is Rbat. From here, the Almohadian troops set sail for Spain; and after the triumph of Alarcos in 1195, Rbat-el-Fath—"Camp of Victory" —received its name. Fez, in hills, is gold: Rbat is a dazzling white over the sea. The bou Regreg slopes down within its sands, between two gentle promontories. On one of them Rbat, on the other Sla—ancient cities, equally white above the sea, equally proud, equally hostile. You can row from the *soukhs* of Rbat to the palaces of Sla in a minute. But these are worlds kept separate in an ageless confrontation. Time was when the two cities were independent; blood stained the sands of the Regreg. Each town slants to the sea upon a mighty dune; and this dune is a divided graveyard.

The ocean has opened Rbat. Its bright streets run with the breeze. Its masonry is less delicate and more resolute than that of Fez. In its soukhs is a tang of salt. The Moors themselves are less shut up. Though their burnouses swathe them and the women walk as hidden in their veils, an Atlantic rhythm has crept within these folds; the somnambulance is brighter.

> "We have lived fair days
>   In Granada, house of delight.
> Among its roses and its roses budding
>   We have sped many a silver night.
> Alas! no more for our enraptured use
>   The dwellings of Andalús. . . . .
> Hush! do not make me suffer more.

We are the guests of a *Cherif*.[1] Two slave girls crouched on the carpet sing for us. The house is modern. But in each detail it is a copy of the classic Moorish style

[1] One of a family tracing descent from Mohammed.

whose glory is Al-Hambra. These might be the days when Al-Ahmar, king of Granada, was friend of the Catholic Fernando; and when Christians were entertained in the Andalús even as we in the Moghreb.

It is a long and narrow chamber, run round by a divan yielding with silk cushions. To a man's height, the wall is mosaic. Above, it is white plaster exquisitely laced in arabesque. The ceiling is carved wood, textured and painted like a maze of flowers, with mother-of-pearl and gold within the toolings. Outside the door we see the court, and hear the song of the fountain. The mansion rises to four stories: upon each floor the balcony goes round and all the windows open in upon it. A girl brings subtly painted goblets; tea fused with mint is poured. Another slave places brasiers of sandalwood. The monotonous wail and rending song has ceased. The singers go in silence, as if they had left with us all that they had. We hear the pulse of the sea: an indeterminate murmur of voice and feet. Two little slaves, with eyes too far to be either friendly or hostile, linger and change our glasses, ere we have half drained them.

"It is because we have disobeyed the Prophet."

A young man speaks. He is the eldest son and his burnouse is white, undecorated wool. He has laid aside his babouches and his feet are bare. He reclines on the divan, resting his languorous head upon a hand more exquisite than the lacework on the wall. The features are subtly virile. There is fire in them, and cruelty. He is a man fine-drawn—but altogether metal. He is twenty: not yet married. His life is the study of Lore at his *zaouïa* and the writing of verse.

"In Al-Koran it is written that we should work—we have not worked. It is written that all Islam should live in peace—we have fought each other. It is written that we should shun luxuriance and vice, that we should cultivate our soil and our minds. We neglect them. It is written that we should raise up our women—we keep them down. Therefore our life is disaster. Therefore the French are upon us. We have been the highest of peoples. Islam and Culture were one. In the old days, among a thousand men, there was not one who did not read. Within a thousand homes, there was not one but had delicate rugs, handsomely carved walls. Now, our houses are dark with smoke; our minds are dark with ignorance. Like the pest unto the unclean body, the French have come."

My host smiled, fearful lest the words of his too serious son should bring discomfort.

"It is an evil hour: and it will pass."

"Are you acting," I asked, "to make it pass the quicker?"

"When we are ready, we shall act. Even as a child when it is ready to walk." The son spoke. And his friend, a philosopher from Tunis, nodded.

"Islam has been cursed with a new childhood. We are not decadent. I know that your historians call us decadent. It is a lie. Measure us by the Law of the Prophet. If it was ever good and great, it is still so today. Perhaps you would find that it was never good. It has been studied by intelligent men—the Jews—and found wanting. We can understand that. But it is not changed: it is not decadent."

I thought of the world fringing the Power of Rome, before Mohammed: a chaos of repellent parts, giving no light. The Arab kindled this anarchy and made it one. I thought of the reeking *Kasbah* of Algiers; of the swarming, inert Marrakech and Fez. I thought of the Monastery city in the Sahara and of the holy Marabout whose Word Arabs came weeks on camel-back to hear. I had felt everywhere a Body, flaccidly receding from its accumulate splendors.

"You are a poet," I said. "Tell me about the forms and the spirit of your verse."

"We have sixteen forms," answered the son. "We have but one Spirit."

"Poetry," said my host, "is more plentiful than trees, in Islam. It is our water-bearer. It is our forest."

"And your greatest poet?"

All three spoke as one: "The Prophet."

The Tunisian explained:

"Amrolkéïs, Antsar, El Bassiri, the poets of El Hariri and El Hamadaín were great. How could there be poetry like that which the Prophet dictated unto his disciples? In those days, Zoheïr was the greatest poet of Mecca. The Prophet had escaped to Al-Medinah. At the annual contest, when all the poets posted their work on the outer wall of El Kaabah, there was none to vie with Zoheïr. And Zoheïr was an idolater, a man of the tribe of the Koreishites—deep haters of the Prophet. But a Sura of the Koran came to the eyes of this man who had been crowned. And he read it, and he tore his victorious poem. And he said: The crown belongs to Mohammed, son of Abd-Allah, son of Abd-El-Motalleb."

"Who are the great poets, now?"

"How, in a low age, can there be high poets? We follow the great humbly. The best of today—whatever it is—in poetry and in philosophy—is found in Egypt."

Mine host led us to the roof of his palace.

"It is night," he explained. "We are not indiscreet." He referred to the custom of Islam which gives the roof as the inviolate playground of the women.

There was no moon. The stars were a swarm of golden bees within the deep blue meadow of the sky. From a hundred open courts, hid lights of houses were thrown up. Each house was a muffled lantern; Rbat was a cluster of hidden lamps peering into the turbulence of stars. The sea slept. Beyond the city walls, the ancient tower of Hassan mused, a gray ghost.

The man from Tunis spoke:

"It is said, O my friends, that Morocco is the tail of Islam. Let it then be known that Islam is a peacock."

Outside the inner city, in the direction of Hassan, there was a small, low group of open lights. Here the houses were not dark lanterns; the houses had windows out upon the street. A trill of horizontal fires came against the upright monotone of Islam.

"It is the Mellah," said mine host, "the Mellah of the Jews."

We went into another chamber. Slave girls brought fresh glasses, candied fruits, dainties from Arabia Felix. Through the open door, the wide night air was a discord from this polyphony of silks and gems, of cedar and spice and ceramic. And there arose the voices of distant women in song. It was the women of the house, locked from the rooms where men of the profane world might come and drink tea with the masters.

The song drifted palpitant and humble. My thought went out to the Mellah—to the place where windows faced outward, where women showed their faces. . . .

c. Ishmael and Israel

Forty men, women, children fill the room with a voice. They are Jews, Jews of the Moorish Mellah. The unveiled faces of the women are fertile, less metallic, harder than the faces of their sisters. The eyes are deeper, their consistency more solid. Gaunt determination holds the warmth of these women like an armor. The men are more variant and less harmonious. A burnouse or red fez in place of the black would pass most of them as Arabs. In their eyes the same cunning, the same swift hardness. Yet underneath dwells a distinction: an enduring spiritual source—a quiet water—of which the agitation of their external lives is tributary.

After the song of the Arab minstrels; after the singers of Fez beneath the Merinidean tombs shouting to the twang of a string; after the fakirs of the Socco in Tangiers who bounce and prance their monkey shines to the lilt of an apish cry, to the crash of a scissors; after the mystic monotone of the Darwish whirling his soul into the Absolute; after the service of the Ouled-Naïl who sway like trees deep-rooted and who shriek like Liliths —now, this Jewish music. Ten women step to the center of the room and squat in a circle around a copper cauldron. They sing, and as they sing they beat with open palms upon the upturned cauldron. Their song is in Arabic; it has similitudes with Moorish songs: there are the ceaseless verses, the narrative design with rhythm and note recurring. But the women are ample-breasted, leoninely gay. The beat of palms upon the copper drum rises like a copper wall about the women and the women's song.

As a mountain torrent carries the rigor of grim heights through a low tropic zone, so this music moves through the Moorish Mellah with its prophetic past. For all its tides of blood and wandering, it is still. The music of Arab races like stripped steeds; that of the Moor jangles like bone, snaps like sinew. Here is a song that dwells wide over fields, tops the cedars of Lebanon, swings with the sun—and yet is but a prayer. Its immobility has voyaged. The prophets are here; and Ruth with her eyes fertile as the wheat; and Judith scabbarded in beauty. And Babylon to which, as Tangiers now, the scum of peoples rose; where magic parded with penury, coins glinted in blood. Spain is here, a perpendicular starkness rising from the low tide of the music—Spain, with her singing seers. And Araby has dropped her gold into a humble song. As in the streets where the street women sing, here is the cry—shrill, lithic: dangling but a moment on the plaint like a barbarous dart upon a mother's breast.

Like the Jews, the Moslems are the People of a Book. The Bible is the compiled and edited remnant of a literature ranging from epigram to epic, into whose making went a thousand years. The Koran is the work of a generation, and of a man. Whatever divergence from the prophetic mouth is due to the disciples, Omar and Ali,[1] it is sure that before Mohammed there was no Koran and after him his text has changed only through processes of natural error. Before the Koran, the Arabs possessed an anthology of verse, lapidic, utterly objective: poems singing the loves and tribulations of the desert. These did not go, like the ancestral heritage of the Hebrews, into their holy book. After the Koran, this strain, celebrating passion, thirst, hospitality and war, went on. The heightened activity of the Arabs enlarged their letters. But the Koran, unlike what came after as before, is subjective. Pictures of Paradise, explicit laws, ways of the

[1] Mohammed is generally supposed not to have been able to read; and his Chapters, brought to him haphazard by the angel Gabriel, were dictated to his disciples. These chapters (Suras) were not compiled until after the Prophet's death.

wrath of Allah, pleadings and campaigns, float in the swim of an inchoate exhortation. There is no reason to doubt that the Prophet did dictate the Koran—and revised it little. The book's substance is an anarchic potpourri of what Mohammed must have thought out for himself, together with what he heard in synagogue and church. There is a canny set of laws: there is an endless repetition of the delights of heaven "where are the gardens under which flow waters" and of the miraculous nature of the virgins there, who are never unclean, being perpetual lovers and perpetual virgins. There is great harping on the unpleasantness of Hell. There are periodic outbursts against the Jews and much gentle reproval of the Christians whom Mohammed wooed with worshipful references to Jesus and to Mary. There is, above all, ceaseless plagiary from the Old Testament tales, whose beauty and significance are usually scrapped in Mohammed's zest to get to his main point. And the point, as a rule, is that Abraham, Moses and Jesus were all true Moslems, that the Hebrews knew full well the ultimate prophecy of Mohammed, that their Book tells them so, and that only their wickedness keeps them from avowal. Finally, the book holds to a running comment on contemporary events and neighboring peoples; and the effect of this, within the holy Script, must have been vast since here was virtually God himself dictating an editorial page on headline stories.

Such matters lay in a great jumble in Mohammed's head; for the Prophet was too great and too busy a man to keep a clear literary mind. And in such jumble they poured forth to make the verbose, extraordinarily rhythmed mosaic of the 114 Suras of the Koran. The book is above all an impressionistic portrait of Mohammed; in Mohammed, of the greatest figure and of the greatest era of the Arabs. Even in translation, it reveals the intense afflatus of a man who, from the age of forty till his death at sixty-three, conquered a world, prepared successors to conquer others, ruled savagely and wisely over a race as unruly as it was naturally keen, won the love even of his foes and the submission of almost countless maidens.

Mohammed was a great statesman, a great captain, a great lawmaker, a great poet: he was not the creator of a great religion. Innumerable mystic and religious men have worshiped Allah and performed the ceremonials of the Prophet. But the Mohammedanism of Mohammed, of the Koran, of the *source* is not essentially a religion at all. A religion is a revealed experience of the relation between a man and his cosmos. If it is not experience, it may be philosophy but it is less than a religion. If it is not revealed, it may be an ecstatic or poetic state, but it is less than a religion. Its conclusion may be suicide for the human spirit, as in some religions of India; its field of consciousness may be narrowly naturalistic or animistic as in the religions of the savage. But no plan for life on earth, however exalted, is of itself a religion; no scheme for reaching heaven. Nor is a system which exploits an already existing sense of God as a means toward a determined human goal a system of religion. This, moreover, is the system of Mohammed. It employs the latent religiosity of the Arab world to a pragmatic end. It exploits the idea of God as modern pragmatism the idea of progress.

Mohammed uplifted a race. Where, in this, is his equal? At his hand an anarchy of tribes filling the desert with internecine blood: and from this anarchy he prepared the force which mastered half Africa, half Asia, Spain— which bound with great houses and great culture Bagdad to Toledo. The religious energy of the Arabs had for ages straggled and fumed in loss; creating but a variety of impotence. The religious energy of the Jews had thrown forth light in the world, and left the Jewish body desolate. Rome? The immense creature, camped about the Latin Sea, accepted Christ in its senility. Its principle of growth had not been Christ; Christ was to help to rot and to transform it. Mohammed studied Rome. He observed this one live element in that immense decay. The religious element. He took it, as the modern pragmatist takes the idea of progress and of science, to express himself and to advance his people.

He lived in a religious age. God for seven hundred years had made a wrangling and a shambles of the marts of the east. God alone, in all Rome, seemed alive. God served to energize Mohammed's act. In the Koran, Allah is a voice bearing no fresh body of eternity or love, bearing no experience of Nature or of a spirit that transcends it: Allah is at best the charged echo of past holy voices, here applied to spur the Arab on. The quantity that gave Islam weight was the force of its leader and the latent might of his race: God was the *n* by which the Prophet raised this quantity to the pitch of action.

And Mohammed is the full rich presence in the Koran. Though God speaks, Mohammed has the eye, the answer, the blessing and the curse for all the ambient world. Mohammed tells the Arab about God chiefly that God is telling the Arab about Mohammed. What else he says is not the crux of the matter. Mohammed is Prophet, to obey him is good, to disobey him is hell, the Jews are a bad lot, Allah is ruthless but to the believer kind—such degradations from the old rationales of faith are not dissonant from religion. Mohammed proceeds, after Moses, to instruct the faithful in diet, in justice, in commerce, marriage, war. His plan of success generates its power shrewdly from the normal appetites: man's dream of heaven, his fear of hell, his love of woman, his thirst for water, his need of forgiveness whenever he has burned his fingers. Here, too, there is no divergence from the usual theocratic Code. But the Koran is distinguished by the relative place of God and of man's experience of God within the system.

Go back not to the Mishna, and the Prophets; but to the barbarous Torah. Science and method are as demoded here as ethics. Blood and corporal anguish are obsessive symbols. Justice is a matter of plagues and trumpetings. Yet is God present. These old fathers would be abstract save for the dwelling in them of a universal principle, called Jehovah. It is He who moves these semi-savage tales. Hunger for a common experience which, being both true and beautiful, is divine, informs the acts of these men, directs their faltering passage. In the suicidal will of the Buddhist, in the Dionysian dance of the Greek, in the metaphysic of Paul or of Plotinus, dwells ever variant this single purpose: the will to fuse (though it be to fuse with loss) man's personal act and his experience of the universal. This is religion. It is not in the religious mechanics of Mohammed.

The Prophet invites Heraclius, emperor of Rome, to join or to acknowledge him. He is denied, of course. But Islam is a "carry-all." It assimilates Mary and Jesus quite as it has garbled the Talmud. It places Mohammed at the top of an agglomeration unified by him from the whirling chaos of the east. Energy, thus drawn from a hundred confusions, thrusts in a hundred directions.

If classic Islam is not essentially a religion, it is an Idea. An Idea in motion. Its motion is horizontal; and its premiss of departure is success. The follower of the Prophet cannot lose. At the worst comes death: death in holy warfare means beatitude and houris. But Mohammed does not lean too heavily on so dim a guerdon. He has genius in the arts of diplomacy and war. He fights innumerable battles, and nearly always he wins. When he does lose, he turns defeat into a strategic triumph. In his first lean years as a Prophet, he has garnered a rare capital for a religious leader: that capital is material success. He loans out his prestige at a usurer's rates. It is clear, soon enough, that to follow Mohammed means victory in arms, means booty, means fresh women.

Health in Islam became a state of profitable war. From the mobile chaos of the desert was created this intent mobility of advance. Islam was a perpetual raid. Its health meant war: and war meant expedition, conquest, ultimate death. The contrary of war, of health, of Islam—was then the dwelling in the present life, and was Peace.

What contrast to the Jew in these brother Semites! Their mobility of steel to the chemic mobility of Judah! The Idea of Islam has indeed for matrix the unrest, physical and spiritual, of the Roman world. Peoples stirred, because the great People were broken. The interior displacement acted like suction on the peripheries of Rome. Dreams of power, opiate creeds went through the windy world, creating new currents, creating and moving new masses. Araby was drawn, so: and awoke. But this Idea of the Arab could not have lived so well within the womb of the world had it been alien to the Arab soul. In the Arab, as in all desert people, worked the impulse of expansion.

Here Arab and Jew are one. Who has seen the desert understands: this indomitable urge born of the sand-sea, to be moving, to pass horizons, to be moving forever. The desert impulse in the Hebrew was sublimated. Not his body, but his god should pass horizons! When the Jews' body migrated, Jehovah became static. Only when the body took deep roots—in Palestine, in Spain, in the Talmud at worst (in America perhaps tomorrow)—could the transfigured Jewish God pass the horizons. But the balance held: as the Jews' spirit spread, their body remained an atom. With the Arabs, it was the body that expanded. Before the Prophet, it had expanded impotently in civil conflict. Mohammed brought this energy to order. But even he knew of no principle of expansion higher than the raid and the empire.

Arabia expanded. Persia, Abyssinia, India, Egypt, the Sahara, Spain became parts of Islam that was Araby in motion. The Jew discovered that to spread in the spirit was to be immobile in the life. Not so the Arab. The Jew learned that only an unmoving and an unmoved God could pass horizons. But in Islam, to expand still meant to move. The law of balance between inner and outer energy was not transcended. The Idea of Islam became all body: all moving, conquering body. Here went the Moslem energy. The energy that dwelt in that hid precinct of creative thought was sapped to a low ebb. In the person of Mohammed, there was energy both for conquest and for the subtler dominance of law and wisdom. He elected that the ideas, the forms, the rituals, the experience, and truth which he created should suffice for all time for his peoples. All their powers might hence be transformed into the stupendous business of outward conquest.

Of course, this was not strictly to be. Many ideas of Islam were born after the Prophet's death. Even the Koran may have been amended. The Moslem architectures, the Moslem philosophies both mystical and materialistic, much of the Moslem ritual, would have been strange to Mohammed. But independent growths of the spirit could not become organic within Islam. For in the Idea, there was the law that only Body of Islam could expand: its thought and vision were create, forever. In consequence, the few new crystallizations called forth by the new needs of Islamic empire became endowed at once with the old principle of fixity, with the sanctity of intransigent stagnation. The body moved. The forms of the body did not move. Wherefore, as soon as the body ceased to add unto itself by outward conquest, it began to rot.

This is the tragedy of Islam. It is writ large in symbols of the present. Fez and Rbat and Bagdad are fetid relics of gone loveliness. Their life has no virtue of rejuvenation; there was in Islam no autonomy of method for the creating of ideas whereby life is recreated. The Arab literary language is identical with the Koran's. Dogma declares that the hodge-podge splendor of Mohammed's script is perfection: who shall dare change perfection? So Arabic literature today is an archaic grimace: a spirit muffled by the masque of thirteen hundred years. And the spoken language, as divergent from the classic as French from Latin, is noisy and yet mute. Moslem architecture has not evolved. The mosque of today is a faithful imitation of some antique model. Prayer has not changed. Science has not changed. The Idea of Islam has forbidden its own growth.

But if this death from inanition is patent in modern Islam, it is implicit in the source. The fruit, only, of the religious impulse lives, for it alone holds the rounding of life's circle. The religious act—be it art or be it ethics—cannot exhaust itself, because each forward step is an approach to the beginning. The man possessed of religion is possessed of a universal principle; and what he does cannot die. The forms and words of his activity may grow archaic—like the sculpture of Egypt, like the gods of the Rig-Veda. But the activity itself is forever an approach to the Source. The farther the religious man goes afield, the closer he will come to the Primordial Fountain, since all his life is plotted to a circle. And if he lose his life, then will he win it. But with the unreligious will, each act is a severance from source. The unreligious is the incomplete. And its symbol is the unreal straight line which moves away from its beginning.[1]

Even in its classic mosque, Islam betrays its unreligious essence. The mosque is a patchwork of details, a mosaic of finery for the senses. The very character of the mosaic is unreligious. For it represents the analytic, not the One. The minaret has no relation with the aspirant Phallus, or with the sublimated Phallus of the Christian church. The minaret is a down-tending structure upon which the muedzin stands, not to send prayer to Allah, but orders to the people.

The religion of the Koran is a caricature of God drawn in the lying lines of time and space.

[1] As mathematics becomes non-Euclidean. it tends toward the religious. In place of the pagan straight-line, we have the geodesic-line which meets its source and completes a body for gravitational and inertial forces.

CHAPTER II

HINTERLAND IN SPAIN

THE sun is hidden from this dawn. The snow range is a crest to the south and east. Air, pouring over, cold and hard like pearls, is the dawn upon Spain. Tidy huertas are green crystals in the dawn. Villages, orange-marged, make a pied flash in it. Fig and olive march in armies up the slopes of the Sierra, toward snow, toward dawn. When the sun stands at last in the ridge, the day is hot.

This is the south. After Guadix, toward the eastern sea, the human world grows dim. The carretera, at the entrance of a town, slides in a slough of mud. Rain is rare and violent; it becomes a torrent from the impervious mountain. Dark men in black grimed capes walk beside laden donkeys. Women herd goats; the tuberous udders sticking on the mud. Children are rhythms in a maze of rags. The eyes of humans are like the eyes of burros.

The Sierras have disappeared behind the depopulous hills. The verdant valleys of Granada are folded back. Villages here are hard like the parched clay. The carretera is a swathe of dust, glittering in the sun. The land is sere as if a flame dwelt on it. The eyes of humans are velvet dark, like the eyes of a dream.

Murcia, now. Even the sparse irrigated huertas disappear. The barbarous abruptness of the soil turns to desert. Villages are a single eyeless street of houses, abject under the eye of the sun. The world is a turmoil of yellow waste. The villages are splinters of the waste. Only, to break the yellow, walls of cactus—a Maya-like green sculpture matching its lush planes with the harsh planes of the clay. Goats, dusty and crabbed, crop an invisible herb. The Barbary fig is the olive and the grape of this land. Villages grow lower, sparser—merge with the desert. Villages disappear.

Under the sky huge mounds of sterile hill rise now; and on their slopes, red and advancing with the mirrored sun, are serried shadows. Caves. Villages of caves. This is below Phœnicia in time. This is Iberia. A Spanish folk still dwells here.

The hills are steep. There is a row of caves, horizontally curved. Above each cave is a tiny aperture for smoke. Then comes another row. In the foreground, the cactus is cultivated for its fruit. There is a hooded well.

It is not yet noon. But the summer sun has turned the heaven into irradiant steel. Light and heat strike like solids on the solid soil, on the intricate levels of the hills. In their rebound, light and heat become polyphonous, weaving the world into their image.

The sun, rising, faints into its own immensity of heat. And the cave villages grow larger. Between them, the sterile hills leap in a monotone against the day's pressure. A cave town flings sheer to the ridge of a pyramidal mountain. A hundred threads of smoke thresh the air like filaments of wire. Caves are dark eyes that hide from the steel heaven. The eyes of the dwellers are caves.

Shadow is cold. Here is a town with houses. Where the sun strikes the street, horses, donkeys, moving forms of people gyre and funnel and become a fume in the sun. Signs on shops, blue shutters, yellow parasols of women tremble and swerve as if they were in flame. But shadow is cold.

Outside, there is desert and the sky has melted. All the steel strokes of the sun, beating down, beating up, are melted: heaven has fallen into waves. Villages live in this fierce element. Men and women, donkeys and goats live in this radiant sea.

Over the brow of a *despoblado*, the sun goes. The desert flattens, like a sea after storm. The sterile hills are farther away, and on the even plain there is grass. The desert becomes a moor. Salt wort suggests the ocean. The road circles, catching the sun again. The sun splinters and breaks on the moor. Huge masses of dried dung, the fuel of these people, catch a last ray. There is a hill, dark-mottled. The hill is a city. At the height, there are caves and dwellings cut in clay. At the base, there is dust: and in the dust are streets.

Sordid wineshops, stores, squat in the dust. All is dust save the people who are clay; clay black-baked in the sun.

CHAPTER III

ANDALUSIA

a. *El Andalús*

In the year of Islam 89 and of Christ 711, an Arab host recruited with proselytes from the pagan Berbers and the Christian Copts, and captained by Târik whose name is a fossil in the rock Gibraltar (*Jebel Târik*) crossed the strait from Africa to Europe. After seven summers, all Spain, even to the Galician mountains, was in the sway of the Prophet. To their new conquest the Arabs gave the name Andalús, which means the land of the west.

Their first pause was in a smiling world. Southern Spain, roughly the part which is Andalusia now, for many ages had drawn the wandering hungers of the nations. Here had been Tartessos, the Tarshish of the thunder of Isaiah, a realm near the present sites of Seville and Cadiz, known as the Land of Silver and whose greatness was synchronous with Crete. Here had been Phœnician Malaca and Gades, cities famous for their gay vice. Here had been Bætican Rome, birthplace of Seneca and of the Stoic mind which in reality was Spanish. Here, from Babylon, came the urgent Jews among the indolent Visigoths. A smiling world. On the breasts of the Sierras, groves of olive and of cork. In the valleys rivers that were veins of wealth. Luxuriant crops, fat kine, orchards and vineyards: shade: and by the alternance of sun and cool a natural culture. Now within this mellowness, the harsh Idea born of the desert dearth.

Historians will give you the facts: how Andalusia did not hold the Arab: how he swarmed the mesas of Castile: how he fanned east to the Ebro and west to the Asturias: how only stubborn knots of Basques withheld him: how he scaled the abrupt wall of Spain and poured down the suaver Pyrenees of France; and how at last, near Poictiers, he was stopped by Charles Martel and driven back forever. The truth is otherwise. Not the Franks, but the smiling south of Spain stopped Islam. When the Arabs faced the French at "Tours," they were turned back already. The desert, the mountains, the incessant war could not weaken Islam. These were its food and its health. But Andalusia was poison. A luxuriant land worked on the spirit of the Arab, causing in the rear a flinching and dissension. This, several years after the "defeat of Tours," caused the return from France.

Often is the question asked: what Islam did to Spain? The first response must be another question: what did Spain make of Islam? Spain was there when the Arab came. She was far older than Islam, far more populous. This Celtiberian base which it is simple and safe to call the Spaniard is a strange people. It is warlike,[1] yet submits to conquest: it is indolent yet dwells in a harsh land: it is inarticulate and savage yet transforms its masters. Carthage has come and gone. Rome has faded, after creating in Spain a spirit that is not found in other parts of Rome. The Visigoths make their easy conquest. They are touched by urban Rome already ere they come; they are no longer the rude Germans of the Rhine. Rome has annulled their savagery. Their nature is rural but their will is urban. Their nature is the foray, but their will is Pax Romana. They have no metaphysical hunger, yet they spend their might defending Arianism against the cross-fires of North Africa and Europe. Their history in Spain is their dissolution; their complete absorption in the mute, indefeasible mass of Spain which they are supposed to rule. When Târik defeats Roderick, last Visigothic king, the business is done. But henceforth, German blood suffuses like a golden glow the flesh of

[1] "The Iberians are the most warlike of all the barbarians." Thucydides.

Iberia which has already drunk the Celt, the Semite, the Greek, the Latin.

There has been no drama. This process is instinctive. Spain lives like a tree with her roots close and her branches harboring the seasons. She has taken to herself the nourishment of wind and rain, the steadfastness of sun. All Spain takes in is Spain. In her own vague life, an Idea has been born, expressive of her chaos. Now, she takes in an alien Idea to work upon her.

The Arabs found their kingdom. In 755, but a generation after their arrival, Abd-er-Rahman I who sits at Córdoba breaks with the Moslem east. Almost at once, the Islam that came to Spain assumes a separate being, grows into a body independent of Bagdad and Damascus. This separation means a transformation. And the cause of it is Spain.

The nature of Islam, we have seen, is like the nature of the pioneer. Pioneer values—motion, violence, acquisition, conquest—bear the Idea of the desert race, moving toward horizons. The Idea is not the horizon nor the water beyond it: it is the moving forever *toward* the unmastered goal. Earth, in such psychology, takes on the delusive aspect of a flying road. And mortal life is synonymous with earth. It is a passing stretch. And it is close to death; for it is unreal and it is dark. The true life, the life of the Idea is that forever unattained, is that toward which our mortal days are an incessant moving. True life, then, is beyond that death which this life truly is. And to attain it, this life should be trampled like a road.

The Idea has its adornments: as in pioneering, they will be simplicity of living and of thought; violence, cruelty, intolerance for all that bars the goal; and the equally violent reflex from these—the narcotics of sleep and sensual relaxation.

Islam's Idea now comes in the land of Spain. And the Moslem hosts who bear it and live to nourish it, settle in the south where settling is easy. And having settled down, they build a culture whose like the world sees seldom and whose causal spirit is essentially opposed to the Idea of Islam. For the Idea of Islam cannot settle down.

Mohammed and his captains knew no such world as this that sends its radiance from Córdoba. Nor would they have found it good. The Prophet would have thundered: "This is blasphemy and failure. This is turning from the commands of Allah. Rather than invent new forms of splendor for your mosques, ye would do well to push on. What? Ye consort with the Jew? Ye are tolerant with the Christian? suffering his monasteries to abide in Islam? Ye turn a peaceful back on the Frank and leave to the Christian Basques the holy labor of driving Charlemagne and Roland from Roncesvalles? And ye study Aristotle? when the Koran holds all wisdom? Ye tolerate schools who explain the creation of the world by natural laws? when I have taught ye of the Hand of Allah." Mohammed was wise. He knew that the nature of the Arab, the Idea of Islam, the conduct of the people must be one, else the Idea would fall. But if Mohammed was wise, this kingdom of south Spain was luminous. Jews collaborated in government, science, art. Christians brought their mysteries and their music; and those who chose to pray in convents were not molested. An architecture was developed. Poetry and thought flourished like grass of the fields.

What had happened to Islam? The Idea born of the desert had become detached from the life of the desert people, when it lay down in this smiling southland. Life relaxed from the stern rigor of the Faith and took unto itself new forms, consonant with its relaxation: Islam whose health was war desired peace.

Meantime, Spain's absorption of invading bloods went on. Christian, Arab, Berber, Copt—each with a past mingling—mingled. There lived soon again in southern Spain, one people: but there lived now three Ideas. The Christian was the least self-conscious, the least active;

the Jewish was an insidious minority; the Moslem was dominant. These three Ideas were fleshed in human beings; and the human beings were virtually one. There were Moslem lords, whose ancestry counted Visigoths and Jews; there were Christian bishops in whose veins flowed Yemen and Berber blood; there were Jewish poets whose mothers had been reared in a Harem. Under all, there was the immemorial base outnumbering the rest. It had been pagan, Catholic, Arian, Catholic again. Now for a while, it was Moslem. Within a hundred years of the African invasion, Spain was once more inhabited by Spaniards.

Yet a new element had arisen, which was destined to grow tragic. The Idea of Islam touched into new intensity the Ideas of Jew and Christian. Jew, Christian, Arab, settled down and married. But the three Ideas, grown virulent, did not marry. They made war.

Islam, meantime, moves from Andalusia north. And as it conquers Spain, the Catholic Reconquest which for near eight centuries holds Spain in blood is cradled in the tiny mountain kingdoms of Asturias and Aragon. Where the Moslem settles, the land becomes Moslem. Often it changes hands in the long war's tides. But the people, like a tree, stays with its roots. Fresh Moslems may perhaps come to live in a province soon reconquered by the Christian. They will become Christian, too. It is one people. The struggle is between a Cross and a Crescent. And the hands which bear them are of a single body.

Islam, battling in the desert north, has settled to peace in the south and fallen from the Idea of Islam. But battling in the desert north it takes its Idea along—its temper and its nature. And these, it gives unto the Christian foe! Rigorous desert traits flourish in Christian Aragon and Castile. For here is desert again, and violence as the matrix of the world. So the Christians of the north, facing Islam in battle, live ever closer to the Idea of Islam. War is an embrace fertile like love. Traits of Christian and Moslem pass in osmosis. And there comes the day when warlike Catholics from the north press on the gentled Mussulmans of the south with true Islamic rigor. And the Moslem south must look to Africa for Moslems close enough to the Idea of Islam to be able to withstand these northern Christians. And the war has no cease, being a war not of bloods but of souls.

We are still in the first scenes of the play whose tragedy begins only when the clash of arms is over. Let us dwell awhile in Andalusia, first home of the Moslem and his last in Spain.

b. *The Eye*

There are places of earth like eyes. They have more than a proportionate share of the light and the fire. They hold, within a fragile cup of space, measures infinitely deep. Córdoba is an eye within the face of Spain.

But Córdoba is dead? This whirl of houses is a husk of splendor, a strew of ancient ash here and there speaking still in remnant eloquence of arch or Square? Córdoba is not dead. Its life is impalpable like that within an eye. Something has lived on in Córdoba. There was vision here: that quickening of the nerves to the spheres of life which we call vision. Here was an eye that saw; and it still sees despite the catalepsy of the ages. Perhaps no eye that truly sees is ever blind. Perhaps if within this cup of the Sierras there was today no Mosque, no subtle nerve of house and street, Córdoba still would be an eye; and if our sense were sharp enough to meet it, there would rise to us yet the Word of its incarnate knowledge.

The Mosque is open to a *patio* with orange trees, palms, fountains whose pallid water runs in counterpoint with the fervor of mosaic and tile. Women with their children stand about, filling their huge earth water-jars, setting them down in the shade of a palm to talk. A girl sings quiet and incessant: like the cool water over the stones her notes diverge from the hard hot day. On the medieval *Puerta del Perdón* the Christian saints and regal arms set up their theme against the Moslem mass of the Mosque. To the sides are colonnaded cloisters. But to the south under the blare of sun in the white sky is the Mosque itself. Nineteen arched gates make way into its open forest.

Hundreds of columns various like trees. They are all low: from their smooth shafts the arches of red and white rise agilely to the ceiling which once was a maze of lace-like wood, inlaid. The movement of the columns becomes horizontal. Pillars of many marbles, of jasper, of porphyry, merge in the sweeping spread. There is no Gothic aspiration. There is a maze of delicate shafts with their heads arched and arabesqued, prancing in cohorts between a dull floor and a dull roof. In the heart of this battalioned whirl, stands the Catholic Capilla Mayor which the Cathedral Chapter placed there in the sixteenth century. It is a formless embryon of gilt and marble. It replaces sixty Arabic columns and its heavy flesh rises far higher than the legion of shafts about it. It is perhaps the greatest monument in Spain of the inæsthesia of Spanish consciousness. But with the worst intentions, it has not broken the spirit of the Mosque. The dance of the pillars moves toward this obtrusion, swirls before it to the right and left, sweeps graciously beyond into the shadows. Svelte and exquisite columns with their double-arched head-dress, with their fleet ankles and shoulders— marshaled like an army—move with the undulance of earth to the *Mihrab* of Abd-er-Rahman and Al-Hakim. The Mihrab is the cynosure of prayer. Before it sits the Master to direct discourse with Allah. The Mihrabs of Córdoba are gems so bright that they make a ghostly swirl of the columns. Individual vibrancies of gem, of mosaic, of marbles frail as sea-shells, fuse into fixity. The Mihrab is the goal of the columns.

So, within Córdoba, stands and lives today the Idea of Islam. Though the Spaniards call it a Cathedral, it is still the *Mesjid al-Jâmi,* open to the fountains and the *naranjeros,* open to the skies. It is a place whose spirit in racing columns bespeaks the horizontal swarm of Islam to the ends of Spain. Islam speaks; and Córdoba, which is far more than Islam, answers. The Córdoban streets press and swerve to the north of the Mosque. They are a compact of stresses doubly held together: the Guadalquivir turning back upon itself and the rim of mountains in whose heights still live the fertile prayers of hermits, hold the streets.

Córdoban streets are not like those of Fez, of the Kasbah of Algiers, of Lisbon. Fez, within its translucent hills and vales, swarms like the entrails of a body. Algiers mounts sinister from the gleaming sea, its streets a blackened coil within the white sepulcher that strikes the sun. Old Lisbon is explosive, gyrant, tragically repressed in its march upward, losing the sky as it comes closer to it. Córdoba is proud. Its pride is intricate as the Talmud; hard and abstruse as the mystic creed of the Sufi; open as a page of Aristotle. This eye that is Córdoba is neither secret nor flinching. And its pride is not willful. Córdoba is unassertive. Its light speaks for it: Seneca the Stoic, Averroës the Commentator, Moses ben Maimun first rationalist of the Jews, Lucan, and Spain's greatest lyric poet, Luis de Góngora . . . such are the light of Córdoba. It is the home of the most perfect Arab Knight, the quiet Al-Mansor who, ruling Spain, decreed Sunday to be a day of rest in deference to the Christians.

Córdoba lies within tumultuous mountains and a lazy river. It is a poise of mountains and river. It is a kingly city within chaos; it is masculine in a feminine land. The Christian Copts brought their woman worship to Seville; the gypsies found haven in Granada for their Black Sea spells. Córdoba forbids such fascinations. It is quiet as its river, dense as its mountains, open as its mosque. The streets turn just enough to throw shade to the patios. Ox-teams survive, yet splash no mud on the immaculate walls. Here a miracle of life has overtaken the lunge and death of Islam: here grew a kingdom of balance and of peace.

For Córdoba is not the rock of Seneca, not the intellectual play of Averroës and Maimonides, not the deep current underneath of mystical devotion. Córdoba is the balance, and the contemplation, of all her parts.

The summer night is cool as wisdom; it is a poise against day like that of Seneca the Stoic against the fever of life. When the sun falls behind the roofs, the town opens as northern towns with the dawn. Day indeed is often fiery night on Córdoba. The good folk have gone to bed; houses have been swathed to keep this white night out. Now, houses are opened wide. Air from the world is permitted to come in to the shut courts where geese patter and women seat themselves at looms.

The people are dark and silent like the dusk. The sky is pale with a glow of convalescence. The houses, serried in the curving streets, are hot. The evening has a magic, it throbs and swells with tacit fervors. The whole of Córdoba is quick under the glow of night. The stone streets are flesh, willfully rigid, of a spirit possessed with the desire to dance. And in the dance are darker intimations: cries, ravage, conquest. But the slow streams of men and women are the sole expression. Are they puritans, then, these Andalusians? They wear easeful masks for faces. The women are clad in black, and their soft flesh within the shrouds seems not the flesh of lovers but of matrons. Even the girls, sinuous walking lilies, promise a snare of momentary passion: their will of men is not to be initiates of love, but to be mothers. All is easeful— the masks on the faces, the dark women's weeds. They have been worn so long! They are like the streets whose stones are mellow and whose curves and windings have the fatality of forest paths. If these be puritans, these men and women, with their heritage of war, privation, pioneering—they whose ancestry is Islam, the Cross, the promised Zion—long since has the hard fruit ripened. They are firm and condignly whole within their city whose maze of streets is whole within the mountains. . . . . . .

This evening, Córdoba, released from day, is going to the Bull-Ring. There is no moon; the bowl of the arena holds a winey night in which the stars are bubbles of effervescence. The seat tiers are deep. Men and women clamber noisily from perch to perch. But the thousand voices

and footbeats are segregate and aloof within the Ring holding this wine of the night. Upon one side, the seats have
been roped off and are empty. Below hang two electric
lamps and cast their naked glare upon a stage improvised
with unpainted planks. The stage is a little tongue thrust
into the arena.

The crowd has come and paid for a good time. But
it is self-sufficient—the strong willed, resourceful crowd
of Spain. Myriad calls and shreds of laughter, play of
hand and foot twine about the Ring: agglutinate: the
groups of clamor thicken and grow wider: the entire Ring
is joined in the enterprise of shouting, shuffling, clapping.
No Spaniards blackening the tiers, but this one sudden
Spain! It has many means of making itself live. Boys
scurry over the laps of matrons: men sing falling cadences
to girls: babies shout. The *aguero* with an earth-jar large
as himself, the vendor of *pastas* and of Arabic sweetmeats,
weave through the mass. But still the Bowl holds its
uncanny silence. The night bubbles at its brim.

On the stage step forth two figures: the lamp-glare
sharpens and deforms them. A man, stout and short,
clad in black broadcloth with a wide purple sash and linen
that is green in the electric glare: he carries a guitar. A
woman, slender and tall: her black *mantón* is like a subtle
fur over the angular brightness of her shoulders. She wears
a large *sombrero ancho*, black as the two black eyes in her
white face.

They stand within the night, within the crowd. The
man takes a chair: the woman remains isolate beside him.
The man's hands brush the strings of his guitar. The
woman's mouth opens, and her breast rises. Under the
laced clamor of the crowd she sings unheard—under the
silent night. . . . . .

A note, hard like silver, high and sharp as an arrow,
rises above the clamor and is heard. Far up, it soars,
surrounded by the stars. It falls. And as it falls, reaching
the crowd, it links itself within the vast confusion. This
rough-hewn Spain falls along with the note: is drawn by

it down to the naked stage, down to the red mouth of the singing woman. The crowd is transfigured. The woman's voice fades into rest, within an utter silence.

The hand of the guitarist is not lean: yet his fingers make a murmur like a breeze: clear in the silence is the music's breathing. The music has conquered: it is the night's silence, speaking; the night's quiet, moving. The woman's body stands rigid, her heels beat a tattoo of subtle restraining: her voice is confident and exultant.

Burden heavy with ages of flesh, bright with ages of dream. Plaint of spirit, rush of blood miraculously woven. A body in dance, rigid as a column; a voice in song, light and swift as a bird. Many Orients are here. In the form, a slender mystic draughtsmanship—Byzantine; a clamor of soul, a submissiveness of body with all its sweetness and its joys merged in the ecstasy of an ideal—Jewish; an intensive thrust, lean, fierce, hunting—Arab. Rising like revelation from the Córdoban Plaza, this Andalusian song of many wills becomes the drama of Spain.

The woman's body scarcely moves. Even as she circles the stage, her arms slowly rising and falling, her heels in periodic showers of sharp strokes, it is as if she did not move: rather the stage, rather the Ring and the crowd move than this plastic fixity of dance. Torment, passion, vision, ruthlessly compress in a thin body.

The music cadence is vertebral. There is a time counterpoint of two adverse factors: a rising lilt, a falling plaint. And they become the skeletal arabesque which is the backbone of the Spanish music. All the voices of Spain's world are laced. The Jew's sensual mysticism, conflict between his homely passions and his cosmic fate, rises in a line more Arabic than Jewish. And the tendency of the music to transcend its scale is Byzantine; it bespeaks the North African shores of Porphyry and Plotinus, of Origen and Augustine. But the stress is more barbarous than platonic. And the *form* is forever Spain. Its elements do not suffice to make this music great. It is greatly moving, because its moving parts become articulate, not in moments, not

progressively, but all at once: in restraint, in defeat—
in the triumph of the artist's will upon them.

The passion does not depart; a woman's body holds it and
we are moved not by the passion but by the unmoved
victory over passion. This cadence is a plaint of agony.
It does not bend her. This peal is pathos. The high head,
the arms crushing the breast, the torrent of heel-notes
rivet a triumph over pathos. The mouth sings languorous
desire; but the body is hard. Sudden the song flares like
a vision from that mouth. But the body circles the stage
in a crisp gayety, the eyes smile, the knees dip in courteous
bestowal.

At the other end of Córdoba, the night lives among the
columns of the Mosque. With arched head and heel of
arabesque, they dance their mystery—a forest of willful
movement under the will-less stars. This woman is a
column too; rigid, and stone-like and adance. But the
dance of the Arab columns is horizontal; it is an easeful
running with the earth. The dance of this woman which
is a dance of Spain, is deep and is high. It is not horizontal. So calm, it touches hell. So still, it reaches God.

c. The Bowels

The Spanish is the fusion of the warring elements of Spain into dramatic wholes. As the proportions of these elements change, the wholes change: and yet are Spanish. Granada, then, is the least Spanish of the towns of Spain; for, with all the elements there, they have remained disparate. Even physically, Granada does not resolve its discords. It is cast in confusion. Two steep spurs come down from the Sierra Nevada. They are divided by the gorge of the río Darro. Smaller, arid gorges break them, they expire in a plain. And within this broken sea of rock and ridge and wood, Granada sits uneasily. One height is Al-Hambra, palace of kings. From its towers the precipice cuts to the river; and in the west rises Al-Baicín, a populous suburb. North, beside the river straggles a gypsy village. And eastward, on another height, is the cascaded, terraced, tawdry splendor of the Generalife. Physically chaos; culturally, spiritually chaos.

For near five hundred years, Granada was the capital of a Moslem state. After the fall of Córdoba, it was independent. And in 1492, when Boabdil fled from Ferdinand and Isabel, there died the last political body of Spanish Islam. For close three hundred years, Granada was the richest and most populous state of Spain. Castile, Aragon, Catalonia were rustics beside it. But the barbarous states spread; and Granada had energy neither to spread nor to glow. The barbarous states had fused their differences in the terrific lust of religious conquest. Castile and León were closer then to the spirit of Mohammed than the Andalusian Town in which the muedzins called his name and the people spoke his tongue. Toledo, Valencia, Badajoz, Seville, Córdoba fell: Granada came to be the last

resort in Spain of the driven Moslems. A veritable city
state it was, going north to Baza, west to Málaga, east to
Almería. Meantime, Spain had converged into an austere
camp. Her forests became deserts, her towns were empty
of men, her women suckled warriors, her churches were
the centers of recruiting. And Granada shone with ease.
In Granada, the wide lands were gardens; husbandry was
an art. The cities sang with ceramic and jewels. The
mosques were models for the mosques of Africa.

Córdoba had been the seat of Arab Spain. Granada
was the heart of the Moor. When the Arabs were too
wasted by peace and thought and quarrel to withstand the
pressing Christians, they turned to the south whence four
hundred years before they too had come, clad only in the
harsh will of the Prophet. In the Moroccan mountains and
the deserts, dwelt still virgin tribes in whom the Idea of
Islam worked with the virulence of birth. This was the
need of Spanish Islam. So the Moors came to Spain to
do what the Arabs had done and could do no longer. The
Moors drove back the Christians. Then they turned and
subdued the Arabs. Arab Andalusia was Moorish.

(And here we must digress for definitions. . . The
greatness of Granada came with the Nazrite dynasty whose
founder, Al-Ahmar, captured the town in 1238 from the
Moorish Almohades. And Al-Ahmar, born in Córdoba,
claimed descent from the pure Yemen Arabs of Kharzrej
and Ansár. Which is important, since it displays the
dangers of speaking, biometrically, of a *race*. The family
that reigned in Moorish Granada was perhaps as Arab as
the dynasties of Córdoba and Seville! And of course, the
very first Arabs in Spain brought with them Berbers,
negroes, Copts. Why then was Córdoba Arab, and
Granada Moorish? . . . We require the names, and for
them there are reasons. The first Moslem invasion was
Arab: for its impulse, its energy, its leadership came straight
from the Arabs. And that first Moslem culture which
from Córdoba held all Spain north to Toledo, south, west,
east to the seas was also *Arab* for the identical reason. Now

come fresh leaders to defend Moslem Spain; and when they have driven back Castile they disperse the Arab masters who bade them in. These hosts come in two waves: the Almoravides—*men of religion*—are Berbers from the Senegal, and the Almohades—*men of the Unity*—are Berbers from the Atlas. It is right to call them Moors since they rose to power in Morocco. And it is right to call their dominance in Spain the Moorish epoch since, after their coming, the culture of all Moslem Spain not only differed from that of Córdoba but was deeply homogeneous within itself despite political chaos.) . . .

In the towns of Spain lived still the Spaniard with his absorption of Semite, African, Latin, German. But the difference of the Moor from the Arab was a change in his Idea and in the ways of life begotten by it. The Christian forces were vastly stronger than they had been. Their own Idea had been enhanced by Moslem contact. They were come a long ways from the invertebrate Christianity of the Visigoths. The first Moslem sweep to Biscay and the Pyrenees had planted a germ of resistance which with the ages grew to be this vital Christian body, a body stripped and ruthless as ever had been Islam. So the Moor could not, like the Arab, dismount from his saddle to invite his soul. The Moor did not become tolerant under pleasant skies. He welcomed no Jewish thinkers and statesmen, he housed no Christian convents. Under the benignity of peace he made no introverted, rational culture. When the Moor rested, it meant that he was weary; and then he invited his body. Arab refinement became voluptuousness; Arab ease became prostration. The energy of the Idea of Islam had by the Arab been transformed into a *contrasting* culture. Under the Moor it became at best a *reposing* culture. And indeed, the Idea did not change. Christian armies saw to that. But the need of Islam—to expand—could not be fulfilled. The Christian armies saw to that, as well. Here then was a warlike energy that could not spread and yet could not transform. It turned against itself. Moor fought Moor. Granada alone

held long to the appearance of a dignified state. And
the appearance was false. Moorish Granada helped the
Christian San Fernando to march against Moorish Seville,
as a century before Moorish troops had helped the Cid
win Moorish Valencia. A hundred years ere its fall,
dynastic quarrels had split Granada into a chaos of tiny
states; the Catholic Kings needed to take it piecemeal in a
series of raids on petty princes.

The Idea of Islam is no more within this lovely world.
But high and low, strewn through the summits and the
troughs of the Sierra, lives the wreckage of the Moorish
body. Across a gorge, Al-Baicín and Al-Hambra face
each other. Al-Hambra! all that may be said of the skill
of the goldsmith may be said of this Palace, with its
scores of patios and halls. It brings to mind, not other
architectures but the triumphs of the Cellinis of the Renaissance, the delicate perfections in Pompeii and in Egyptian
tombs. In minute and marvelous grace, it transcends them
all: and yet it is a building!

Within the *patio de los arrayanes* there is a pool enclosed
in myrtle as a sapphire within emerald. Overhead is the
soft pale sky. Beyond the *sala de la barca*, arched like a
ship, is the Ambassadors' Hall, its dome an incessancy of
carven woods, columns and walls so tooled that they seem
lace threaded with gems. Myriad patios on either side
are myriad surprises of wood, plaster, stone that flows with
arabesques and softens to the creaminess of linens.

Some architectures make one think of man; some make
one think of God; some, of the tragic struggle in men's
flesh between the man and the god. Al-Hambra exiles both
the earth and heaven. That a palace lacks high poetry,
movement of aspirance, is not amiss. But Al-Hambra lacks
as well the sense of being made for men to dwell in.
It is cold as a jewel and as a jewel hard. Yet unlike
other jewels, it adorns no breast and no altar. It is faëry.
Yet unlike other visions of surprise, it does not entice the
mind. It is no outward form of the old dreams. Nor is

it strong, save as some stellar gem, fallen in the mud of our world, has its impregnable strength. It is immaculate of men. It is too far from man, too far from God. It is not strong, yet it is not poetic. Poetry must pay its tribute. If it sing a blade of grass, a kingdom, a divinity—yet it must make its tribute to the world: man in giving music gives himself. Al-Hambra, for all its matchless grace, is incarnate of no warmth, no joy, no agony, no love. . . It is a jeweled monster; a sort of dissociate birth of human will. Although its tints are magic, its curves delicate as a woman's mouth, its forms courteous, and its stuffs transfigurations of the elements into the radiance of silk and the sweetness of wool, yet it is but a fragment. Its rapture parts not from itself. It is Narcissus. It is a *Golem* of the Moors.

The rock of Al-Hambra falls into the river and on the farther side rises Al-Baicín, antiphony of Al-Hambra.

In the days of the first Nazrites, here was a place of noble mansions. But when the Moslems, exiled from conquered towns, poured into Granada, Al-Baicín became what it is now—a swarming city. This is as near to the Kasbah of Algiers, to the dense Attarine of Fez as you may come in Spain. The town is a lay of alleys maggoting up the breast of the Sierra. The throngs are dark, aburst with energy. Eyes are gentle and give forth no light. Faces are locked as if in obscure struggle of themselves. This folk is neither gay nor sad, savage nor kind. It partakes of the ineffable nature of the houses. What it is, what it has to say—as with the houses—is detached from the hour, is a minglement of nostalgia and obsession. An incommunicable town, knowing no tongue save an archaic one: its houses speak not to us but to their own old shadows.

A patio stable with its mangy mules, a gigantic oven where bread in memorial Moorish shapes is thrust at the end of a pole . . such are the words of the streets. Beneath the language which the people speak, this rhythmic word of the streets.

Al-Baicín has a soul. What Al-Baicín lacks is body! Groveling life within an ancient molder of walls, patios, wine shops black as warts—this life so halted, so disgraced, so blind is life that lacks a body. And there, polished clean of the clamors of the spirit, shines the body on the opposite hill—soulless Al-Hambra.

d. *A Goddess and Don Juan*

The air is spiced with murmur, throat call, peal, with stirring of feet, clink of earth-jar; it is a weave through which the horse's hoof, flick of whip, *ar-r-ra* and *shuh* of driver make a swathe. Singing cry of a girl, crying song of a girl cascade to church bells. . . Silence. . . A little square (Castilians say *patio*, Andalusians say *compás*) holds an alicatado fountain: thin water within a sapphire bowl wavers, splinters, fades like stars at a dawn. All about, the wings of a vast Church. Fortress-like they rise, rise in terrace, in forest of sculpture, in buttresses that sweep out of sight. And straight above, a tower. It is the old prayer tower of a mosque—*al-minar*: the muedzin post which the Christians call Giralda.

In the compas, it is cool; high overhead within the well of the walls, the heat of afternoon is writhing. Heat cannot pierce the eight foot walls of the tower. A pavement, so gradual and wide that a coach could follow it, climbs to the peak. There are windows to tell how you climb. The Cathedral, resonant with statues; the stucco palace of the Bishop beside a compas sleepy and cool like a virgin at dawn; a slant of street with houses dodging sun. . . Cathedral roof, a groined and columned symphony with transepts trilling in overtones away; a knot of buttresses that scale a higher wall you could not guess was there; a grove of turrets against the town, green trees; a line of river; town itself keen in the gyrant air . . guitar-like music under the voice of the sun. A scarf of hill, treeless and red. A court within the sapphire day like rubies and emeralds—the *patio de los naranjos*—a frame of creamy walls holding the rows of orange trees. The top of Giralda.

Seville: No, this body is Isbilíya. Town of the Visigoths, the Yemen Arabs and the Copts, alcázar of the Moorish Yusuf who built Giralda, town whence Ferdinand of Castile with the aid of his friend the Moslem of Granada drove countless Moslems in 1248, bringing in other men who said Christ, not Allah—said it in the same Mosque rechristened, in the same town, under the same sun, from the same Giralda.

The repeopling, the christening could not avail against the might of this past. Christ dimmed again; Our Lady grew. Our Lady who was Isis ere she was Mary: consort of Osiris, Horus, Khem, ere she sat with Jesus. And in her hand, through Seville, through Andalusia, a lily that does not grow in Spain but grows indeed on the Nile . . lily or lotus or more simply still *la flor* in all heraldry, all holy craft of the land. For Islam had passed to Egypt and won the Christian Copts who were in heresy for that they adored a living Trinity and had no Christ on the Cross, a trinity older than the Pyramids with the new Christian names. And now, for an age, their trinity disappeared. But Our Lady became Fatima, daughter of the Prophet and virgin although she bore miraculous sons. And Arab and Copt march on to Spain. And the Christian saint comes south. And the mosque of Seville is again the church of Our Lady. And from Seville to Rome goes the first urgency to make a dogma of the Immaculate Conception. . . . . .

The town is so very thick with houses, where are the streets? Those sharp cracks weaving through the roofs are streets? The roofs are live, bewildering planes. White flat roofs under dominant chimneys. Roofs that run with their walls. Roofs that are clusters of rush. Roofs that are little gardens for goats and chickens. Roofs that are vineyards. Roofs that are nurseries. Roofs that are streets on which stand huts of turf. In a court, is a palm; its round head sends green star-rays to the sky.

The town is so very wide; solid it rings you. The breaks are breathings for a palm, or a wide wall with crenellated top or a tiled dome like a jewel in the breast of Seville. Thick town . . intricate, turning roofs. Until the sudden stop! Seville does not linger. There is thick town, then huerta. Country gardens are perfumed brasiers. A wandering ribbon of low trees marks the sleepy river creeping down to the copper wall of sunset. . .

It is cool now. They have drawn to the roof tops the canopies that shield the streets. Now let you go down into Seville.

Varying weathers fall upon Seville. In summer days, she smiles resilient and cool within a fire that shrivels the river. In winter, under a slatey sky with her streets drenched, she is smiling still. Weather and invasions come upon Seville; she masters them all.

She is an Eastern goddess unknown of the Greeks, whose cult is sung with cymbals and in blood. She is no Semite; she is the antistrophe in this, as in all things, of her great brother of the north: Toledo. Within the huddle of her streets, lives clarity; within her sudden and esconded curves, glows coolness. She is immeasurably far from the hot Jew and Arab. Seville is Pagan. But her pagan spirit is uniquely hers. It is not dark and carnal like the Sumerian; not analytic, open-eyed like the Greek; it lacks the Italic will. Nor is it Berber. This spirit has a spirit; the Giralda. To see Giralda from the town is to see both the tower and Seville. Everywhere al-minar follows. It is cool in the sun; in the damp of winter it is gleam. On the river's margin where vessels coal, it is a yesterday when ships had sails. Its simple face is strength above the prone complexity of life. Variant, it is constant, sovereignly self-contained. It mirrors men's perceptions, who can see of it at each moment but a flash of time. It stands for Seville whose traits and deeds are facets of a Crystal.

This fixity, this intricate appearance within fixity is the deep trait of Seville. Her genius, her emotions, her religion are in fixity for they are held unwavering to herself. She looks not at Spain nor the world. Not like Venus does

this goddess walk and give herself to men. Not like
Astarte, thirst for the blood of others. Not like Isis is she
concerned with the cycles of sun and planet. Seville loves
only herself; and the moon and stars are brilliants for
her hair.

The narcism of Seville is fecund. The gorgeous litany
of the Semana Santa is but the most famous of her arts.
Religion is but the most obvious pretext of her self-worship.
Seville abounds in dramas and in altars of her self-delight.
Wander through her streets, commune with her churches
and cafés, watch her ample daughters dance to the splendor
of their own high breasts; read the legends—Don Juan,
La Macarena. An hour will come, perhaps at dusk in the
park along the river, when she will tell her secret:

"The Guadalquivir is my scarf of saffron; the
orange blossoms sing the chant of my flesh; the sky is
a mantón of rose and purple on my white shoulders.
Church and God, love, blood and death are castanets!
I am Real. I am the dancer. I am Isbilíya."

Sierpes, chief street of the town, is a bit of a way
with a crick in its middle: too narrow for horses and
mules: the lines of shops and clubs face each other across
a slender sidewalk. When the good weather comes the
doors open; the clubs and cafés pile chairs pell-mell upon
the street. And Seville sits down and looks at herself.
Drinks coffee, Manzanilla wine, and looks at herself. Eats
mariscos and looks some more at herself. Athwart the
Sierpes, other streets are a maze of tiny shops: shops small
and delicate like toys, shops secret and uncommercial like
the good Majas [1] who keep them, shops with too deep
modesty to display their wares and too little will to have
much wares to display. Reticent, charming shops like

---

[1] The native women of Seville.

the hearts of simple folk, so full they are of warm darkness. In such a passage, crammed with stores (for these central streets are merely passages), in the very heart of a world of dolls, lottery tickets, pastries, newspapers, umbrellas, fans and pipes, is a Chapel. It is open to the street and it reveals within a long recess its garish bower of candles. The throng crowds by. Dark clad, the women; drab, the men with wide stiff hats and a clank to their high heels. They talk of little things; eyes hold to the unconscious rhythm of the throng. And as they pass, they shift their talk an instant into prayer; or they make the sign of the cross; or they kneel. So Seville prays to herself.

In the Parish church of San Gil, there is the figure of a woman. Is it some crude artisan's idea of a prosperous Maja? The dress is modern on La Macarena—idol of Our Lady. And La Macarena is the most vaunted, the most puissant goddess in Seville. At Semana Santa, in her garish dress, she parades the town. The Majas of Seville throw themselves before her; and sing; and pray. And as the Doll, who is both Mary and Maja, moves through Seville, the streets are paved with the breasts of the Sevillanas, loving their own image.

The Gardens of Alcázar are a geometric maze of tiny verdant patios. Each stands at its own level, a gradual step lowering with the flow of water. Each is a little bower with tiled floor, an intimate garden holding to its charm in the great sum of gardens. The patios make a mosaic. The design is severe; it is a heritage of the analytic Moslems. But in Seville, the mathematic form is snared into an idyll.

Hundreds of churches in Seville. Many of them are bleak rococo monsters and their interiors gross piles of gilt and scarlet. They are not bad taste in Seville. Murillo is not bad taste in Seville. They are parts of a ceremonial. Seville's love is great enough to hold and to transform them. So, in the compas of the Convento de Santa Paula, a noble Gothic portal stands with a palm tree; so the rococo dome of Santa Catalina blazes to ceramic; so the

Plaza Santa Cruz becomes a faëry quarter, its rows of ancient houses painted like the flowers and the birds that hang from the low casements; so, even the Casa de las Dueñas, home of the bloody Dukes of Alba, winds behind its iron gates into quaint patios and palms and archways.

Each street has its garland of self-praise. A color of façade, a jewel of ceramic, a tiny unsuspected court elbowed between the blank backs of two houses, from which oak doors lead into other courts—communities of painters, artisans, teachers of the dance. And each season has its pretext for self-song. The Semana Santa and the Feria are the most famous rites: in Holy Week, the spirit of Seville meets Seville's body in orgasmic climax. But other seasons have not less typical embraces. The Velada de San Pedro comes in summer. There are no foreigners and the rich townsfolk are north in the Basque country. Night follows a day's fever. And now the people open their doors, throw wide their canopies and go into Seville. The servants carry great hampers of *fiambres*: cold sea food, mostly, with jars of Jérez and Manzanilla. They proceed to the popular squares, Alameda de Hiércules, Plaza de León, Plaza Encarnación, near the Mercado where with cool night comes the stir of odors . . . greens, fruits, cheeses. They spread themselves, the good folk: they eat and play.

La Plaza de San Juan Bautista de la Palma is not as large as it sounds. A dozen families fill it: it is a pretty stage for the Sevillan drama. Overhead are the crisp stars. The houses, painted cream, blue, pink, fade in unlighted shadow. In the center is a pavilion cut into tiny booths for *churros, pasteles, bombones, patas, mariscos, bocadillos, fiambres, vinos, cervezas, gaseosas*—myriad tidbits *de media noche*. Nearby sit three men and a woman. They play the guitar, the mandolin, the fiddle; and the woman sings. She wears a buff shawl that is caught tight over one shoulder and tighter still under the other armpit. Rondures of breast and stomach press the lashed silk. She is a *gitana:* she comes of an immodest race, but ere she goes among the crowd for coppers she will place a black shawl over the revealing buff one. Each of a dozen groups has its place in the Square. They eat, drink, dance and court within their private precinct. They are as unconcerned as if they were in their own private compas. But their gayety is richer; this open sharing of a public place is the sharing of a rite.

You have seen a young girl in some peasant road step *endimanchée* from her house to the sun. The velvet bosom of her bodice rises. A jewel at her neck, a ring on a finger, an eye gleam brighter than the jewel make of her a song that runs with the Spring sun and the grass. You know that the peasant girl loves and is loved. Love has wrought this miracle on her flesh. And so, in Seville: the miracle of her streets is the same alchemy. She is adance with the magic of fondness; she is gay in a perpetual Spring of self-delight.

Near the Guadalquivir and not far from the Torre de Oro, a dodecagonal relic of the Moors who built their castle on the waterfront, there is a baroque structure. It is the *Hospital de la Caridad*. In the seventeenth century Don Miguel de Mañara was a caballero in Seville; a knight so dissolute that legend makes him the Burlador, the true Don Juan. This the nuns of the Caridad deny. But the day came when the Lord miraculously spared his life from the assault of a noble seeking to avenge the honor of his sister. Don Miguel avowed the will of God and his sins; and caused to be built this Charity as witness, through perpetual good works, of his atonement.

Above the chapel there is a chaste stone hall; a stair, spreading from above like the train of a regal robe, leads to the carved door of the Consistory. Here hangs the portrait of Don Miguel de Mañara. The face is darkly sensual and brooding. The chin is obtrusive, the eyes have the rigidity of a madman's. He sits at a table, and behind him in the room there opens a fantastic landscape. It is radiant and nubilous, a landscape of vapors rather than of earth. And on the floor beside the table and at Don Miguel's feet, squats a boy and looks at him and smiles. Pedro Salinas, the poet, has a theory about this portrait. Don Miguel is mad, says he: the landscape, so amazingly like the "spirit paintings" of our day, is his vision of madness. The boy is the sane boy—the Sancho Panza—laughing at the madman.

Whatever the painter meant, whatever the historical connection of Don Miguel with the legended Don Juan, here at least is his true interpretation. Don Juan is the most conspicuous symbol of Seville. Since Tirso de Molina in the seventeenth century made a play from the old ballad and folklore sources of Don Juan, poets and playwrights of many lands have retold his story.[1] The modern mood has freshened him again with new psychology into a modish legend. But it is futile to approach Don Juan save through the spirit of his town. The Don Juan of Tirso, the first, remains the greatest. For Tirso placed his hero in the proper setting. Tirso was no analyst, but he was a poet . . a great dramatic poet. And his plastic presentation needs no analysis to reach the truth.

Seville—auto-erotic, self-rapt goddess—has a god. Her streets, her churches, her festivals bring you her lord. Don Juan is not the full-grown lover. The true lover dwells within the spirit and body of his woman as within a world holding heaven but earth too and hell: and he enfeoffed to them all for that they all are the true world which he loves. The true lover is constant; he has seen his woman so deep that he has found infinitude within her; and how could he desire to transcend it? What holds him to her is not pleasure: pleasure is but a moment in this eternity of love. Anguish, anger, the black shades of disappointment are also in his woman and he accepts them also. The true lover is rare, rarer than genius. But Don Juan is

---

[1] Italian imitations of Tirso were innumerable. Doubtless through them Molière took his turn. Mozart, Byron, Zorrilla followed. Among the moderns who have rewritten him is Rostand. Tirso's real name is Gabriel Téllez (1571?-1648).

one who loves in woman his own senses, his own victory, and seeking ever these fleet constants of himself moves ever on from breast to breast. The true lover is rare because the full-grown man is rare. Don Juan is common because infancy is common: the state of seeking only oneself, of taking life as a flowered highway along which appetite and ease run gayly in pursuit of their own image.

Like his mother Seville, Don Juan is restlessly pagan, hunting in countless dramatic scenes a tribute to self-adoration. Each woman is a mirror to himself; love of each woman is a pageant in which he enacts his triumph. When the glance has been enjoyed, what is the mirror for? When the pageant is past, what are its faded garlands? The real is Don Juan! That he may be forever fresh, that his triumph may be forever clear, undulled by custom, there must be new mirrors, new pageants—new women.

Under Don Juan's lyric words, there is coldness; under his exploits, there is abstraction. His passion is but the spark, ere it has kindled life and made life passion. And his deeds are fantasies, for only he is real and the women whom he meets he never knows, knowing only his desire. Therefore, his deeds like the landscape in the portrait of Mañara are abstract.

All the elements of Don Juan are in Seville. But Seville is greater than her son. His worship of himself in the white bodies of women is true Seville. The constant shift of his deeds, like facets in the crystal of desire, is true Seville. His orgiastic use of blood, of mysticisms, his encounters with statues, necrophiles and ghosts—are Seville of the Semana Santa. His ultimate sinking into the peace of self-absorption is Seville. But the town is ampler, deeper. Don Juan conquers only women. Seville conquers Spain.

This is her ultimate secret. She too—like Córdoba, Toledo, Greco, Cervantes—is a living whole fused from the hostile elements of Spain. But the peculiar chemic proportion of Seville makes all these worlds and wealths the single gesture and the rite of her self-adoration.

She is the pagan goddess, ample limbed, with hair in which brood darkness and the laugh of the sun. She leans over her Giralda. She stirs her head and her arms in a half somnolent, half ecstasied dance, seeking her own image in the water. . . . .

e. The Gypsies Dance

Below Al-Baicín the bodiless soul and Al-Hambra the soulless body, there is a gypsy town. The sparse waters of the Darro run at the level of the road. And on its other side the land mounts like a wall. Here, under the hill are caves, the dwellings of *gitanos*.

Heavy women, their bare arms clinking with metal and stone ornaments, their breasts slung in crass colors, call out for gain. The eyes are shallow and sly; the mouth that smiles is like the straining of an unsmiling substance; the oily hair throws off the glance of the sun. Men are rigid and yet slender; they lack the easy harshness of the women. Their bodies have melancholy and fatigue; as if an endless joust of appetite and song had worn them.

The cave becomes, inside, an ample room, narrow, cool, long. Walls are white plaster. Floors are fine-beaten clay. Chairs, tables, lamps, make this modern ease fantastic against the crude stone mouth of a cave within a hill. Men take tambours and sing; women dance.

It is a cave of storms. The blasts of many roads, the seas and forests of untempered passions shriek in this music. Tambour, castanet, foot stamp, hand-clap, raise the world in a maelstrom. And the Spanish cadence gleams like a strip of sun upon the barbarous clouds.

The *gitano* music is impure, and heavy. It has crude curves and broken surfaces. Its timbre is inexact, its form aimless. "Time" is the best of it as if this race had its true ritual in the beat of feet upon the endless highway. Time becomes a hurrying *crescendo* that splits, turns back, gallops against itself so that it never really moves. The women have an easy grace upon the easy floor. Full bodies swing and swerve in a sensuous complacence. They step to the singing men. And the song of the men swirls like a colored smoke about their hair, about the eyes of the women.

Foot-beat under song ribs it, volumes it, controls its wild delight: holds the *gitanos* together: is their soul. But this softness and spirit of the music is within; it speaks soothing to the *gitanos*, making their faces good. The outside of the music is coarse and motley. We . . all the world . . know but the wrong side of the weave.

f. Spain Dances

Andalusia is the youngest part of Spain. Its land came last from the receding waters; its Christian culture came last from the receding Islam. Its tongue is the youngest of the many forms of Spanish. Galician, Valencian, Catalan, were sister languages of the Castilian: like the dominant form, they sprang from the medieval Latin and for long were rivals. Andalusian stems, not from the mother tongue, but from the Castilian. It is of a later generation. Immigrants from the north gave birth to the fluid, fresh speech which is still heard from Almería to Cádiz. For in the days when writers like Rojas were consecrating Castilian prose, much of Andalusia still spoke Arabic.

There is a reason therefore for the vigor of this land. The cells that make the newborn body are old as the world. Youth inheres in the fresh fusing. In new environment and combination, they are renewed. So Andalusia, ancient of parts, has this organic youth. In this birth, the great factor is Castile. Castile came down with its fanatic will to make Spain one—to make Spain a theodicy in Christ. Castile turned Moor and Jew into the sea: and replenished the fields with farmers from the north. Coming down to make this youngest Spain, Castile caught the rejuvenation.

The body of Andalusia is bright with morning. The ancient capitals reflect this dawn. But the small town is its best image. Villages in Andalusia are gems of white and orange on the green breast of the huerta. Men and women live in a mirage of which their houses are the crystal setting. They seem to know that any day their Saint (or Our Lady) will lift them into heaven. (These villages would fit well into heaven.) They live—and their stone world lives—in an expectant mood. Life becomes a symbol and a pageant. Passion is the breath of a prayer; blood is the paint of a picture. The *pueblo* entire is platform for the Dance.

. . . .

Far worlds bespeak us, before the dancer herself. The music plays; and in the distance, the click of castanets. These castanets are gypsy; they came to Spain from regions of the Black Sea. The dancer walks quietly forward, playing an obbligato with her castanets, not to the music (she has not been married to the music), but to the march of her feet, to the swing of her hips. She wears a yellow silk mantón: a mantón de Manilla that went from China to the Philippines and thence to Spain to become the Andalusian shawl. The *bailarina* bows and listens to the music. In her hair, like the crest of a mythic bird, stands a *peina* of tortoise shell. Most Andalusian—this arrogant Gothic comb. She hears a cadence—Andalusian too— whose strain is of the Jews and Arabs. Her body is still; the torso faintly turns and the arms wind upward to her head. There is no mistaking this rigorous control. She has answered Semitic song with a gesture of Castile!

Her dance begins as this response, almost this opposition to the music. Sinew of the north confronts the fluid south. Two dominant forms embrace in warfare: a music, limned like prayer, rhythmed like heartbeat, and this fierce coldness on a woman's body, which is the Word of Castile. The dancer is a column, articulate of spirit: a live plasticity: with the moods of eye and waving hand flung like a largess to our sense.

There is a pause. The two dominants of the dance (the north and the south) fall momently apart and reveal a third. It is the personality of the dancer herself. She is woman: very woman. She is large, almost heavy. Her arms are full rounded; her head is poised; her bare shoulders are a magnificent molding of firm flesh. From the waist, the skirt thrusts almost at right angles. It is a cascade of gold down to the ankles; and as the dancer whirls it flares out wide, revealing the gray stockinged legs which are a minor almost girlish note within the sumptuous dress. Her feet stamp; the skirt flows; the torso, lashed in purple, stands heroically still, its silence an articulation not alone of the tempest within but of the will to subdue it. The arms float languidly to the head. The castanets click their dry commentary. Purring, shrilling, silent, they are a gloss subtle as Talmud page, as Arabesque, upon this whirl of sculpted fire which is the dance of Spain.

The castanet came, probably, with the gypsy from the ruined culture of Byzance. It was known to the Greeks and Romans. In the hands of the *gitana*, it is—as perhaps it was in the Dionysian rites—a heightened bloodbeat to the music: simple, single dimensioned, metronomic. Here it is an instrument subtle as a voice. It is a running, rhyming prose. Like the arabesque—a decoration evolved from the written language—it retains an intellectual power. The line and music of the castanets are apart from the dance. While the arms flow like birds wheeling, while the body becomes a throat of song, here is analysis forever present.

The action in the dance is drama. The bailarina moves in a tiny square. She draws intensity from subtle signals of torso, shoulder, limb, hand: this intensity she transposes to an undulous swing carrying her now far about the platform. She is horizontal and relaxed. She turns her naked shoulders forward; the castanets click almost silently beside her hips that roll in a slow ruminance. She faces about; her caress comes full and forward. The music tears with its down cadence against this mellow mother. Plaint and passion weave a subtle net that draws her forward (the castanets are still). Suddenly, she is held in rigor. The fertile mother of the south is sacrificed to the harsh north. The gorgeous breast, the hips, the arms like songs of love, are tortured in a vise of passionate control. She is the drama of women giving up their sons to the Reconquest, giving the man of their marriage bed to battle with the Moor. . . But the mood does not last. Cas-

tanets trip lightly. She dances fluidly, widely; her heels
strike high; her golden skirt rises and frees her legs. The
castanets are become as the chatter of children. From the
new relaxation of delight wells more energy, and comes
again the tragic transformation. With the emotion, rises
the ruthless will locking at last this pleasaunce in its hostile
grip. The music is now a battle. Song, body, castanets
fuse in the war of passion and will, of nature and of
reason breaking on each other. And above this symphony,
the dancer's face is silence.

So do all the motions of this drama converge into a
plastic movelessness. The dance itself is not drama; is
less kin to the dances of Europe than to the sculpture of
Egypt. One thinks of the stones of the Nile in whose un-
subtle substance live flame and intricate vision. One thinks
of the Maya reliefs of Yucatan whose myriad planes twine
to harmonious flatness.

Since the dance is a true classic art, the need of personal
genius to express it is reduced. The true genius here is
the tradition. Spain dances. Unlike the other dances of
modern Europe, the dance of Andalusia is a norm: and the
true dancer is a normal woman.

The good bailarina conforms strictly to the type of
the good *andaluza*. She is handsomely stout, with broad
pelvis, full-developed breast, strong, regular features. She
lacks sensual erethism. She is indeed the matron, rather
than the prostitute. And the matron is fitted for the classic
dance, precisely because of its normality, because it has been
purged of the romantic, the brilliant, the superficially sensual—the accidental. A "romantic" Andalusian dance is
nonsense.[1]

The classic bailarina is, then, a quiet woman. Her
body is splendid without obvious incitements. Her cos-

[1] The desire to conform with foreign notions has produced a
Spanish export in which the true genius of the Spanish dance is lost.
To see Seville or Córdoba, you must go to Andalusia. To see the
Andalusian dance, you must do likewise.

tume is lovely in form and color, but it is too heavy and too complete to be sexually arousing. She conforms to an ideal of plastic motion in which all the romantic elements of the dance—lust, madness, nakedness—are sublimated into social symbols: love, prayer, vision, sacrifice. And all her movements (again unlike the dances of Europe) merge into an almost static mold that has the ultimate finality of sculpture.

The true Andalusian dance is solitary; and except in the special case of the *cuadro flamenco* it is an æsthetic error for more than a single dancer to occupy the stage. The true Andalusian dancer (with the same exception) is a *woman*. The true Andalusian audience is a *man*. The relation, however, is not sexual, save perhaps in a remote Freudian sense: it is matriarchal. And this too is normal, since psychologically, Spain is matriarchal. The dancer is mother, teacher, priestess. She holds the stage alone, and smiles on the men who sit beyond the music. This smile is a physical caress, reticent, unconsciously restrained like the caress of a mother. It must win her men, else her ultimate word as teacher and as priestess of Spain's mystery will go for naught. The men, with the brutal candor of the Spaniard (and of the child) will turn from her and make a clamor of talk to drown her out. But the true *andaluza* wins her men; and gives her message which is the message of all Spain and Spain herself: this quickened fusion of many hostile worlds into a single Beauty.

. . . .

The cuadro flamenco is a brilliant dilution of the Andalusian dance. *Flamenco* means Flemish, and is applied strictly to Andalusia. The use harks back to the age of Carlos I and Felipe II when Flanders was part of the Theodicy of Spain and the best will of Castile and the best blood of the south went into the wars with the Low Countries. It became Andalusia's pride to share in this mad religious struggle.[1]

[1] Of the many explanations for this strange use of *flamenco,* that of Federico de Onís strikes me as plausible. He believes that *flamenco*

The *cuadro* is a "team" of perhaps two men guitarists, four women and one man dancer. The men are clad in trousers that rise like cylinders to a high black band above the waist. They wear white shirts and the coat (which is often absent) is cut in the front like our evening dress, and tailless. The women are soberly gowned. The shawl is brown or black. Only the slippers give a flare of red. The hat is the stiff *sombrero ancho* of the farmer whose more romantic, more flexible offshoot is our "cowboy Stetson." The group sit in a half circle. The guitars thrum almost absently. The men and women seem to be examining one another. A woman rises and goes to the center of the group. She dances. The other women and the single man from their chairs with clapping of hand and foot-beat mark a skeletal obbligato.

To the more pigmented music and more volumnear forms of the other Andalusian dances, this dance bears the relation of a steel-engraving to an oil painting. It is a climax of the bare Castilian *motif*: the warrior will of the Reconquest which lived on, after the Moor had disappeared from Spain, in the Inquisition, in the Holy War against the Dutch, in the rapt butcheries of Mexico and Peru—in this flamenco. The dance makes saccade angles against the lush weave of the music. It is too graphic, too linear: it remains in the realm of draughtsmanship and drama.

The dancer does not move from her central square. Feet beat intricate tattoos, the body is poised stiffly, the head turns, arms swerve up and down in a sort of wistful memory of ease, while the fingers click an osseous pointillation that is a shadow of the castanets. The lyrical release of the arms is held to the verge of vanishment. The guitars make a music like dry wind in autumn trees. The maternal verdure of the women, fixed in their chairs, is

was first applied to the dress of Flemish courtiers of Carlos I. Nobles of Spain imitated these styles; the people of Andalusia finally adopted them, and so at last *flamenco* was applied to the song and dance accompanying a style.

sacrificed wholly to the stripped will of the dance. One thinks of fields turned into the desert of Castile. The fertile and the pagan are almost gone. And the protagonist of the flamenco is a man.

He comes from his chair only after each woman has danced and has retired. He is short, neither stout nor slender; there is no gallantry about him. His face and his dark body are stamped with seriousness. He has watched the women through their arid figures with eyes like the eyes of a master. He is no lover: he is the priest of a rite. Now, he stands moveless within the weave of the music. Sudden, his feet break in a shattering tattoo from which his body rises in subtle suppressed waves. Even the lyric holiday of the arms is absent from his dance. They are still at his side, or they are held in fixity near the shoulder. The body is vised; the head does not swerve. Feet and legs make a dance, perpendicular and juiceless: bereft of rhetoric and gesture, they bespeak the hoof-beat of armies, the vigils of the desert, the absolute symbol of the Arab Darwish. All of Spain that is not this male message of Castile has been crushed out. . . .

The distinction of flamenco is only of degree. The Andalusian dance is impersonal and abstract. All the movements of the soul and body of an intricate race are essenced here into a ruthless form. The appolonian is channeled; the dionysian is mastered; the dramatic is cleansed of episode; the lyrical is exploited as a mere carrier of life to sculptured unity.

The Andalusian dance is the converse of the art of the Russian ballet in which the pure materials of plastic movement are exteriorized and denatured into the melodramatic. In the Russian dance, the means is the art; the end is the personal, the pathetic. The Russian dance is analytic, episodic, realistic. The Spanish dance is organic and essential. It is the one great classic dance surviving in our modern world.

CHAPTER IV

ARAGON

a. The Atom
b. The Way of the Atom

a. The Atom

From the Mediterranean to the Atlantic, the north boundary of Spain is mountain. To the east it is called the Pyrenees: a wall of snowy rock that falls, save for a space above the fertile fields of Catalonia, into the desert of Aragon and Navarre. Westward, the wall is lower and has another name: Cantábrico. It too is wild, but the more moderate moisture covers it with pine and its fall southward is but a step to the high meseta of León and Castile. Within this barrier that like a jagged knife cuts Spain from Europe lived the Christian Remnant before the Arabs. And from two fastnesses of this wall—where the Arabs never gained a foothold—went forth at once the *Reconquista* which for eight hundred years, thrusting, expanding, retreating, made war upon the Moslem and at last after innumerable shifts of fortune drove him out. The western point of the Reconquest's birth lies in the perpendicular rocks of the Asturias. This is the cradle of the Kingdom of León, which, thrusting from the Cantábrico, became Castile. To the east, the nucleus of the long "push" south was in the bleakest and highest Pyrenees of Spain: the Ribagorza and Sobrarbe whose hard squat Iberian chieftains were the first kings of Aragon. Not till the last decades of the fifteenth century, at the end of the long battle, did the two Christian forces join and become Spain. During seven hundred years, they had waged war against Mohammed; they had grown great in Spain; they had flung their power northward across the mountains, eastward across the sea to Italy and Greece: but they had lived—Castile and Aragon—separate from each other and for the most part hostile.

Within the Pyrenees—the stratified chaos north of

Huesca and Barbastro—the atom of Aragon lives above the splendor it has given forth. Here, if anywhere, is the aboriginal Spaniard—unchanged as his mountains. The Iberians who were pushed north from the desert or south from Acquitaine into the Sobrarbe and the Ribagorza found themselves in a sort of Continental crow's-nest, high above invasion. The Romans did not tarry here, nor the Visigoths. The Arabs were beaten back, south of Jaca, and had to veer to the east to enter France. For countless ages, these primeval men beside the river Aragon lived uninvaded, until their atomic energy grew to be explosive and they became invaders.

But they are still the atom. They live in the crannies of mountains, in the steep stretches of valleys torn by torrents. The sky above them is shut in by rock. Northward the Pyrenees stand ordered and columned upon France. But in their southward march they become a delirium of broken walls. They symbolize the cacophony of Spain. The little villages perch on a precipitous bench of mountain or are lost within the immense sweep of a moor. They too are stone. The houses are gathered fragments of the heights. Often there is no wooden door. Windows are tiny apertures of space. The houses huddle so close that they appear to be a single rock, whence rise the blind walls of the church—fortress rather than church —like an irregular edge. Another such obtrusion seems the entire village upon the high face of the mountains. If it is low in a valley, still the monotone is there. For the moor is gray and mournful like a stone; and the furze of summer makes it but faintly fluid as if from the blaze of the sun. The rushing river sends splinters of gray fume over the teeth of its rapids. Stone. . . . .

From these stone towns come the creatures who have built them. Small weazened men they are, with heads like nuts and eyes like iron. They have no sensuality and no art. Indeed, they too are fragments of the fragmented mountains: atoms of rock who have detached themselves and learned to walk about. They are silent, impenetrable.

They have the mineral virtues. They are strong, they are steadfast, they are inexpugnably honest, they are brave. To dislodge them from the inertia of their world is as hard as to lodge an idea in their heads. And as they walk about, their slow and clumsy gait perfects the sense that they are walking stones: that this human venture is a masquerade: that presently they will cast their uncouth manhood and go back into the eternal mountain sleep.

They wear black leathern breeches slashed at the side and ending well above the knee. In the split at the side and below, the drawers bulge white or gray. The calf is enclosed in heavy leggings of white wool, doubly lined with buttons. The feet are wrapped in a cloth and shod in a sole of wood or wool that is thonged with leather, and bound about the ankle. About the waist is a huge sash—*faja*—coming down thick on the buttocks and serving as the pocket. The jacket is short. The aboriginal Aragonese wears no hat: a handkerchief slanted athwart his head absorbs the sweat of his labor and leaves the cropped crown free. When he wears a hat, it is an adaptation either of the *boina* of the Basque or a lumpish variant of the pie-shaped hat of Castile. His invention has not gone so high as his head.

The effect of the costume is farce. It is elaborate, intricate, unmanly. The bulging drawers, the sash so fat about the buttocks exaggerate the shortness of the body. The man is lean, hard, small. And he drapes himself in clothes that are centrifugal and fussy. The sense of masquerade persists. This man is a stone—an atom of the horizons. With his assumption of a soul, his body has felt cold and he has elaborated this uncongenial mess of wool and leather. His head, however, is still too mineral to need a hat.

His woman is not stone: rather she is the clayish soil that with the stone makes up the slopes and moorlands. She is the earth—dark brown and gray—from which the stone is hardened. She is the earth, the earth-bed of her man. She is silent: when she is young, she has the savage and swift mellowness of the mountain Springtime. Her dress is black. On feast days, the black becomes vermilion, deep blue, green. The thick, rough wool, dyed to one color, falls from below the armpits where it is caught in a tight bodice: falls widely, unheeding the waist, into a flaring skirt. It is a dress that has the dignity of the primeval Springs: its mood is fecund; it is not human enough to be aware of waist, of hips, of breast. Unluxuriant, unvaried, it has the bloom of wholeness. The women of these mountains are the loam on the wastes.

Here is a better model for Adam and Eve, than the pretty Italians, the mystic lovely Byzantines: this rudimentary pair, the man decking his stone simplicity in a clownish gape of drawers and breeches, and the woman, earth-mooded, earth-whole, chording her man and bearing him along.

They have left paradise, and now the world works on them. Christianity has come. They build monasteries —mountain fortresses for God. Strife has come: invasion or threat of invasion. And for these, chieftains, nobles have sprung up who are no longer content to shelter in the little villages of stone. Walled towns make their appearance: such towns as Jaca, pure Iberian name and indeed but a medieval structure for the Iberian blood. Jaca looks up the valley of the Aragon toward France. It sees the primordial hamlets clustered in the moors and on the heights. But Jaca itself crowds sophistications within its turreted walls. The walls themselves are the same gray granite and the streets, narrow and high, are stylizations of the passes northward. But Jaca belongs to history. These houses know of treaties and rebellions. Life has moved into Sobrarbe: now Sobrarbe moves. The mountain citadel is the sign of its moving. It will go south to the valley of the Ebro. It will flow with the Ebro and be part of Spain. It will challenge the world. . . .

The valley of the Ebro—Nile of Spain and historic artery of all her bloods—is still below. The way from Jaca down is short but steep. The wall of the Pyrenees, in a few miles, drops seven thousand feet: but drops, not as northward upon smiling France—drops to desolation. Aragon which began as mountain wall becomes a yellow waste: and save for the narrow corridor of the Ebro, all Aragon is this. It is the bottom of what was once a sea. The rocks of the Pyrenees, of Catalonia, of Valencia and Castile are the rim of the dry bowl through which the Ebro trickles. The soil is still subaqueous: marl, clay, gypsum, alkalis make its sterile surface. Salt lies free on it. Even the heather and grass of the upland moors do not live here.

But the Aragonese lives here: and here is the second stage of his progression. Sere towns lie in the sere waste. The houses are clay. There are wooden doors, but windows of glass are still rare. The peasant chooses the desert bottom for his house. South and north rise the walls of the Sierras, naked as flint: and the winds sweep through his narrow passage, bringing the rigor of the rocks into the air he breathes.

This low tier of the world of Aragon has no clement weather. It has no spring and no autumn. Winter is a rigid siege: summer is fire. When the weather shifts between the seasons, the winds make a runway of the valleys. Frost, flame, storm are the angry cycle. And its dwellers are worthy of their weather. They are not degenerate like the inbred natives of Las Hurdes between Extremadura and León. Nor are they spiced and strained with eastern bloods, like the cave-dwellers of Murcia and Almería. They are simple human stock extraordinarily coarsened. Dull-eyed, crude-lipped, slow-moving, slow-talking: they lack the mineral sheerness of the mountain men. The air that they breathe is not snow-swept. Their flesh has no crystal tarn for neighbor. They live in a roadway of unleashed elements. Dust, clay, salt, drug their air and clog their pores. But there is something else. There is the roadway, and the mobile spirit of the roadway. Movement and action infuse this brutish people.

b. *The Way of the Atom*

The men of the mountain and the desert store up great energy within their core: the outer world harries, arouses: the virgin force grows aggressive. East of Aragon are two rich and fluid lands: the Christian Principality of Catalonia, the Moorish Kingdom of Valencia. Frankish Barcelona rivals Marseilles and Venice, in ships. (Ramón Lull, Spain's most original schoolman, lived here: he wrote in Latin, Catalan and Arabic, books on love and wisdom. Chasdai ben Crescas, Spain's most original Jewish thinker, lived here: he founded a new Prophetic lineage which three centuries later grew to be Spinoza.) Farther down the coast are the lush huertas of Valencia: a great port facing south as Barcelona east, a seat of Moorish culture.

As Rome once the subtle nations to her east, tough Aragon comes to control these affluent worlds. When in 1149 Ramón Berenguer IV of Barcelona wedded the daughter of Ramiro II of Aragon, the mountainous kingdom did not lose its sway. Catalonia became part of Aragon: and the currents of its open life the veins of the uncouth inland realm. A century later, Jaime I of Aragon with Catalonian help conquered Valencia. Valencia had been in Christian hands before: El Cid had won it rather by treachery than arms. But after the great freebooter's death, the Moors came back. Now that Aragon sits down within its valleys, Valencia is Christian forever. It loses even its name of tributary kingdom. It becomes simply part of Aragon. Catalan blood has helped win it—for Aragon. Now Catalan, Valencian, and Castilian, led by the Great Captain of Córdoba, win Sicily and Naples—in the name of Aragon again.

Aragon of the desert and the mountains has in its stone‑

like men an energy which informed the mental mobility of the Catalan, the sensuous fervor of the Valencian: prevailed upon them, dominioned them and made them tools at last to its own activity in Europe, to its ultimate partnership with Castile in Spain. Within itself, Aragon has little else. It lacked the elements for the creating of an indigenous culture. Aragon the core remained prehistoric: its history is its power to accumulate forces about it.

But this elemental virtue through its very neutralness served to fuse the diverse natures upon which Aragon worked. The initial urgency was Aragon: and Aragon was the name of the amalgam which resulted. When at the close of the fifteenth century the nation of Spain was born, its eye toward Europe was Aragon. Isabel of Castile was the spirit and the religious motor of that birth. Ferdinand of Aragon, with his infusion of Frankish-Catalan and Jewish bloods, was the diplomat and politician who turned the mystical Castilian dream into a European fact. Aragon took its place in that polyphony of elemental fusions which was Spain. But with this difference. That fusion, in Castile, Galicia, Portugal, Andalusia, had a preponderance of parts native to these provinces. In Aragon the fusion was of outer elements. Aragon was the port of Spain: it had become a power in Europe. But its own integral rôle in the cultural life of the Aragonese nation was that of a catalyst in a solution.

Although historic Aragon is dead, in the capital city, Zaragoza, the process is revealed. Zaragoza is Spanish: yet its parts speak all of the east, of the south, and of the north. The streets have a dark fluidity which suggests Naples. They are not rigid and bright like the streets of Castile. Their warmth is freeflowing like a blood under the swarthy stones. They brood, they rot: they are not transfixed in contemplation of their unity, nor in rapt service of their own high fate. They are not noble, not inspired streets like the most sordid in Avila or Burgos. Italy's ageing paganism darklies them: and the Moor's mobility which lifts Valencia into a dance gives them an elusive charm, a play of light and shadow which Naples lacks.

Upon the dusty shores of the Ebro where the trees bend in a gray burden to the tawny waters, Spain speaks through Zaragoza. Here stand two monsters, the cathedrals. Nuestra Señora del Pilar is a long pile, drear as a Jesuit college, dull as a bull-ring: and from its mournful mass rise suddenly, inappositely, the huge *azulejo* domes, their hypertrophic rhetoric gleaming of Andalusia and Morocco. Within is a church in the style of Louis XVI of France! The other cathedral is more mellow, but not less hybrid. La Seo is Gothic. There is a Romanesque window: the façade is rich in Moorish bricks and tiles. The columns are Gothic; the walls are exuberant tissues of plateresque. Yet the whole is harmonious, is impressive. It is Aragon. There is here something at once pagan in mind and Christian in mood. The cathedral indeed is like the Latin Sea: a converted heathen whose thought holds to the limits of youth and from the Christian infinite has taken a boundless and vague melancholy. This crossing of sun and shadow is Aragón. Light is here—in eclipse: storm—sun-tinged. The immutable atomism of the Aragonese shivers in contradiction. The sun of Italy breaks into motes, dancing on a grave: the Spanish burden of death becomes the irrational refrain of a gay song.

In La Seo, Aragon works its transformation upon elements chiefly of France and the east. In the *jota*, the basic material is Spanish. What is known as the first jota is a birth of the defense of Zaragoza in 1808 against the forces of Napoleon. It swears to the Virgen del Pilar that the men and women of Zaragoza never will be French. Jota songs and variants of its dance are legion throughout Spain, and its musical elements hark back to Arab days. The formation of the jota is the couplet; the music is an adaptation, in three-quarter time, of Andalusian *cante hondo*. The classic southern song becomes romantic. Its abstract lines, devoted to the elemental passions, become vehicles for commentary verse in which religion, politics, wit and satire are barbarously mingled. The tragic music of Spain is lightened, aerated and then, by the ultimate twist of Aragon, it is once more sicklied with a haunting gloom. But the gloom is pagan, not Christian. It is empiric. Its fluidity is of the east, but its will is a release come from the north.

The dance of the jota is a diluting, a quickening, above all a flattening of the sheer pure figures of the southern dance. The body loses all relationship with sculpture. It is given up to that easy dynamism whose language is the leap, the skip, the pirouette. It has abandoned the dynamism of the soul whose infinite motions conform into an almost motionless figure. The classic dance of Spain, drenched with a facile nervousness from Europe—this is the jota of Aragon.

So the prehistoric atom begets this baroque romanticism of Aragon. There is nobility here. These are the people who fought the establishment of the Inquisition: the heroic defenders of their land against Roman, Visigoth, Arab, Frenchman. But the toughness of Aragón is vulnerable, if not to its invaders, to its own conquests. Valencia and Barcelona become conduits through which a motley of elements pour in. The alliance with Castile brings another bewilderment of forces. The primitive stuff of Aragon has no *organic* response for these racy cultures. They overwhelm it: they form an amalgam *about* the rigid core. And the harmony of Aragon is indeed one of flashing dissonances: brilliant, appealing, evanescent. It is a surface fusion, and its charm is flight from an impenetrable center.

Triumphant Aragon disappears in the living peoples it absorbs, in the great neighbor with which it is allied. As cultural beings, its vassals all survive it. Its own primal core survives it. . . .

These men of the Sobrarbe and the desert have been too ruthlessly hardened by their world to receive the juices of spirit. Like a steel mirror, they reflected for an hour the suns of Italy, of Araby and Spain. This is the greatness of Aragon—a swift reflection in which affluent worlds were fused in the reflector and took on the form of the reflector's contour. But the worlds swung past, life shifted: the light no longer fell on Aragon. Its surface becomes dull once more, and unillumined.

CHAPTER V

CASTILE

a. *The Castle of the Cid*

THE valley of the Ebro is a vein of green, deep within
wastes of earth and tiers of mountain. Northward the
Solana, sudden as a fort, stands before the snow-clad
Pyrenees. Southward the sierras of Aragon and Castile are
walls of flint upon a yellow floor. Slender and sinuous,
the Ebro leads up to the head of Spain.

This way came the Romans, met by the nut-hard
Aragonese and the Basques of Navarre. Here the Visigoths were fought and were absorbed. When the Arabs
faced north of Andalusia, they veered to the east: and
the Ebro was their path back to Spain's center. Commerce and nurture went this way: but were the servants
of War. Signs of War still mark the valley for its own.
Encased in desert and rock, the towns rise above the
plethoric vineyards like parts of the stone world. War
has brought the desert ranges down and has made cities of
them. The Valley, pressing up through Aragon, through
Navarre to Castile, is clad in armor of rock towns. So
weighted, it could not keep pace with the world. It was
great when mountains were barriers and when a river was
a highway. It has remained as the past sealed it. North
of Zaragoza no great city lies within the valley. It has
become an agricultural, above all a viticultural center.
Haro, Logroño, are towns of the wine-growers. But even
when new houses are put up, they are made of the eternal
rock—the warlike rock of the past.

At Miranda the invader leaves the Ebro, and stands at
the climax of Castile. The south is a breakage of treeless moor. In the crevices of heights, small towns hide,
and church steeples are indistinguishable from the rock.

But the earth mellows. Angles are replaced by curves. Wheatfields plaid the rolling slopes of hills. There are dingles, copses. This is the head of Old Castile—the part of the hard land where men lived best, and where they first united against the Moslem to call themselves Castilians. This is Burgos: *La cabeza de Castilla.*

.   .   .   .   .   .

Bristling castles, castle-like sierras exist everywhere in Spain. Why is just this portion called Castile? Look at Burgos, nestling in the bosom of a hill and green with springtime. The río Arlanzón has leaped from the savage Pico de Lara. But when it reaches Burgos, it is gentled: it is an idling pleasant little river. And the folk of Burgos have built along its banks an esplanade, a park of meticulous shrubs and gravel walks, a street of clubs and cafés where music, at nightfall, answers the tripping water and the wheatfields bending in breeze.

The town goes up from a seven-sided Plaza. It is stone, but mellow. Its streets are criss-crossed with surprising squares, irregular in shape and level. Old houses bearing shields seem to stoop as if time-softened in the mounting swirl. The cathedral stands waist-high among roofs. Its grandiloquent splendor is town-bound. Only the loftiest windows catch the free heaven for the nave. The doors of the cathedral open on many levels. Far up in the transept is a golden window topping a stair of carven oak: and this window is a door upon a street. Burgos begins to terrace up less gently. Houses, streets, arched galleries over steps are all one stone: but everywhere the gray walls crack: lilacs bloom in every crevice. Windows are open: flowers wave in them. Black-gowned women make shadows. In the gutters which are clean, play children, warm like their mothers, lyric like the lilacs. . . . . A running bloom in Burgos mounts with the streets until they match the steeples of the churches, until the harsh high churches are engulfed. A green hill dappled with cherry is the height of Burgos. And here is a castle.

It is a famous Castle. It belonged to the first Counts

of Castile, ere Castile was a kingdom. It witnessed the marriage of Ruy Díaz de Vivar, *el Cid*, to Ximena: and in its shadow stood the Cid's *solar*, his "city dwelling." It dominates the town. But it is ruin. It appears to have no importance. A paltry mass of rock it is, weeds in its cracks, gashes in its sides, and its top agape with earth and shrubs. It stands alone upon the top of the hill and crumbles into dust. Behind it are shanties: asses, dogs, hens possess the theater of its glory. The walls that once enclosed the city go down irrelevant now from the castle ruin: their cubos and bastions droop into a row of modern tenements, one spot of which is a tavern—a noisy mouth— filled with the red coats and red calls of soldiers.

What is this castle in the life of Burgos? A disused memory. It stands above a town whose fluent smile is turned away from it. Surely, it is no symbol?

Nor does the Cid's spirit, more than that of Burgos, appear to chime with the ruin. The Cid lived in the eleventh century. Shortly after his death, he was immortalized by the poet of *El Cantar de Mío Cid*, probably a Christian menestral, residing in the Moor country of Medinaceli. The *romancero* painted the Cid afresh. He was a mobile scoundrel. His king, Alfonso of León, distrusted him and ordered him forth from his seigneurial seat Vivar. Ruy Díaz was penniless: but he possessed a trunk whose iron-thonged flanks you can still admire in the chapel of Corpus Christi of the cathedral. He filled this coffer with rock and sand, and sealed it. By his friend, Martín Antolínez, he caused it to be carried to Raquel and Vidas, rich Jews of Burgos. "These are my treasures," he told the wily Jews. "I am exiled. Guard my wealth for me as security and loan me six hundred marks. The contents of my coffer are worth vastly more; but I am a simple knight and I need cash to pay my people at Vivar, and to lodge my wife with the monks of Cardeña. Six hundred modest marks."

The Cid crosses into the Moor country of Aragon and begins his raid on the Moslem. Like the Jew, the Moslem is free game—a wilder sort of boar. God sent him into the world for Catholics to prey on. The Cid is out for spoils. It does not occur to him to convert a Moor: he strips him. But he is canny: he never quite strips him bare. He wants him for a friend as he turns his back to go on other raids. At last, the Cid captures Valencia, by guile rather than arms. He is a rich man now! He has sent gifts to mollify Alfonso, and to Ximena and to the monks of Cardeña. (Of course, he does not repay the Jews.) But he imports a bishop to Valencia del Cid, one completely fitted out with all the latest golden implements of worship—quite as a millionaire of Pittsburgh imports a chef from Paris. Listen to mío Cid reflecting on his luck.

> All these winnings the Campeador made his.
> "Thanks be to God who of the world is master!
> "Before I was poor, today I am rich;
> "I have money and lands, I have gold and wide
>   possessions,
> "And for sons-in-law I have the Counts of Carrión,
> "All battles do I win, it is the will of the Lord.
> "Muslim and Christian hold me in great fear.
> "Yonder in Morocco where are the Muslim mosques,
> "They might open to my attack. Who knows? per-
>   haps they have
> "The dread that I may come: but I am not so minded.
> "I'll not go seek the Moor; here in Valencia I'll stay.
> "And let them bring me their wealth: with the help
>   of the Lord
> "They'll keep on paying me—or whomever I dele-
>   gate."

This is the constant temper of the first hero of Castile whom the changing mood of Spain was to turn at the last into a fanatical crusader. He has conquered another Moorish town:

"Hearken to me, Albar Fánez, and all my valiant
knights!
"With this castle we have won great spoil;
"Many Moors have died; few do I see still living.
"As to survivors, both the men and the women, there's
no one who will buy them
"If we cut off their heads. Nary a bit would we
gain.
"Let's save them for ourselves; now that we are the
masters.
"We'll lodge in their houses; we'll make them wait on
us." [1]

The Cid reminds us vividly how far his Spain was yet
from the ultimate, classic Spanish character, four hundred
years after the battle had begun between the Moor and
Christian. In the Cid are all the elements of that character—in their raw, chemically unfused state. But in
the sense that Isabel was Castilian, and that the Castle
is Castilian, he is not Castilian and he is not Spanish. His
spirit is pagan and is European. No such light-hearted,
almost comic bellicosity exists among the Semites to whom
warfare was a solemn, religious matter. The Cid is the
knight-errant, the medieval sportsman, stripped, however,
of the mystic and amorous sentiment which Christianity
later put upon the freebooters of the northern forests.
The Cid is cheerful and fluid as any pagan: but he has
a trait which no true Teuton knight possessed: his extreme concern with money. The Cid fights like a Goth:
but he figures like a Phœnician. And, like an Arab, he
keeps moving.

From time to time, the Cid is minded that he is fighting
for the Lord, that Christ is his captain, and that the Moor
(aside passing alliances and friendships) is his spiritual foe.

[1] To the reader who fears the difficulty of the old Spanish, I
recommend a modern Castilian version of this perennial poem in
which none of the flavor is lost: it is by Alfonso Reyes, the Mexican
poet, and is published in the *Collección Universal* of *Madrid*.

He gets this notion from the Moor himself: and it is well to realize how weakly the Christian has adapted it after four centuries of fighting. Meantime, the Arab who had crossed the Strait in a flame of religious passion, cooled and lost his sectarian, desert ardor. Spain was become a simmering chaos with no clear elements. Christian and Moslem were often in alliançe. The Ideas of Cross and Crescent resided unalloyed only in monasteries. The process of osmosis whereby the Christian was to inherit the religious fanaticism long lost by the Moslem did not reach its climax until the Age of Isabel.

The Cid—gay, ambulant, fluid, mercenary pragmatist of arms—lived under the shadow of no Castle. The Castle of Burgos had as yet no spirit for its bristling body. It was not yet Castile. But though the Castle's body is a ruin over Burgos, and Castile is wrecked among the modern nations, their spirit lives. It created a hard kingdom to tower over Spain, to dominion the world, and stratify at last the Spanish soul.

What is a castle?

It is a shut place that commands by its shutness the open place about it. A castle is builded of the stone of its world: it rises from the stone of its world: it *is* the stone of its world. A castle is austere toward the world which it defends. It is invariable, forbidding: its strength is that of a perpetual shutting-out of all which lies outside it. Sun beats on the castle wall: inside it is dark. Moon melts on its bastion and bathes its county blue: it is harsh and rigid. Water and wind make song of the green hills: the castle is silent. It is lord of its county because it is apart from it. A castle is hot in a cold land: a castle is cold in a hot land: a castle is high in a low land: a castle is full in a land of dearth: a castle is dry in a land of verdure.

Within the castle walls, anarchy may flame: the walls are law enough. The walls are spirit and sanctity enough, so that within life may be mad and fleshly. A castle draws on the affluence of its world to save its world: it lifts itself into a desert peak, that the low lands may flourish: and then it sucks the land.

Castile becomes a castle. The chaos of running passion and idea hardens: Christian Spain, weary at last of ages of dissension, steals the discarded fervor of the Moor: becomes one passion, permanent and crystal, to withstand all others. Upon the crest of Spain forms this stony essence of her will. The actual struggle dies: the Moslem world droops away toward Africa. But the spirit of the struggle becomes rock.

A castle to defend the soul of Spain; and Spain's soul at last a castle. The walls raised to minister to an open land grow higher, grow ever more remote from the reason of their being. Become at last a reason unto themselves.

See the castle now, stirred from its mooring in a fertile world! The fertile world itself must turn into a castle! This will of service destroys the served. This vision is so intense that it is blind. The castle is become an unleashed monster, mobile as the Arab or the Cid. It lives—to be a castle. And it devours the spirits and fields of men which raised it up in order to protect them.

The castle, become Spain, moves through Europe: moves across the sea. Its shut erectness is the measure of good. Its sunless cells are the measure of light. Its turrets are the church. Its trampling march over the pliant earth is music. Its dream is to make a castle of the House of God.

b. The Stones of Wisdom

The Province of Valladolid in Old Castile is fertile. The plain has the aspect of a verdant sea swept by long tides, the hills. In Spring the fields of wheat and barley unfurl their delicate green illimitably to horizons where white clouds stand like enchanted caravels. In the soft grass and the turf, velvety with rains, the flowers sparkle like myriad splinters of sky. And on this vastness, under a solid Dome, towns stand as sudden islands.

Such a town is Medina del Campo—City of the Field: a huddle of clay huts about a bastioned castle where Isabel the Catholic loved to live and where at last she died. The plains are at low ebb against the walls of Medina. They recede with their lush rhythms from this ruined arrogance which once housed Glory. Medina is like a penniless hidalgo. The town's pride—the Castle—is a molder within the walls. And the town itself is a lay of sordid houses on mud streets, a conglomerate life of stamping peasants and braying mules and women occult like the hidden fires of their kitchens.

West of Medina del Campo lies the Province of Salamanca. It is the southern spur of the kingdom of León which Castile absorbed in the eleventh century, and it is contiguous with Portugal. It is less fertile than Valladolid. That sea-like plain roughens and grows abrupt. The Castilian *borrico* is less frequent; and likewise the crude *carro* which it draws with the driver bouncing on its rump. Here is a land of oxen. Slow and inevitable as the day, they swing and steam beneath their wooden yokes, drawing the stone plow through the rocky loam or the cart with axleless wheels on the harsh ruts of a road. The cool young grain-shoot trills less in this land.

It is a world of flocks. Sheep fleck the hills; goats cast their jagged shapes like living stones within the stony valleys. It is a world of ranches—of *dehesas*. Bulls, reared for the bull-ring—*toros bravos*—browse in great sweeps of meadow.

The ranch house is of stone. It is large and bleak; if the dehesa breeds good bulls, it is rich. *Toreros* come to study their victims, for when the bull is not "game" the *espada* is helpless. There are many bedrooms for guests: the dining room is a long hall in mahogany or oak with crystal candelabras, lofty leather chairs, sideboard glittering with colored glasses, a bull's-head over the door and portraits of great toreros on the walls. But the house is cold; rustic and crude it is, like the harsh earth of León. The livable room and the living room is the kitchen. The owner, in *zamarra* and *calzón*, smokes his rank pipe by a vast open fire. (There are few stoves in this land.) A medieval spit, great enough for the whole side of a beef, stands in the blue-black chimney. And through the Castilian winter, when the wind is unbroken from the Cantábrico to the Sierra Morena, the ranch house is a cavern, but the kitchen is warm.

The hidalgo has changed little from his ancestors who fought the Moor at Zamora. With him is his son, who incites the savagery of the bulls as a gardener incites the color of rare flowers; and his son's wife, a mellow creature, quiet as the low flame of *encina* that heats the *garbanzo* jar upon the hearth; and her child, also, taking the breast of a nurse. The other servants sit, too, before the fire in that equality which alone a feudal sense of caste makes possible.

Salamanca is a land of little cities, of tight, insulate worlds with a thousand or five hundred souls. A crude land and a people whose spirit the land encases. A crustaceous people. . . . A tiny river is nearby, else there could be no town. The houses ray out upon the turf like regimented snails. Windows are spots in a chalky shell. The door, within a triangular cut of the house (as if the reclusion made it less penetrable) is massive oak impounded with iron or with copper. It is divided horizontally, so that the housewife can open the upper half and talk and trade, and yet be locked within her tiny castle.

She is locked ever within herself. Her garb is black. When she goes forth to market in the village square (here bulls are fought on holy-days), there is a black shawl over her black hair and very close to her eyes. The face is beautiful. The skin, color of parchment, ages silken soft. The jaw is round and unassertive. The nose is straight, the mouth is thin and large. Passion, here, and right are not separate claimants to her soul. All this peasant woman's will and all her duty unison from girlhood to the grave. Service to God and service to her man, the sacraments of communion and of love, the tasks of household and of motherhood . . are one and have one word in her plain mind. They are life itself: like God a unity which miracle divides into three persons. And she is like her hearthfire, this woman of Old Castile: fecund and ensconced. She is the light of her shut home. She has jealous distrust of sun and of the open air. They are her rivals and she bars them out with her tiny windows and her divided door.

Her man moves slow through a strange outward world; for he is wholly embraced by the close of his home and his woman. He wears knee-breeches of hide that are tight as a skin and box his rump into a rigid square. He wears a coat of raw sheepskin with a gap for the head and gaps for the arms. For shoes, he has a bundle of rags cased in sandal-soles and thonged. His hat is either the black skull boina of the Basque or the true sombrero of Castile—pie-shaped, velvety black, with the center pyramiding up to a peak. You see him best when he goes astride his ass. A crude plaid muffler (*tapabocas*) stops his mouth. The woolen manta regally folds from his shoulders to the flanks of his brute. The burro trots sharp and perpendicular. The man is movelessly erect, untinged by the mount's rhythm. Even a peasant, even on an ass, he seems a caballero. His head is sternly forward; his hands do not stir; he is silent. His world is a coarse world. Winter is a blast and summer is a blast; the short spring covers his field with mud more than with flowers. This his encasement. And within, a balance like a tree's of sun and earth and weather. He wages an intricate but instinctive warfare within the Hand of God. For God makes the sun a sear or a dim mockery; and God makes foes of the men of the world. Unto the bloody Moor of yesterday there has succeeded the bleeding Noble. Yet he has won of this complexity a peace simple and deep. He lives in a profound seclusion. Love and work are his hearthfire. And from their secret place he can look out, his eyes old in understanding, his eyes bright with the irony of distance.

Within this land of unkempt fields studded with encina, land of wild bulls, of towns shut from the sun and the wind, there glows a jewel that has warmed the world. It is the city of Salamanca. It lies in treeless mountains. Northward Zamora bristles warlike, westward Portugal turns an unfriendly back: and all about, Castile. Sierra de Gata, Peña de Francia, Sierra de Béjar, Sierra de Gredos . . . from such wild quarries has come the mellow stone to build a scholar city: the city of the Wisdom and the Love of God within the crude dichotomy of Spain.

Salamanca is its University. Here in the first splendor of the Reconquista, Christian kings foregathered wise men of Israel and Islam and joined to them the aspirant scholars in Christ. The school was founded by a king of León and chartered by a saint, San Fernando of Castile. For two centuries, learning here was universalistic. Here, in spirit, Ibn Gabírol the Jew became Avicebron, and his book *Mekor Hayim* the Latin *Fons Vitæ* which nourished Saint Thomas of Aquinas. Here the teaching of Averroës the Moslem was absorbed for Rome. The Mussulman Avempace and Tofaíl—Platonists—here went down before the Stagyrite phalanx which included Ibn Ezra, Ben Maimun and Gersonides. Here was prepared food that later fed Albertus Magnus; here were married east and west as a thousand years before in Alexandria. For the body of Catholic Europe was bone of Greek logic, flesh of Jewish faith and eye of Arab science.

Here, ages later, when the medieval unity of Rome drooped and split, when Protestant heresy was annexed by the new State wills of the north, the Church of Rome was saved. From Salamanca came the theocratic polity of the Catholic kings which fused the modern will of the State to the old idea of the Church. From Salamanca spread the religious energy which won all South America and part of North America to Roman Doctrine.[1] For here above all, were nurtured the Spanish mystics who made possible that last great conversion: Cristobal Colón, Pedro de Alcántara, Juan de Avila, Luis de León, Luis de Granada, Juan de la Cruz, Teresa de Jesús, Iñigo de Loyola—that various athletic group who by book or preachment, by crusade or compass revived Rome. In Salamanca, at least in spirit, the Medieval Synthesis was reborn: and in spirit has subsisted to our day.

The earlier, more liberal Salamanca which had so immediate a share in the real splendor of that Synthesis is not this town still glowing by the River Tormes. The Salamanca of today is that of Isabel and Ferdinand, of the sixteenth century—of the Jesuits and the fanatical revivers.

Unlike most of the great cities of Castile, it rises gently from the meseta. And heroisms of the mind, rather than of blood, speak in the smolder of its ancient body. The River Tormes is urbane, almost European. It passes waving willows and lush fruit trees; washes the shaded soto where the monks met to platonize with Luis de León upon the Names of Christ. A Roman bridge leads low to the city.

---

[1] It must not be forgotten that the Jesuits of France who contributed so greatly to the creation of the Catholic strongholds of Canada were the instruments of a spirit and of a method born in Spain.

Here once stood a granite bull by means of which the wily beggar knocked wisdom into the head of Lazarillo. And the streets climb up through the mud. Walls crumble with the hillside under the town. An ancient church stands on the bank surrounded by the mire; and houses, foul with age, their carved seals moldered, limp like proud beggars up the sharp incline. The Cathedral is a soft gold crest in the sun: at its feet are waves of convents, consistories, churches, schools. The central streets are paved with cobble stones. The houses are low and the glass of their windows is out of place, so new it gleams within the soft senility of walls. Dogs, children, refuse clutter up the streets. Everywhere one feels the elemental base—a hill—on which this young culture of Christian Spain has builded. In the churches, five centuries are confused. The Old Cathedral is Romanesque; with its chaste columns and its nave a petrified forest, it stands beside the scintillance of the plateresque New Cathedral. Nearby is a Dominican convent in which a queer mariner named Columbus found refuge and support in a scheme rejected by most of the Crowns of Europe. The seventeenth century baroque of the Churrigueras flaunts its high monstrosities beneath ornate ceilings. Much of the gold arrogance of this convent is a result of that mad scheme of Columbus. But the man himself is closer to the streets; for here one still encounters at least in spirit the pícaro, the monk half-saint, half-satyr, the immortal Celestina. A Jesuit convent rears its chill harsh walls in the town's heart: a symbol of the ruthless might of the Company of Jesus, of its enormous logic. And everywhere, the alleys limping up, limping down, between the homes of the Church.

This Salamanca, fixed in the eras of Isabel, Carlos, Felipe II, has aged; has not changed. The dirty streets are the same; the low blind precincts of the poor (Cervantes lived here once) and the dominant recurrent periods of church and tower. Life's anarchy is here controlled by learning. Every crooked street is righted by a convent;

every lurch of alley is stopped by a square. And the whole town is mastered by the Plaza Mayor—a square as correct as a schoolman's syllogism. Its sides are unvariant four-storied walls; it is colonnaded equally and equally façaded; it is the noble, proper heart of a town which has argued unity in Christ through seven rank chaotic hundred years. . .

The buildings of the university are the least of it. In the Library you may find manuscripts by Alfonso the Wise, glosses by thirteenth century Jews, Arabic illuminations of Gazali. You may sit in the same chill lecture halls where once great masters taught humanities and where but yesterday Miguel de Unamuno "explained" Greek after the universal measure. But Salamanca is an ancient seer whose word has gone forth to the world, while the body shriveled and the blood grew bleak.

More of the university is the tropical gold work of the Dominican altars; is the stupendous grace of the two Cathedrals; is the immense glower of the Jesuit on the hill. More, the sedulous symmetry of the Plaza within the coil of gutters. More, the glow of the yellow mellow stone within the desert fastness of Castile.

c. The Water Bridge

The æsthetic sense of Spain is social, instinctive, unconscious. Her master works of art rise like isolate acts from the trammels of her life. Her cities are among them: and none more perfect than the ancient towns bristling upon rocks within the Castilian desert.

Choose your day well for visiting these communal works of Spain. Salamanca needs sun: its warm gold stones speak graciously within an azure sky. The Escorial is best in rain: its chill stones shrink from the blue-gold of the Spanish day, but under the drift of breaking clouds it glows like fossil fire. Segovia sings most clearly in a wind. Great clouds like armies plunge from the Sierras and invest the Castle. The sun makes sudden sallies on the Cathedral. Then gloom once more on the town, like repentance after violence.

Castile, here, is a chaos of mountain and of desert. The Guadarrama is steep over the lofty town. The desert leaps and dips in a cacophony of planes. Elsewhere in Spain, it is Spring. But April in Segovia is stormy. The mountains are still clad in winter. In the pockets of the surrounding valley almond trees and cherry are in bloom, making little perfumed furls of mist against the barren earth. The sky is neither spring nor winter. A great wind rages. Momently, heaven changes. Titanic mounds of cloud are flung like eiderdown from peak to peak: the sun is a swift flash between dark purples. Rain in melted diamonds glances across the valley in the oblique shaft of the sun: is gone: a copse of poplar sings suddenly green and yellow under gray. The volumnear motions of the hills seem to be waves of a seismic sea, swept by the wind and roaring with its might.

Segovia fills the height of a long rock shaped like a ship within this stormy earth. Below one side pours the Eresma, with its melted snows. The valley rises on the other beam, purple and bronze soil, blue sage, rock . . rises to a village that lies flat like a dory on the breast of a wave . . rises again to the sky where the clouds drive wildly. Segovia's ancient walls are bastioned, pierced with knotty towers and gates, and topped with the typical round cubos which Rome gave to Spain. The walls bind the precipitous rock which holds a park and the Alcázar, the usual pile of tessellated towers that gave Castile its name.

This is one end of the town. The rock goes higher toward the center. Houses are a clutter, unanimous like an army in the moment ere it comes forth to attack. A romanesque church, a feudal tower rise from the stony mob like leaders. And in the town's heart, stands the Cathedral. Its interior is intricate and cold. But in the façade of the city, it is perfect. It is the climax of Segovia rising to meet it. To the right Alcázar is alone, facing the waste of the meseta; alone above the river and the rock like a lord of the city. But now, the streets mount, an aspiration makes them one: their goal is the Cathedral. Its base is lost in the streets. Rise free and clear only the two thick towers and the crest of the gigantic nave. The Cathedral is a ship breasting the sea of the town: even as the town is a ship, breasting the hills.

Down from the Cathedral in the direction away from Alcázar, once more the city falls. No regular descent. There is no metric rhythm in Segovia, save for the mind that stands outside of it. An Olympian eye sees the vast bowl of the Guadarrama: and on the tide of turf and rock, the city riding like a frigate: and in the town, this regular rise to the Cathedral. But each of these general units is a chaos. The plateau is an intricate context of heights, villages, farms and valley-spots suddenly sweet with orchards. The wave on which Segovia rides is itself broken into rising, falling crests. To make a hundred yards of horizontal progress, the voyager must go up, go down: slipping through alleys that swerve, climbing steps that lift him into hidden *plazas* where an old church spreads its romanesque cloisters like wings, or a palace with faceted walls stands aloof from a plebeian throng of houses.

So, laboriously the voyager makes his way to the other end of town. There is a Square. The Aqueduct of Rome, immemorial and chaste, rises from the Spanish market. *Plaza del Azoquejo:* it is a name that recalls the soukhs and bazaars of Islam. Within its sordid taverns, fish-shops, stands Rome.

Segovia's chaos disappears. Segovia becomes a drama rigorously styled. As the town bristles under the wind and the mountains, so has passion run riot in this town. Here lived Juan Bravo, leader of the *Communeros* who arose through Spain, in tragic presentiment of disaster, to oppose the Austrian Karl who became Carlos the Great. Here lived the stubborn burghers who shut their gates against the young Queen Isabel. Segovia is crude, coarse, anarchic. But Spain's unconscious art has made it perfect, weaving the elements of its cross-grained will into a living balance.

This is the work of the Roman Water Bridge. Two thousand years ago, the Empire built it to carry from Fuenfría to a reservoir not far from La Granja. The distance was great, so the Aqueduct was long. No aspirance, here, no thinking about symbols. The pragmatic, confident Roman thought not of miracle: the passionate Segovian, building his chaos beneath these Roman arches, looked for miracle elsewhere. And the miracle is born of the unwitting marriage of these wills. . . .

Roman aqueduct and Spanish town offset each other and create, once more, the complex unity of Spain. The Square is a boil of braying burros, muddy motorbuses, lottery vendors, beggars, drinkers. Above it and across it spans the double tier of arches. They are vast granite blocks, pieced without clamp or mortar into a soaring lacework. Hundreds of feet above, swings the upper rim. The town clambers after it on steps, becoming at the top level a hidden maze of low houses. The Bridge, dwarfed here, disappears into the wall of a convent. Its massive granite shelters a patio with a pump, grapevines, geese—and a young girl stringing red clothes on the branch of an encina. Upon the other height from the Plaza del Azoquejo, the Bridge grows gradually less steep as the town rises slowly. Rome's cool stones run ever closer to the Spanish streets, singing against sordid wineshops, almost touching a schoolhouse dismal as death, skirting a square where boys play at *pelota*. Rome is now a single-tiered, a stolid marching music. It turns at right angles and runs along a road lined with indigent shops. A *bodega* opens its dark fragrance as it passes: pigskins filled lifesize with wine sprawl like bloated corpses in the shadow of this march of Rome. The town is behind: the sedulous arched mass moves like a resistless army into the ground that rises toward La Granja. . . .

The Aqueduct of Rome is Segovia's youngest life. Its stones are immense, but its grace makes wings for them. Its tiers and terraces are an ordered song. Horatian is the balance of these pragmatic blocks. The mountains of Castile are old. The barren soil of Castile, stripped of its loam, is old. Segovia is old. It is a spilling of energy, a thing of chaos. Segovia comes to dark and tragic life within this Measure, sure and at ease, of the cool will of Rome.

d. The Miracle of El Greco

South of the Guadarrama lies New Castile. The world flattens to the vast plain of La Mancha. Towns stand like tiny toys on a table. It is a calm before storm: vineyards and wheatfields stop against the wildest pass of Spain, Despeñaperros of the Sierra Morena. Here Don Quixote like his idol Amadís went into penance and prayer; here the Arabs passed from Andalusia to the high Plateau; here at Las Navas de Toloso they were pushed back and down five centuries later. Within a land of fierce extremities, none is more telling than this sudden chaos rocking to the sky between two mellow plains. In the upper one, La Mancha, the eye is lost between the infinites of earth and heaven: it ceases to feed logic to the mind and the soul starves in a waste of vague realities or, like Don Quixote's, leaps to the realm of visions.

North of La Mancha, another climax. The Tagus flows lazily west, carrying silt and loam from gradual hills serrated with the olive. The land is wide-browed. Its lack of trees gives it essential peace, as if it were in contemplation of its own fortunate ease among the embattled mountains. Now, swinging westward with the river, the land catches a spiritual fever. Fields grow rockier, hills abrupt. Rondure sharpens to angle; horizons shut. Something like a geological convulsion takes the body of New Castile and turns it into a steep, a tumultuous storm. The land becomes a maelstrom, swirling into a single rock—Toledo. The Tagus maddens too. Bending south, it cuts into a canyon, one of whose walls is Toledo and the other a rocky world to rim it. The river circles; deep in a notch of stone it becomes a purpling torrent. It cuts a precipice, it leaps a rapid, it reverses northward seeking again the long plains that lounge westward to rocky Portugal and to the sea.

Toledo is cold upon its sudden height. Across the gorge that makes it almost an island, olive groves, symmetrical as in the ancient prints, draw verdant stripes in the red face of the hills. The country houses and the chapels mark the swift slopes like little steadfastnesses nailing their chaos. But in this geologic gyre and husbandry, Toledo stands unmoving.

To the north where the plains lead to Toledo and where alone there is no fending water, are walls. So an unbroken rigor belts the high town. Here is the ancient Puerta de Visagra, unchanged since the Arabs put it up twelve centuries ago upon a Roman stronghold dizzily maintained by the Visigoths Athanagild and Leovgild to capital all the land. Gigantic stones not polished by time. Three separate tiers of bastion and of turret. And within the Gate's shadow like a womb of rock, delicate Arab arches. Behind, the street leads with a promise of gentle curves into the harbored city. Children gambol in these monstrous walls; their calls are flowers suddenly alight in a bleak winter. Women sit before painted doorways and send voices like velvet strands into the silent granite of Toledo. But life cannot prevail against this protecting death. Nearby is a new Visagra (a mere five hundred years). Arms of Carlos V and a statue of San Antonio furbish its forbiddance. Through its round arch, you see two pointed towers with their *Mudéjar* tiles aflash in the sun. But the tiles are not verdant and skyey like the tiles of Granada and Seville. They are colorless, and they are cold.

Toledo is a coil of streets, like the Tagus stormy and like the rocks precipitous. Men and women live in Toledo. But they are void within the intricate death of convent walls and church, and convent and convent again. Rather than men and women of the sort who come together in the ache of flesh, and of their ease bear fruitage, there seem to live here creatures of prayer and dogma. Children indeed are scarce in these streets that are the bodies of a Creed and a Rite. When there is open, there is waste. When there is color, there is irony.

San Juan de los Reyes . . church, college, convent . . stands on the westward buttress of the Toledan mountain. The rock cuts to the river. The ancient bridge of San Martín loops high above the rapids, thrusting its road away into a waste of dust. The Gate of San Martín stands in a slanting square; and it is naked for the walls are gone. So desert comes into Toledo. Within the city Gate, here is the face of mountain. The streets stand on it, despite their ages, insecure and shallow. Desert is not hostile to them, so they have let it in. Was it not there before them? Let it come back to serve as the refrain of their bleak rigor—of their denials. And the Church which the Catholic Kings projected and then for-got—San Juan of the Kings—shrills with its painted statues in this desert: Gothic, Arabic, and baroque against a hardier silence.

Farther on is the Judería—what is left of this Borough of Jews who ruled Toledo when the Arabs came, and who throve thereafter in Toledo for seven hundred years. The rigid mood goes on. The Castle of the Jews has disappeared: but where it stood, beside the Paseo of a synagogue, falls the escarpment, dark and sheer, into the rushing river. On the farther side, the mountain is a wall. Water foams through the notch. There is a tower stand-ing on a thrust of rock just above the waves. Halfway between the river and the Jewish homes, this ancient prison has survived and fronts with its bars the desolate interstice of stone. Churches and chapels stud the variant heights. And all about, the rise and fall of streets, shut in and clamorously silent, cold in the neutral tint of the Sierra.

You must cross the river. The Puente de Alcántara is a bridge whose subtle dichotomy of arch and gate marks in plastic terms the way from Moslem Musa to Christian Philip. Best strike down from the Cathedral to the ferry. These are the oldest and the poorest streets. And here are children—naked children, and naked patches of rock and turf within the filth of alleys. Dark, over-ripe, mute. These streets on the mountainside are as the hive of some subterraneous bee whose honey is bitter-black. The people are blind. They behold neither the river below that flows to the sea, nor the Cathedral above that touches God. They live compressed within the surging forces of Toledo. They live in a limbo of balance. Their obscurity is poignant, within so aspirant a world. The ferry is a round and ancient bark with a carved prow and two unwieldy oars to pilot it, for better or for worse, athwart the current. And above the precipice of the other side, is the rocky chaos where El Greco sat to paint his city. . .

Rigor, rigor inflexibly holds. Toledo's streets are stone veins imbedded. The Alcázar is a higher rock above the rocky huddle of the town: its rectangular loom is a peak of the mountain, polished by the sun. At the summit bristles the Cathedral. Towers, turrets, crested pediments, flying buttresses and chapel roofs are pressed aloft by the Toledan wave, and rise from it like foam. All of the sharp volutions of the streets, even the sheer Alcázar, converge and aspire into this jet of granite. And over the Cathedral is the sky—God's empty answer to this blast of icy aspiration.

This is one Theme of Toledo: the word of traditional Castile and of her castle towns. The mountain is refuge of friend, menace to foe. The face of the Christian warrior is set. Moor and Jew are driven out. And all the Toledan world becomes a symbol of the mood that drove them. The soul of the Spaniard becomes a castled mountain; masters its chaos by turning it to stone. And what will not ply to immobility, it shuts without the draw-bridge. . . . One theme of Toledo. But a typical Castilian town—no more—is not Toledo. Castile surpasses itself. Spain grows universal.

Color, flame, live too in the shut town. They are everywhere. And in their protean form, they are one. Halfway up from the Puerta Visagra stands Cristo de la Luz in a rough field of rocks. In 1085, the conquering Castilians passed through the Arabs' gate. Their titular head was Alfonso VI. But Ruy Díaz de Vivar, the Cid, rode first. The streets then were not different from now. Crude stone paved the steep, and the gray houses hid their eyes about the inner verdure of their courts. The Cid came to a little mosque. His horse fell to his knees and the Campeador could not avail to budge him. At last, he dismounted from the rapt steed and strode into the mosque. He beat away the gold-encrusted Mihrab and disclosed a Visigothic chapel. In the altar place, before the Christ, was a brass lamp; and it was burning even as it had burned three and a half centuries before, when Musa walled it up to make his mosque.[1]

The mosque stands first in the unkempt garden. Its entrance is double-arched. Through the three columns topped by a lyric arabesque, lies the round depth of the altar. Upon the walls are paintings of ascetic Christians, lean with the Byzantine projection of their color into the life of their forms. These paintings were recent when the Arab came to Toledo in 711. They are recent today —in the Toledo of El Greco.

Cristo de la Luz is delicate. Its counterpoint of German, Byzantine and Arab themes makes it a song wavering flute-like from the stiff music of the Castilian town. On the other slope, in the Judería that leaned so fatefully over the gorge of the Tagus, are other dissident jewels. Two synagogues have survived. One of them consecrated as a church under the tutelage of Santa María la Blanca, later became the asylum for penitent prostitutes, later a barrack for cavalry and a stable. The other was

---

[1] Must I assure the reader that this is pure legend? The historical Cid was probably raiding "on his own" in Valencia when his king, who had exiled him, entered Toledo.

made over by the Catholic Kings to that most unjewish of cults—the death (Tránsito) of the Virgin Mother. Builded by the Jews, the houses speak across the stormy ages of the Jews, their builders. The sultry masquerades to which they have submitted fade away. This is Toledo indeed. The Toledo of Abraham Ibn Ezra, descendant of Gabírol and forefather of Spinoza; of the munificent and tragic Samuel, treasurer to Spain's most cruel king; of Ibn Daud, Talmudist, and of his great foe, Jehudah Ha Levi.

At the time of Paul, there were already Jews in Spain. Like the Phœnicians and the Greeks before them, they became protagonists of Spanish urban culture. The Visigoths who inherited the land upon the Roman death, were an agricultural folk. Their will to control this peninsula of cities failed, because they lacked the spirit of the city. At the end, when disaster neared they oppressed the Jews —masters of urbanity—for economic reasons. It was natural, that the oppressed should welcome the Arabs: and that the Moslem captains, aware of the possible ally in a hostile land, should overlook the chief hate of their Prophet by welcoming the Jews. Jews were placed in control of Seville, Málaga, Córdoba, Granada, Toledo. Under the Córdoban Caliphate, they throve and Spain became their land. Jewish Wisdom crossed the sea from Babylon and founded the first Academies of Europe.

During four centuries, the Jew was a master in Spain. But it is doubtful if his number ever equaled half a million. He was a leaven and an enzyme in the land. He was artisan, tradesman. No guild of the cities failed to count him in. He was physician and teacher. He became scientist and philosopher. The majority of Jews lived, of course, in the humble circumstance of a farmer or a weaver. But a few grew great. Jews became diplomats and statesmen for Moslem and for Christian princes. As the modern economy gradually evolved, they became ministers of finance; they waxed wealthy. And with their power they builded in the towns of Spain centers of lib-

eral, luxuriant culture whose like was not then in Europe.
They were masters of many tongues, masters of many
illuminations. When Arab Córdoba had rotted and the
courts of Italy were yet swarming knots of bandits, the
Jews of Spain dwelt in a world which embraced Asia,
Africa, Europe. Indeed, they were among the eyes of
Portugal and Spain, yearning across the seas. They were
cartographers; they were promoters of trade. And from
Gabírol who was born in Málaga in 1021 to Hasdai ben
Crescas who died in Barcelona in 1410—a period of time
nearly as great as that which separates the Discovery of
America from our day—they traced an incessant thought
in Spain.

The modern State sounded once again a Jewish doom.
With the birth of its fanatical will came persecution.
The Jews' internationalism was a subtle, psychologic poison.
The servants of royal unity became aware of an enemy
in their household—of an enemy in their blood. In 1391,
Spain—the liberal theater of ideas whose like had not
been known since Alexandria (for here argued men who
believed, not in abstract gods, but in flaming Prophets and
in Incarnations)—lurched to one modern way of progress.
Massacre rose from Seville to Toledo. A century later,
the Jews were ordered to give up either their faith or
their home. They had been in Spain for centuries; their
urban genius had helped build Spain's cities. They had
kindled a fire to warm the world and to illumine heaven.
They were artisans in the body and in the mind of their
land. They were ordered to die. For to leave the home
of Spain or the home of Bible and Talmud was no mere
uprooting. Probably not much more than a hundred thousand left. The moiety stayed and were lost in the great
Catholic amalgam. Their organizations for action and
for thought were reft from them. They had no halls or
synagogues. They had no language. Worst of all, they
had to abandon—those who stayed—the immemorial
forms of feeling which were Jewish and in which they
were beginning to mold (witness Crescas and Leon He-

breo) a new Enlightenment, a new Naturalistic religion! An end . . not the first, not the last . . came to Jewish Wisdom. And while Europe whose spirit they had nourished rose in Renascence to the bloody dawn of our "liberal" age, the Jews sank down into the very night of mumbled ritual and superstition from which they had upraised their oppressors.

As they pass from the stern city or are lost within its rigorous stones, the Jews give to it a color and a theme without which it would not be Toledo. By their acceptance of death, they have won life unceasing: and here in Toledo which once gave them death, they have bestowed a spirit which has not died.

The house of Samuel Levy stands, gracious and simple, in its garden. (El Greco lived here.) The arched columns of Santa Maria are unhurt. The Tránsito still breathes, darkly, like a rose over-ripe. It is a rectangular building, higher than wide. Its walls are white under the cedar ceiling. Around runs a frieze, margined in Hebrew texts. Above are arches in relief, *rejas* that suggest the Arab, and a higher line from the Old Testament. But the base wall of the synagogue is its full glory. It is a façade wholly of Hebrew. (Two Castilian seals thrust in to mar it have no more effect than a spot on a sublime illumined page.) The letters of stone make a warm intricate music. The æsthetic inspiration is Arab. But how these Jews have deepened and dimensioned it! The arabesque is a delicate, wavering line; without denseness, without integration. It is like a silhouette, against a desert sky; it is like the trail of life on desert sands. The Hebrew letters are slower, less emphatic, more volumnear. They are far mellower in curves; they are far deeper. They build, in this façade of a Toledan synagogue, a poem that is history. They march on the stone surface of a wall, resolute, self-effacing: symbols of a world whose spirit seems by miracle to survive its body.

Color and aspirant light, throughout Toledo. How has it survived? Not alone the Cristo de la Luz: not alone the Judería. Athwart the Cathedral, in a little Square, is a building—the *Ayuntamiento*—bright, warm, almost fancifully gay with towers. (El Greco builded it.) There are Churches like San Vicente, Santo Tomé, in which a wall grows suddenly glorious in color and sings above the dolorous shadows. (Here, El Greco painted.) Even the Cathedral turns traitor to its stones! The cloisters are a perfumed close. The choir has rows of wood-carved stalls that shout their sensual delight against the heavy columns. And in the Sacristía hangs an altar piece—an *Expolio*—that is a sunny jewel. A genius—from across the sea—has infused this conventional matter with prophetic spirit: space moves, spirit grows manifest in flesh. A red-robed Christ becomes a ritual flame, transfiguring the human shapes about him.

And this, in Catholic Toledo, the stone grim city! Because there came a man to dwell here in whom dwelt the old Prophecies, and who resolved them into shapes which Catholic Toledo could not deny. Color against stone, fire against rigor—this had been the Argument in Toledo, until Isabel and Cisneros put a stop to it, by blotting out the one in favor of the other. A simple resolution. Moor and Jew go forth. Dogma and Conventual remain. The Cardinals of Toledo—Popes of Spain—espouse the iron purpose of Castile. And the long blank walls of the streets with their hidden monks and nuns—these seem the victors of Toledo.

Comes, now, in the last quarter of the sixteenth century a young Cretan painter to make his home in the town. His name is Doménico Theotocópuli. He has studied in Italy with Tintoretto. He is a wanderer. He learns that there is much gold to earn in Spain, and little talent to earn it. A handy place in which to make a fortune. He comes and stays: and although the fortune proves shy, Toledo becomes immortal.

The question of the actual blood which flowed in El Greco's veins is of no consequence. Child of the Mediterranean *Völkerchaos*, there must have been echoes of many voices in his soul. Maurice Barrès [1] plays with the unestablished notion that he was a Jew. The certainty is the prophetic spirit of his work; the certainty is the vision of the East with which he dowered Spain. He came to Toledo, disciple of a realist in Florence; and he produced an art as opposed to the paganism of his master as it is close to Isaiah.

The spirit of Israel and Byzantium does not die in Spain, because a Catholic has come to make it flesh of the body. The Jew may go into his alien ghettos; the Arab may rot in the Levant. Here is a man to blaze their truth upon the walls of churches—and with a color so wise, that the walls crumble ere his word grows dim.

The work of El Greco was misunderstood by his own age and scouted by the criticism that came after. The wonder is, that it was tolerated—the invasion in it of a world condemned. Manuel Cossío [2] has explained this plausibly by the personal prestige of the man. His contemporaries, failing to grasp his apocalyptic and "inaccurate" are, were moved by the deep power of the man and by his own self-confidence. His work is the crowning plastic of the West. More and more, as the walls of his stiff world molder, El Greco is seen to express not alone Toledo, not Spain alone, but the Christian Synthesis of Europe at its highest luminous pitch.

His æsthetic is one of incarnation. He possesses an idea, dynamic, mystical. He makes his figures immediate forms of that idea. Not symbols, not representations—not even emanations in the separatistic sense of the Brahmins. The spirit *informs* these heads and torsos, much as the spirit informs the Substance of Spinoza. This is an æsthetic to be found in Egyptian sculpture. The archaic Greeks knew it and the classic Greeks, growing analytical, abandoned it. It has come closest to the West in the word of the Hebrews. Isaiah, Hosea, Job, the Song of Songs, the

---

[1] El Gréco: ou Le Secret de Tolède.

[2] Author of the authoritative life of El Greco, and one of the world's few truly great art critics.

Psalms, and the Alexandrian Pseudepigraphia rose, all, from a like æsthetic law. Byzantium rewon it wanly in its painting. El Greco's idiom is close to the Byzantine. In his essence, the fierce passion of its flaming, he is far closer to the Hebrews. This does not mean that Doménico Theotocópuli had Jewish blood. It proves rather that Christianity had Jewish blood, so that the Toledan ambiance of Semitic rhythm and Semitic thought could call forth for Rome a vision very close to the old vision of the Prophets.

El Greco must be regarded as a partaker, crucially, in the Toledan scene. Thus only can the mystical culmination of his work be understood. In Toledo, two antithetic Themes: a will of rigor and a flame of the East. What mystery shall fuse them? In El Greco, two dominant traits: volumnear color, movemented form. The mystery is at hand! Color creates plastic mass; mass, formed through configuration into bodies, creates a flow. But the flow is not of fluid; it is of fire. Fire flows and is steadfast; an essential object and an immutable circumambiance mold its motions to immobility. So now the flowing of El Greco's forms. Massing colors, thrusting shapes, parabolas of expression round spherically into a balance *with no outlet*. Ecstasy lies within itself. Life aspires—to life. Here is the vision of a Mystery which like flame flows forth from God, is held to God and is a form, in its commotion, of God's immutable, immobile essence. Here is a Mystery not transcendental, not neoplatonic. But Dante and Spinoza would have hailed it. And Toledo's stones could be transfigured to express it, without loss of their own nature.

Thus did the essence of El Greco's art resolve the two themes of his city. Once again, the God of the East upon the body of the West creates a masterpiece. . . . . . .

e. The Tomb

The ultimate Word of Castile. . .

A gray rectangle on the bleak Sierras. Behind, upon three sides, the immense mountains. Below, the rock and clay that join Madrid to Avila. Four stories of gray granite. A delicately arched slate mansard roof. Upon each corner a tower and three more tiers of windows tapering through the slender roof to a ball and a cross. Within, sixteen patios, making the design of a Gridiron: symbol of the gridiron upon which San Lorenzo, patron of the Escorial, was roasted. This Gridiron is cold. A mighty central patio, its walls of invariant granite broken by the church façade which rises within the building like a prayer wrung from the rigor of that stony life. Doric columns, gigantic and harsh figures of the Hebrew kings standing upon the pediment. Two towers at the corners, and within, a Dome lifting above the building like a Tomb and making death the dominant of this invulnerable music.

The Escorial stands on a stone platform whose inelastic might is emphasized by the severe cropped hedges. The green of the box, the green of window-sills and shutters chimes faintly against the silence. To the south, under the granite terrace, is a little pond. Its square surface mirrors only granite: that of the monastery walls or of the Guadarrama.

Within also silence. A monastery with its cloisters and chapter halls, a church, a college, a Palace . . in square stone rigor. Walls are thick like fortress walls; rooms are vaults; floors are bare. Below ground is an octagonal chamber of vermilion marble piled to the peaked ceiling with coffins of kings. And beyond, like the streets of some lugubrious town, are the vaults of the Infantas—a procession of marble mansions, body-large. This city of the dead holds the Escorial.

Eastward slopes a little park, and south from the artificial pool there is a lawn. It ends in a granite front flush with the grass. This brief pleasaunce is like a spot of verdure within desolation. Against it rises the Escorial, framed by the scoriant Sierras, based and topped by death —the profoundly stylized and essential form of the bleak Coronal of Castile.

It is the masterwork of Philip II. And Philip is a masterwork of Spain. The Spanish will to forge a unity from the warring elements of its life won no darker victory than his. He was the great grandson of the Most Catholic Kings. He was the true heir of their impossible purpose. His Empire spanned the world. Never has there been its like. Portugal, Holland, Franche-Comté, Austria, the Americas were bulwarks of his House. He strove to make of this delirious chaos a unitary Word to bespeak Christ. He gave his country's blood and his life. He took at their full value the accoutered lists of his imperial titles. He was the Catholic King; let his land express God. He was Monarch; let him know his children. His personal correspondence immensely regarded every city, every hamlet, every estate in his realms. Each curate of each parish was invited by the King to send detailed reports of the persons of his flock. But the curate might err in perspective. Each report was tested and criticized by another. Philip lived in the scaffolding of a Dream. The Dream was good, for it was to create and rule a unitary world. But the scaffolding was warfare, intrigue, laborious documentation. For peace, he went to war: for light, he plowed the dark. He spent his years and his people: and at the end he felt death.

This was the hour when the Escorial shaped in his dark mind. The pretext was the desire of his father Carlos I, that the kings of Spain possess a worthy tomb; and was the victory over the French on San Lorenzo's day. But the work that grew was strangely different from the plan, and far profounder.

The will to unity must come to this? Philip had dreamed of a monument of Life: a Spain that was to be the symphony of continents and seas, of a hundred peoples and a hundred tongues fused in the grace of Christ. Now, in the ardor of his maturity and in the glamour of his bloody conquests, Philip knows he has failed. Unity . . the health of Unity . . must be sought elsewhere. Not in the piling up of worlds but in their giving up; not in life but through death.

Many-mooded death. Death of the senses, death of the mind, death of glory, death of the will to live. From his imperial splendor and from the ranges of his kingly sway, Philip steps forth an ascetic. He will have his Solution within the ken of his eye—this master upon whose realm the sun does not set. He is the lord of the earth; and lives with one last mastering desire: to build a tomb for his glory.

Philip searches the waste fastness of Castile, until he finds his site: this barren spur of the Sierra below whose rock spreads the desert. Now he calls his slaves—they are the painters and the architects. Juan Bautista de Toledo and his successor Juan de Herrera, builders of the Escorial, are tools in the fever-cold hand of the king. Their plans are studied, revised, rejected. Their ebullient moods are flayed, their dignity is slurred. They are slaves—mere cutters of stone—they are tools.

And so, in a land of bastard architectures, where the Gothic is deformed, where Renaissance and baroque and Oriental forms are puddled and hypertrophied and belied, rises this masterwork. In its brutal chastity, speaks the tragic spirit of him who made it. The Escorial is to unverdant, fanatically ordered Spain what the green tragedies of Racine are to open, sweetly measured France.[1]

. . . . . .

[1] Like many other major works of art, the Escorial has its imperfections. The murals on the vaults of the Church are absurd;

Across the valley on a wooded height is a rocky bench known as the Seat of the King. Here Philip comes each day and watches the Escorial grow before him. He fears he might die ere it is done. He drives his slaves the artists; imports whole corps of them from Italy and Flanders. And when he is stricken with the illness which he thought his last, he is carried in a litter from Madrid, eight dolorous days upon the bleak meseta. He seeks the bare cell that is his Palace in the Escorial basement; he lies in the bedroom built beside the Altar so that he may hear Mass from his pillows. And so indeed he died. But still he sits each afternoon upon the *Silla del Rey,* and watches.

Below him, the sun goes down and a cold moon rises. Below him a patch of lawn and a flume float within this world splintered of granite and twilight. A wood of encina stands like an army of cowled saints. They are gnarled, gray-armored in moss, and their leaves are little refulgences of prayer, holding the sunset above the sodden ground. They look up, as Philip looks, toward the Escorial. It is matriced in jagged rock; it is sheer from the sun and the moon light. . . .

the murals in the cloisters of the Patio de Los Evangelistas are monstrous; and the pretty interiors of many of the Palace chambers are impertinent. But the blame for these defects does not lie with Philip II: they are the deed of successors. There is another flaw in the Escorial more significant. and miraculously appropriate. It is the presence of the *San Marcial* of El Greco in the Salas Capitulares. Philip ordered this painting; and when it was delivered he disliked it and refused it admission. The story goes that El Greco insisted on being paid. Philip paid him and thrust the work into the cellar. It is customary, on this point, to make sport of the bad taste of the King. El Greco is the greatest of Spanish painters; the *San Marcial* is perhaps his greatest picture. But Philip was right. This luminous and parabolic life did not belong in the frozen rigor of El Escorial. Today it serves with its gyrant aspirant forms to offset the brooding stillness in which it lives: a flame in an impenetrable night.

CHAPTER VI

THE DREAM OF VALENCIA

Spain, with face turned east away from the sun, takes her afternoon siesta. She has dined well. Soup of seven meats, codfish, the seven meats, cheese rich as manure, Galician greens, Toledan mazapan, Sevillan *dulces*, wines from Málaga, Jérez and La Mancha, heroic tobacco from the Canary Islands, fill her. She was hungry. For her day had been active. She had served and fused the wills of many peoples: swift Phœnicians, heavy-headed Romans, meteor Greeks, Goths with wild hair and tender eyes, intricate introvert Jews, Arabs with convictions about the materiality of Cosmos, Moors whose blood was fierce like Atlas avalanche, sportsmen like the Cid whose charity was of the sword, whose religion was of the moment, mystics of Castile parsing Christ with Horace, Spaniards at last . . Torquemada, Isabela, Celestina . . makers of the dominance of Castile. So Spain was hungry and heartily ate: was weary and heavily slept. And her dream was a city of the eastern coast.

Its name Valencia. Its streets a Carnival. Its life a Masquerade.

Medieval towers stand over streets that shrill with modern shops. Great Gates of Rome pinion the labyrinths of Orient. Arches of Islam throw into shade white mansions built by American concerns of sewing machines and fountain pens. All masquerade. The people speak a tongue close to the French languedoc: they ride in Citroens and Fords. Put no trust in this, they are not European. These open knots of barter, these entrail alleys, murmurous and fluid, speak of Fez and Tunis. Fraud again: this is not Africa. Islam puts a mockery on Rome. Judah redargues the Castilian dogma. Moorish marts belie the modern measure. Avenues of villas stretch straight from the town in gleams, and end in rice swamps: near the bungalows toss galleys on the tide, with sails like the sails of Carthage. Masquerade.

Here is the market place. *Lonja de seda,* the silk exchange, is Gothic. (The mulberry trees are thick upon the huertas.) But the base from which the Gothic rises is a Moorish palace. And from the noble height hangs Arab ornament. The gargoyles indeed lean down like muedzins —fossil muedzins with a frozen Allah on their lips. Under the holy walls, upon the floor, squat merchants: they masquerade for Greece of the Völkerchaos, for Talmudry of gain. And their commercial heads bathe in the light of a fairer east—the Sun.

Outside are throngs. A church façade, rococo overblown from the French Renaissance, echoes the shouts of women at their sheds. Oranges in tons, winesacks like human bodies, dates from Elche, potatoes, flowers, donkeys towing *tartinas* . . all produce of the lush Valencian huerta. The women wear great red aprons and have purple eyes. . .

Valencia in chaos is a masquerade. Greece, Carthage, Rome, Alexandria, Mecca, Fez annul each other here. Turbulent Valencia does nothing, says nothing. It is a dream of Spain, laden with her ages.

END OF PART ONE

PART TWO

The Tragedy of Spain

CHAPTER VII

THE WILL OF THE CATHOLIC KINGS

Young Isabel, sister of the king, sits in her castle tower at Medina, and looks beyond Castile: looks south to the Moorish realm, Granada; looks east and north to the kingdoms of Aragon and Navarre; looks west to Portugal. "Let there be Spain," says Isabel of Castile.

Her own land is riven in chaos. Ferdinand the Saint who won Córdoba and Seville from the Moslem was a strong monarch. But Alfonso the Learnèd was not wise in ruling. There have been two hundred years of banditry, of baronial insolence, of royal wavering. Castile is a quicksand upon which no will can march. Only the penniless submit to taxes. Nobles are outlaws. Rome parcels out appointments in the Church to alien lackeys. Prelates of Spain go their own way with their own crimson armies, or sulk in arrogant safety in their fortress-churches. Tolerance has begotten anarchy. Ideas annul each other in the too free sun. And God, with many faces, turns against Himself.

Isabel, looking from the bastioned windows of her tower out upon Castile is a luminous quiet heart in the storm. King Henry, the Impotent, is fertile of disaster. His favorites juggle with the scepter, scribble upon the royal parchment commands of idleness and of ambition. One of his favorites, Beltrán, has begotten on the Queen a daughter: and Joanna's growth is the growth of fresh dynastic war. Alfonso, the king's brother, claims the throne and writes his claim on the sparse wheatfields of Castile, making them desert. Portugal pushes: France plots and watches. Each fortune has its army. Each church is a castle. Each mountain is either an ambush or a throne. "Let there be Spain," says Isabel of Castile.

She will be queen: but in her own way. And her way,

like her will, is her rapt possession by the spirit of her land. Her brother, Alfonso, has died: his faction demand of her that she assume the Crown and drive out the impotent king. Isabel refuses. She bargains with Henry. While he lives, he is to rule. But his pseudo-daughter shall renounce: his adulterous wife shall return to Portugal: Isabel shall be acknowledged heiress of Castile. Henry gives his word, and breaks it. He is neither friend nor foe. He is a symbol of Spain's brackish chaos. Isabel holds to her castle. She is almost penniless; but she has for confessor a couched eagle, Cisneros, who is to second her mysterious work. Isabel learns that her brother the king plots to imprison her for the sake of Joanna whom the heir of Portugal has married. Isabel summons Ferdinand, heir to Aragon, to come and wed her. She is thinking of Spain; and her articulate will has convinced the old King Juan of Aragon, Ferdinand's father, that she is going to win—and that the union is good.

Disguised and penniless, Ferdinand crosses the hostile land and reaches the princess in Valladolid. He is seventeen: a lissom, romantic knight, the impact of whose bloods—Latin, Goth and Jew—has kindled a swift fire in his face. He sees this girl, tall and stately and one year his elder: her ruddy hair is a braided glow about her brow, the great blue eyes are a sky for the large rigor of her features. He enters the mansion of her love, to dwell forever within the sway of her will. For her will is Spain. He is brilliant, sharp, ubiquitous: but her will has place for him. Let him move from Italy to Peru: he will yet be within the will of Isabel.

The married boy and girl are fettered by penury in Castile; and like a breath to move them wait the death of Henry. He dies when Isabel is twenty-three. Portugal marches eastward for Joanna. His great army is a shadow in León. Isabel's faction dwindles. Ferdinand, wise consort, proposes peace with Portugal at the price of Zamora and other bastions of the west. Isabel refuses. She is pregnant. She makes long night journeys on horse, to her

recalcitrant towns. She pleads before rough communes and
proud *ricos hombres*. She spends her woman's strength
—she and Spain will suffer for it—but she does not entail
her still shadowy queen's power. She makes recruits.
She has a good field general in her husband. Portugal loses
heart before this hearty mother of unborn Spain. The
stubborn towns of Castile rally to her. In 1479 Juan
of Aragon dies: Ferdinand becomes king: Castile and
Aragon at last are wedded with their monarchs.

"Let there be Spain," is the rhythm of Isabel's thought.

"We have not yet won Castile," she tells her husband
on the march to the long, last war for the conquest of
Granada.

From ages of invasion and dissent, Spain has become
this throbbing swarm of aroused centrifugal impulse.
Ideas, races, communities, men: a boiling tumult to be
summed and stilled. Spain longs for peace: Spain longs
to become Spain. From her multiverse of wills, she has
willed a symbol: this person, fair and strong. She has
willed Isabel who is the flesh of Spain's will.

Isabel is one possessed. Her vision, thought and sense
move in one cycle. To her, physical love is not this tenderness between herself and her man: it is a joining of
Aragon and Castile. To her, physical fecundity is not her
woman's flower: it is the providing by a queen of counters
for dynastic matches.

But she is deliberate and wise. She has more than her
will and the weapon of her body. She has ideas for
weapons. The modern State functioning under an al-
mighty monarch, the medieval Church with its source in
Rome and Christ, and for her people Justice: this is the
triune tool whereby to weld the anarchies of Spain into
her Spain at last.

Strabo already wrote of the separatism of Spain: Rome
suffered here as nowhere else to unify her conquest.
Spain lacked a nervous system and a base: she had to be
subdued bit by bit—and so held. Since the Romans,
twelve hundred years have stratified the chaos. Each new

strain of blood, each fresh disposal of culture and of faith has become a claimant. The Spaniard bears in his nerves the variance of a past—all anarchy of dissent and self-assertion.

The Catholic Kings sit weekly in open court and dispense justice. The nobles are leveled down: the commoners are lifted. Finance is once more farmed from plenty, not extorted from indigence. Rome is compelled to relinquish to the Kings the right of nomination to high office. In all of this, the monarchs meet Spain's intricate problem with the conventional measures—those which are unifying France and Britain.

In Spain, this is mere prelude. Spain's chaos is more organic, and is unique in Europe. Isabel follows the logic of her weapons. What disrupts Spain is not banditry, not the insolence of nobles: but Spain's free life of inimical ideas. All else is consequence, not cause. To the south is a whole kingdom of the Moors. Everywhere live Mussulmans and Jews. More insidious still, there are the converted Jews—*los conversos*—who under cover of acquiescence spread the poison of their immemorial discord. When France was truly Catholic with Saint Louis for king, her Dominican friars backed by Pope Gregory set up an Inquisitional Tribunal. France showed her mettle against the Albigenses. Isabel has even a closer precedent to hand: Aragon defended herself against the heretics in 1242; and six centuries before, the Visigoths made protective laws against the Jews—the accursed Jews who freed themselves from oppression by letting in the Arabs! They are the same Jews still: few in number, but with the strength of ferment. They turn Christian: they achieve power and wealth: they marry with the nobles: they become princes of the Church. And their anti-national nature, their passion for free thought and independent action rot the weak royal fabric. Isabel applies for a Papal Bull: the Inquisition is set up, not against open Jews and Moors, but against the subtle and treacherous *conversos*.

Granada, decomposed under the affluent Moors, falls to the Catholic Kings. The Inquisition, captained by Torquemada, sends thousands of souls upon their way to Heaven and fills Spain with the anguish of torn bodies. Her roads are safe, her nobles and churchmen buckle under; the last Moorish prince has crossed the Strait to the Moghreb. And yet Spain is not One. Spain must become a Being, rapt and single, serving Christ and conquering for Christ. She who is the symbol of Spain's will strives to make her land in her own image. Spain, like her, must become chaste and absolute: a Catholic people as she is a Catholic woman.

The Jews are offered a merciful alternative: to be Catholic or to quit the land. Isabel argues that the *conversos* will lose their secret virulence if they have no nourishment from open Jewish neighbors. In 1492 a goodly fraction of the Jews of Spain "exchanging a House for an ass, a Vineyard for a coat," leave the cities where they have lived for ages. Ten years later, the Moors of the conquered kingdom of Granada, meet the same fate. Again, a host of intellectuals, artists, tradesfolk is bled away. The peasants do not stir: they become Catholic with the same inert response which had made them Moslem seven centuries before, or Arian under the Visigoths, or pagan under Rome.

Isabel looks at her work—and nods—and is not satisfied. She says: "We do unto the body of our beloved land as Christ did unto the possessed: we have cast out devils. But this is not enough. True disciple of our Lord, Spain must take up her burden and go forth: must forsake comfort and family and the long-sued peace: must bring His Word to all that dwell on earth. Spain is Christ's true apostle. France turns away in trickery and ambition. Henri IV, Louis XI—how far they are from Saint Louis! Italy is helpless. Spain is the well-beloved: Spain is Israel, and Rome's right hand. Let my king, Ferdinand, go with his hardened troops to Sicily and Naples.

"But even this suffices not. The Apostles did not stay

among the Jews: they went out to the Gentile. There is more than Europe. Can this strange religious mariner, Cristobal Colón, be right?"

Isabel ponders what she has heard of Columbus. He is the author of a book of *Prophecias*. He has found and plotted in the Old Testament his rationale for a westward route to the Indies. God perhaps wrote down in Isaiah, not alone Christ and the Word of Christ in Europe, but Spain and how Spain shall bring the Word to the East. Columbus a prophet? (He says there is gold in the Indies. Spain needs gold, for her crusade.) He is the friend of holy men in Spain: the Dominicans bespeak him and his cause. He has been rejected by Juan II of Portugal, by Henry VII of England, by Anne of Beaujeu, Regent queen of France.

"Let Colón go westward to the heathen east," the Catholic Kings ordain. "Let him carry the Christian word to the heathen, and bring back gold to carry the Word farther."

Isabel's will is religious. She is a woman incarnate of an idea: passionately eager to make all her realm, all the world flesh of her purpose. This means that her design must be practicable, also. Kingship is acceptance of the immanence of God. Isabel thinks she understands, looking over the turmoiled centuries of Spain: those of the Reconquest from Moor and Arab. She knows that the *mind* of these shifting wars was of this world and for the spoils of the earth. She knows that the Cid at times fought Christian, and that Saint Ferdinand could not have won Seville without the aid of the Moslems of Granada. God used mundane weapons for His purpose. No archangel did He send to drive Târik and Al-Mansor from Santiago, but mercenary treacherous knights who knew of the Infidel that he had gold, rather than that he spat upon the Cross. And unto this day, the Moor is respected in Castile! He is learnèd, liberal: he has fought well and lived well. Isabel accepts the strange ways of her Lord. She, too, must use mundane weapons. Ferdinand is ambitious: let his lust be a weapon. He is sharp, swift, hard like Toledo steel: no king of France can outwit him, no Italian cardinal withstand him. Isabel cherishes the good tool. A more conscious tool is Columbus. His ships have blundered on a new rich continent. His fortune has foundered: he is in chains—as were the older prophets. But the wealth is Spain's! His mariners are bullies—worldly tools of the Lord: yet even by them the Indian can be saved. Even by them and their greed, Rome can bring grace to the Indies. Isabel accepts the immanence of God, in the lusts of her servants.

She is a tall, fair woman. In the camp, in the castles that raise her constant journeys across Spain—Córdoba, Valladolid, Medina, Burgos—she lives the frugal life of the campaigner. She has paid for her forced night rides: the heaviest price, perhaps, is the feebleness of her children, none of whom survives to inherit or give an heir to Spain, save the mad second daughter, mother of Carlos the Great. The queen's splendors are reserved for display that shall bespeak her greatness to the world. When she enters Avila or Seville, it is upon a tide of gold and rubies. But when the doors shut upon her castle and the drawbridge rises, when she is alone with her family or her confessor, the jewels and the cloth of gold are gone: a woman, resolute and stark like the Castilian mountains, looks within herself for God's next message.

She is the spirit of Spain. Her husband, often unruly, often rebellious, is muscle, skill, craft—he is not the spirit of Spain. Her spiritual father, Ximenez de Cisneros, whom she chose for confessor because he had no respect for a queen, and whom she exalted to be Primate of Toledo because he abhorred all greatness—he is the nude projection of her conscience upon the widening splendor of her realm. Beneath the sumptuous robes of Cisneros is a shirt of hair. Deep in his vast castle is a cell, a bare and bedless floor on which the Primate sleeps after the penitential rope each night has lashed into his flesh the words of Christ. He is a formula of her immaculate will: but he is not the spirit of Spain. His fanatical asceticism is too simple. Spain, like Isabel, is turbulent and complex.

What pouring of flesh and spirit upon Spain, since the Phœnician, the Berber and the Celt first made the Iberian fecund! A subtle chaos. For Spain is a diapason of hostile forces, needing each other to survive: the embattled parts have long since found their balance, and each is in love with itself.

Isabel works like an artist. She has her vision. Her instinct and experience evolve for it a form and for herself a method. She takes her material ruthlessly and transfigures it with a cold passion. But for a deeper reason, Isabel is an artist. This design which is her vision and her will and to which she conforms her world is her world's will and vision. The creative circle is closed. For he alone is the true artist whose personal will is the will of his land and of God: only in this marriage of wills can there be true creation. Isabel makes Spain over into the image of Spain.

Behold the saintly, the murderous woman! She is the face of irony, and her smile is tragic. With what tender hand she sets up the Inquisition: "Unity in Christ, enforced by the power of the modern State." With what warm eyes, she bids her marauding mariners godspeed: "America brings recruits for Christ—and gold for the winning and holding of more recruits." How fondly she gives her insane child, Joanna, in marriage to the heir of Hapsburg; how resolutely furthers her husband's ambitions in the east. Spain, kingdom of God, surely cannot embrace America and neglect Europe? Infidel Africa, false France must be surrounded and crushed—"Austria, Artois, Netherland, Africa, America," she counts the organs of her embodied Christ.

And the heart of the Body, Spain herself, with Portugal long since joined by blood alliance: it must be pure and solid like the heart of the Queen. This is the kernel of her work. Isabel looks back upon her life and finds again her measure and her method. She will create a race of Spaniards whose every unit, man and woman, in intimate thought shall strike a single note: so that this note, myriad-repeated, fill the world. Spain, mother and child of chaos, shall become the archetype of unison on earth.

Isabel is ruthless, she is unafraid: she is certain. Such feeble virtues as tolerance, freedom, joy of life—Spain was celebrated for them beyond all Europe—must be given up. Shall Isabel spare her land, when she has not spared herself?

She was young and tender. She has known what it is to lie in a man's arms. She has been a mother. She has sacrificed love to become a captain. She has lost her children, unborn or born, because of her forced marches in the saddle. She has mortified not alone her lusts and vanities, but her gentleness and sweetness, to become this Weapon of the Lord.

Let Spain do as much. Let there be laws against the wearing of gold braid: against display of luxuriance and ease. Let there be laws against the idleness of doubt, against the vice of willful search of truth. (Rome has the truth!) Let there be laws against any wavering whatsoever from the pure unity of Spain. And what element offends against this white simplicity, let it be cut away—though the land bleed.

Above all let there be no peace. Isabel's art reaches its ironic climax. Spain's hunger for unity was the hunger for peace. Disunion and multiplicity had made perpetual war. Now unity was achieved, the Spanish rhythm—which was war—went on. The new ideal nourished the old mode. Spain is the apostle of Christ. Spain has become a state to establish Christ on earth. Let Spain not rest. Christ brings not peace, but a sword.

The vision, a theodicy: the form, the Church of Rome: the dynamic means, a State. In the impossible marriage of these three elements lies the tragedy of Spain.

For seven centuries Christians have fought Moslems.

Their motive was conquest of power. But their pretext became the Cross. The opposing Crescent determined this. The Cross grew, because of the faith of the Moor. Very early the Christians found it well in their raids against the Mussulman, to enlist the Presence of the Church. The priest became an auxiliary soldier: he brought the poetry and spirit of a religious slogan to enhance the fleeting motive of the Raid. And now at last the slogan has come true! Saint Ferdinand took Seville because he wanted more land. But Isabel sends ships to the Indies because she wants more Christians. A millennium of brutish restlessness has mothered this religious restlessness of Spain which would embroil the world till all the world be Christian. Ages after the Crusades of France and England, ages after the decadence of the Arab, the troops of Isabel become crusaders.

A modern State with a medieval God. In France and England, the medieval God has already vaporized away. England breaks literally with Rome. France dissolves her bonds into mere gesture. *The modern State must have no God but itself.* It must create its own pragmatic, its ethic, its metaphysic, finally its religion upon the unitary plan of its own health and progress. France knows this: henceforth the State of France will act unhindered by any ideal external to its future. And England knows this. Two mighty States move forward with a unity of program and of control born of the need of the State.

But in Spain, the State is not cause and effect, not ideal and goal, not master and dispenser. In Spain, the State shall be the tool of a Vision hostile to the State's essential nature.

The State must be materialistic, possessive, selfish. Spain's ideal is visionary, creative, altruistic. The State must steal and hold. Spain's ideal spends. The State murders to enhance itself. Spain's ideal murders to enhance Christ. The State is anti-individual. Spain's ideal makes and controls by law the yearning of each soul.

Isabel is an artist: she has the logic and the integrity

of the artist. But in the form of her work live elements
that disrupt and that belie each other. She makes of
Spain a modern State: she sends this monster, lustful,
treacherous and dull, upon a Christian errand. . . .

CHAPTER VIII

THE WILL OF SAINT AND SINNER

a. Irony and Honor

THE Catholic Kings have builded ruthlessly: absolutism, the grace of Christ, intolerance, universal justice, arms and prayer were to make Spain one. Now each of these qualities takes form and grows personified in Spain. Each is imbued with Spain's imperious will to be whole and one: each grows great with this spirit: each wars upon them all. Spain was chaotic and diverse. Her will to be one serries her into antitheses. Her will to union breaks her into extremes. Irony works on Isabel's fair fabric.

Perhaps the land itself is symbol of the process. Spain is desert—and garden; flat plain—and mountain; great heat—and winter. Spain is Europe—and Africa. In her events, she reveals this first ironic state of fusion—the splitting up into opposites of action. Columbus, mystic captain who charted his voyage in the Prophets, becomes enchained in the lust of avarice. His men, sent to Christianize the Indies, enslave the courteous American and sack his cities. Spain's past transforms! The Cid, that playful knight, becomes crusader. Saints turn knight-errant. Moderate Stoics (like Seneca, or Marcus Aurelius whose father was a Spaniard) inspire the ascetic fury of the hermits. And the humane Arcipreste de Hita, Castile's first poet, is turned into an apologist for license.

In her pageant of extremes, Spain's Middle Class is crowded out. The land has warriors—and beggars; nobles and rascals: saints and scoundrels. Charity is practiced with the sword and the mystic walks with the thief. Santa Teresa answers La Celestina. Don Quixote sallies forth with Sancho Panza.

One spirit moves them all. They have each the same whole pride in Spain, the same faith in her destiny, the same mind that Spain is their inheritance. The Spanish mystic is no aloof and transcendental man: he works for Spain. The Spanish rascal is no shallow rascal: he has the almost metaphysical conviction that Spain must feed him. And every Spaniard, from prostitute to saint, from king to beggar, moves within a sense which reveals this terrible will to *social unity:* the sense of Honor.[1]

The Spanish sense of Honor is the need of Spain to resist the social chaos of her land. The member of an integrated world completes it with self-approval. Self-approval the Spaniard does not need. He was a person, long before he had a nation. The Spaniard knew what was right, what was true. His need was to make others know as he did: for in this social conformity, he would feel himself at last the member of a group. The *pundonor* was the point of contact whereby he graphed, not his place in Heaven, but his place in the world. The stress was upon others. And this was the trait of a land in which individual unity was achieved; in which rights of personality needed no insistence; but in which social unity was lacking and was longed for.[1]

This need was so intense that it inspired a literature and informed a religion. Æsthetic worlds were built upon this impulse and it infused the writings of mystics as well as the histories of rascals. Spain in her great Age— a pattern of sharp-limned individuals—was symphonized in the key of Honor.

[1] The relatively great importance of honor to women in all lands is perhaps to be explained by analogue. The inherent social sense in women (beyond the family sense) is weaker than in men: hence their need of social approval is the more intense.

b. The Mystic

The mystics of Catholic Spain who in act and word gave utterance to the will of Isabel rose from a high tradition in the land. They were indeed the fulfillment . . as was the Queen . . of a religious vision older than Spain herself. When Salamon B. Judah Ibn Gabírol was born in Málaga in 1021, there was not yet Spain. Gabírol looked about him at this land in which three continents and three religions were embroiled. And he said:

> "Thy Glory is not diminished because of them that worship aught beside Thee. For the intention of them all is to attain Thee. But they are as the blind: they set their faces toward the way of the King; and they wander out of the way."

Gabírol the Jew wrote hymns which were included in the Sephardic ritual. But the book which sets forth his vision of God and life reveals no specific creed: it was too universalistic for the Jews who neglected his philosophy and soon lost even the Arabic manuscript of his work. Two centuries later, the *Mekor Hayim* reappears in the Latin version *Fons Vitæ*: Aquinas combats its intuitionalism, Duns Scotus leans on it. The Arabs Ibn Sina and Ibn Roshd were naturalized in Europe as Avicenna and Averroës: now Ibn Gabírol, stripped of his race and sect, becomes Avicebron: one of the sources of platonic faith in modern thought. But it is an error to confound Gabírol with the followers of Plotinus who supplied the principal attack upon those fossils of modern rationalism, Maimonides and Aquinas. There is an element in Gabírol which the true neo-platonist lacks: an element both Semitic and of Spain. It is the element of Will, immanent and purposeful, in his conception of divinity. Life to Gabírol is no mere fated emanation of the Godhead as to the true North African and Hindu mystic: nor is it an unreal envelope about truth, as to the followers of Plato. Life is the form of God in matter: the willful imprint of divinity on earth. This concept gives to the rapt activity of the mystics who embrace it an earthward, a practical direction. If the world is pattern of God's will, the highest human spirit cannot in the highest vision transcend the earth or grow detached from it: he must work in earth and through earthly deed enact God's revelation.

Gabírol, first of Spain's literary mystics, founds this tradition which at the end is to produce in Spain a lineage of mystics who are men of action: a lineage far removed indeed from the commoner progeny of mystics who, as they approach God, leave the terrestrial life. The early Moslem thinkers outdid even their Jewish partners in the great Courts of Córdoba and other Andalusian towns, by this tendency of their doctrines. But their universalism became materialistic. Stressing the monism of nature, they lost sight of God as the *informer:* the Prophet Mohammed shrank to a sort of intellectual agent of the will, what the Spaniards called *intendimiento agente,* a power more physical than of the spirit. There were exceptions. Avempace, the Moslem platonist, for instance, who was born in Guadix a little later than Gabírol. And his disciple, Tofaíl, whose novel *Hai-ben-Jochdam* is a spiritual *Robinson Crusoe,* an extraordinary proof of the immanence of God. Hai, an infant, is abandoned on a desert island. A doe nurses him. The bare demands of material survival sharpen his reason: and from the purity of intellectual understanding he achieves religious revelation. His body has evoked reason, and reason evokes God. Now, at the end of his days, an aged saint comes to the island. He has reached by simple faith the same religious certitude as Hai by the exercise of mind. The circle is rounded. God is the end of all ways, and is the way of all thoughts. But the rational monism of the Moslems was not protected, like that of the Jews from a sheer materialism which made many thinkers at the Court of Abd-er-Rahman contemporaries at once of Democritus and Haeckel. The immediate plateau from which arose in Spain the Catholic mystic heights was Jewish.

For many ages, the Spanish Catholics [1] contribute little to the medieval Scripture whose prophets were men like Abelard, Albertus and Aquinas. The long line of Spanish Jewish worthies droops: while in the north the subtly variant seed of Roger Bacon and Duns Scotus flowers at last into the twin rebellion of Protestantism and of rationalism. It is with the age of Calvin, of Francis Bacon, of Erasmus, that Catholic Spain finds voice at last: and in a way which is an act. By means of this late flowering in the south, modern Europe is a natural issue from the womb of the medieval Church. Rome is saved until the seed of Rome's successorship is planted: international law is founded: America is discovered and is peopled.

The tradition of such men as Gabírol and Tofaíl seemed dead, when it spoke suddenly afresh in the work of a Spanish Jew. And of this man's influence, Menendez y Pelayo says in his classic work on the Ideas of Spain: "All the Catholic mystics, from the Dominican Fray Luis de Granada to the Jesuit Nieremberg accepted the æsthetic of Leon Hebreo integrally, knowingly."

His true name was Judah Leo Abravanel and with his father, a statesman and a thinker, he left Spain in the exodus of 1492. He was a young man when he settled in Italy, and it is very possible that his *Dialogues of Love* were originally written in Italian.[2] The oldest text of this epoch-making work is an Italian prose full of Castilian uses.

[1] There was of course Ramón Lull, the great scholastic poet and mystic of Majorca.

[2] A. S. Oko, the Hebrew scholar, is certain that the original was in Italian. José Ortega y Gasset, Professor of metaphysics in the University of Madrid, assured me of his personal conviction that an original Castilian MS. was lost.

The originality of the work of Leon Hebreo rests chiefly in the fact that here for the first time ancient and medieval thought achieves a modern form. The stuffs of the *Dialogues* come up from Plato, Plotinus, Crescas and the Kabbala: but the grace of the Renaissance, the humanism of Venice and of Florence are within them. Here is the doctrine of the Eternal Recurrence which Nietszche strove to incorporate in European thought. Here in germ is Spinoza's explanation of the union of the individual with God and of the unity of substance. The *Dialogues* are so universalistic that they do not refute the legend of their author's conversion to the Christian faith: and they are so poetic that they constitute indeed a lyrical threshold to the Pantheism which Spinoza was to architect for Europe. To Crescas and Leon Hebreo comes Descartes to produce Spinoza: comes the spiritual body of the Spanish will to produce the Spanish mystics. Castilian grows to be the literal and literary word of a nation resolved to win the earth in order to establish God upon it.

Perhaps the most powerful writer among these mystics [1] was the Augustinian monk, Luis de León, whose lecture hall with its narrow wooden benches honeycombed with the knife-marks of his students, one may still see in Salamanca.

---

[1] A mighty lineage of masters who made of the Castilian an immortal language. Among them are the Dominican Luis de Granada; the Franciscans Juan de los Angeles, Diego de Estella, San Pedro de Alcántara; the Carmelites San Juan de la Cruz, Santa Teresa, Jerónimo Gracián, Miguel de la Fuente; the Augustinians Malon de Chaide, Alonzo de Orozco; and the Jesuits Nieremberg (Juan Eusebio) and Alonzo Rodríguez. . . At the same time a literary æsthetic was developed (Ausias March, Fernando de Herrera de Sevilla) whose creative liberality rings refreshingly modern, beside the poetics of Boileau. Writes Herrera: "So long as a language lives and is spoken, it cannot be said to have run its course: for its constant tendency is to surpass itself and to leave behind what was formerly esteemed. We must constantly essay new forms. . ." This was the spirit which made possible El Greco and Góngora and Cervantes. It was one outcome of the monasteries and of the religious universities of the Age of Isabel. It proves how strong, in a way, the Renaissance was in Spain until the reactionary time of Philip II.

The prose of Abravanel is luminous, pigmented, mobile. His dialogues remain a string of separate gems, variously valued, inorganic. The prose of Luis de León—far superior to his verse—is integral and substantial as the will of Spain. Abravanel was an uprooted speculator. León was a Spanish Catholic immersed in the business of his age. He is indeed a mystic only by reflection: a classicist at heart. His work is less parabolic, has fewer flashes than the *Dialogues;* it is indeed less open to the sun and stars. But it is far more plastic. Spain herself moves in his sentences and knits them whole. The author is a passionate believer: so is his land, so is his Monarch: so becomes his people. There is no separation between the dreams of the close of Salamanca and the sea-bridging policy of the Castilian State. Luis de León, preaching to his students in a narrow hall within a narrow city, is linked with Italy and with America.

The process of art is the endowment of a particular experience with the full measure of life. The work of art is a fragment of word or substance informed with the wholeness of spiritual vision. The mystics of Spain were fated to make art, or to make deeds. For here theology was heir to centuries of universal vision. The mystic remains a Catholic and a churchman. The Inquisition narrows his forms of speculation. He is a part of Spain. But all Spain's cosmic will is in him.

This will is in the great work of Luis de León: *Los Nombres de Cristo.* Three Augustinian monks set forth from their convent across the river from Salamanca. One of them has found a shaded grove on the río Tormes: here, shielded from the fever of the sun, they rest and exchange discourse on the names of Christ. The subject is rigidly dogmatic: the treatment of the virtue of names has the Pythagorian and Kabbalistic note which Plato and Aquinas equally would have rejected. Yet in this stifled frame, an artist quickens a magnificent world. The monks with their conventional background, the old town in flame of summer, the river panting through its fringe of trees, the athletic freedom of the mind in search, the passionate reality of God—all Spain is in this antiquated book. Her extremes of waste and verdure, her turmoil of race, her traffic and speculation, her panoply of vision—Jew, Christian, warrior, priest—converge into the substance of prose. The delirious delights of logic scaling the battlements of God, the southern arabesque whereby the abstract thought becomes design make it glamorous and moving.

León's career was action. He was a teacher, and his words were on the quick of deed. This is why the Inquisition took note of him and subjected him to five years of imprisonment and torture. The Inquisition, for all its folly and corruption, was the coefficient of Spain's unity. In any organism, thought and act are joined. This was true of medieval Europe: it was true of Spain alone in Europe after the modern dawn.

A younger man than Luis was Juan de Yepes whom Rome later canonized as San Juan de la Cruz. Like Luis de León, like Teresa and Loyola, Juan met with persecution not because he was a mystic and a poet; but a man of action. Haggard, fanatical, almost disembodied, this spirit had body enough to pass like a scourge of flame through the dark cities of Castile, cleansing monastic evil; and like a breath of sweetness, comforting the sick. He, too, is incarnate, in his particular phase, of Spain's whole will. He is a saint: rapt and ascetic. His voice is the voice of spiritual vision. Yet it, as his life, is marvelously fleshed: a sort of slender fire. The peculiar plasticity of Spain is clear in Juan if one contrast his life with that of Saint Francis of Assisi, or his work with that of Porphyry and Plotinus. Grace here has a hard edge, is the handle of action. This reforming flesh fuses the sweetness of Saint Francis with the acumen of Savonarola. Juan is very close to Christ. For he is ruthless and practical. His charity like Christ's is sharper than a sword.

John of the Cross shares the *graphic* quality which Spain through her unitary will breathed into her various parts. He is abstract—plastically; he is Idea—incarnate. In no wise is he transcendent. Chained down to rot in some hostile convent cell, he is still concerned with persons and with convents. A titanic pressure—Spain—seems to have columned all the world into this lean, bright figure.

His song is like him. The simple words hold an immensity like the deep nights of Spain. Love of conquest, of gold, of glory and of power—the turbulence of Spain is not within them. Yet the essence of will and power, making this intricate turmoil, lives in his poems like a resolution of many chords in silence.

Juan's preceptress and ally in their task of purifying convents was Teresa de Ahumada, known to religion and to letters as Santa Teresa de Jesús. Teresa's town, Avila, stands for her: stands for the woman of Spain. The unbroken walls, the elliptical towers, the crenellated parapets and gateways, symbolize her virtue. Within, Avila is mellow and is fecund. Her walls shut her safe from the thrusting mountains of Castile. Avila is ordered, within chaos.

Santa Teresa is the mystic, as organizer: she is yet another part of the will of Isabel and Spain. The religious houses of the land are dissolute and weak. Against the hostility which her sex aroused, against the distrust of the Inquisition, Teresa moves through Spain, cleansing and creating hearths for the luminous life. The world, to her, is a household. The Master is Christ and he requires service. Her imaginative powers . . in which the Arab glamour is not wanting . . make so vivid the delights of service that the convents of Spain become as magnets, sapping the humbler households of the land. To Teresa, the soul also is a home; and her book *Las Moradas* is a picture of its chambers. "As above, so below." Christ, the bridegroom, enters the household of the soul: and at once, the humble household becomes Heaven. Teresa's convents are literal heavens upon earth: they are the dwelling of a Lord whose passion fails not. Spain's will pours a sea of energy into this fragment of her deed. Teresa's work is homely; and so is the rough plastic language of her books. *Las Moradas, El Libro desu Vida* articulate the sense of the common Spanish matron who makes of her bridal bed an altar, and of her religion a marriage.

Teresa is no merely powerful reformer: she is a creator. In her hand, the broom and the account-book become mystic weapons: even as in the hands of Torquemada the wrack; and in the hands of Columbus the rudder and the compass.

He was born in Italy; and the question of his descent, Italian or Spanish or Jew, is unsolved and has no bearing. Christopher Columbus in his historic rôle belongs with the Spanish mystics. We have lost his book of *Prophecias.* But we can reconstruct the trend of the argument which, having failed to convince the "practical" Courts of England, Portugal and France, won over the clerics of Spain and at Córdoba moved the Queen to send him westward.

Like the platonic Jews, Columbus idealized his route and made a symbol of his navigating passion. Like Philo, he mapped out his scheme in Scripture. Yet another phase of Spain's organic will was served by this devout seafarer: and through Spain, yet another need of Europe.

Medieval Christendom is in dissolution. Much energy is released; and needs an outlet, and cannot find it until this mystic mariner, Christian and medieval, finds America. Down to earth pours the energy of Europe: the Vision and Body of a Gothic Christ no longer hold it. Down it clamors, seeking earthly forms—seeking an America, indeed! But Columbus is a Catholic. And Isabel, the Catholic Queen, smiles on his adventure, aiming to spread the Church to India. And what they do—this mystic seafarer, this rapt good monarch—is to give to Europe an escape for its too-long stored Catholic might: to give to it a land in which the blood of the medieval Christ may be sluiced, may be lost forever!

Irony marries with heroic Spain.

c. The Jesuit

In 1491, there was born to a family of noble Basques in the Guipúzcoan castle of Loyola another mystic instrument of the Spanish will. Iñigo Lopez de Recalde had the crude upbringing of the gentlemen of his race. He learned to write Castilian; he served in the Court of the Catholic Kings; and he became a soldier. He was a good soldier and the eyes of his superiors were on him. At the age of thirty he took part in the defense against the French of Pampeluna, capital of Navarre. A cannon ball shattered his leg. During the long convalescence, grace came to the Basque captain. He renounced worldly arms and took the staff and habit of a religious beggar. He pilgrimaged to Rome and to Jerusalem. At thirty-three, he began to study Latin. His austerity and that of a few comrades whom he had attracted and whom he held for life brought him the usual displeasure of the Holy Office who discouraged any swerving, even in the path of piety, from the common norm. Loyola met distrust in the University of Alcalá: on his arrival at Salamanca, he was jailed on general suspicion of being either too holy or a fraud. Thence, still seeking theology, he went to Paris and to London. Everywhere he was coldly received, and forbidden to speak on religious topics. He was forty: he had abandoned a career of arms: he was not even a priest. But he had friends: they formed a band of seven including another Basque, Francisco Xavier, a Frenchman and a Portuguese. In 1534, they took a private vow of chastity, poverty and devotion. Three years later, Loyola was ordained a priest. Since his conversion at the age of thirty, eighteen years had passed, and they had been for him a constant wrack of suspicion and of impediment to his purpose. He waited eighteen more months ere he judged him-

self worthy to say Mass. And not until then did he
put forth his plan of a Company of Jesus—a cohort of
religious soldiers—to defend Christ in the world and to
spread Him. Pope Paul III recognized the Order in
1540. Loyola against his will was elected General in
1541.

Like its name, the *Compañia de Jesús* was military in
form and method. One year before Loyola's conversion
at Pampeluna, Martin Luther had burned the Papal bull
of excommunication. Europe made this simultaneous gesture of antithesis. The north lurched from the medieval
Body: and Spain took its fate unto herself, girded her
loins to save and spread the Church. Born to war, converted in an experience of war, surrounded by the strife
of faction, Loyola never ceased to be a soldier. He conceived Christianity in martial terms. The Church needed
defense and aggrandizement. The nature of the man's
career and the will of his nation shaped the Company
of Jesus.

At its head was a General, with power as absolute as
that of a commander-in-chief in war. The Church was
at war. Monastery and convent were Christ's infantry.
They did not suffice. They were even losing ground.
The new Compañía would be the cavalry: an arm best
fitted for skirmish and attack.

"Let us think all in the same manner; let us speak all in
the same manner," said Loyola. His Spiritual Exercises
were the drill of his cohorts. So the militant ideal of
Spain, serving in her armies the will of Isabel, found this
new and compact body. The sword had become a mystic
instrument. Now a body of spiritual fathers turned themselves into a sword: took on the traits and ethic of the
sword. Like Spain's, the forces of Loyola spread at once
to Africa, America and Asia. And at the end, the Society of Jesus, like Spain once more, locked in too perfect
oneness: its strength hardened and grew brittle: its heroic
faith became a stifling armor.

About a hundred years after the founding of the Society of Jesus, a young Frenchman, Blaise Pascal, wrote a series of Letters which have focused all the distrust and misconception aroused by the aggressive Body, and from whose subtle blows it never has recovered. *Les Lettres d'un Provincial* is a great literary work. A man of genius, spokesman of his race, exposes the presence in his land of an organism monstrously alien to the spirit and rhythm of France. His intuitions are metaphysically deeper than his logic. Pascal does not know that the Society of Jesus is a formulation of the will of Spain: his points often are departures from false premises as in his invidious handling of the Jesuit doctrine of *probabilism* or of the famous Jesuit sentence: "The end justifies the means." Small matter: Pascal wrote a brilliant laughing prose whose beauty has not faded; and more, almost unwittingly he defended France against the invasion of an alien will. Although his arguments were often false, although his irony was unscrupulous, Pascal from his vantage-point was right.

The will of France has been adverse to that of Spain: France has worked from a social sense to the creation of a personal conscience. She has moved from the group-mystical to the personal-rational; from the Gothic church to the modern realistic; from social vision to the individual; from Substance to Essence; from France herself to man. Blaise Pascal is an exemplar of this pattern of his people's progress. He and the Jansenists reveal the effort of the conservative French to transform the old Catholicism into an individualistic faith that shall be consonant with France's future. Pascal's sense of Grace as a determined individual gift of personality places his conflict with the Jesuits on its fairest ground: it is the will of social France for personal autonomy, at odds with this invasion of personalized Spain whose will is to create a social spirit.[1] Pascal, Racine, Descartes are the last great

[1] The Jansenist belief in predestination and the Jesuit doctrine of free will appear to contradict this. The paradox is only of the sur-

minds of France to believe in the persistence of their nation's progress *within* the Church. Calvin, greatest of
the Protestant thinkers and a true Frenchman, marks the
break. France accepts a destiny outside of Rome which,
in this logical people, swiftly leads to a destiny outside
the whole structure of Christian revelation. Pascal and
Racine within the Church, Calvin in a church of his
own, Montaigne the skeptic, begin not by accepting man—
but by the desire to create him. The social body exists:
the individual soul does not. All French classic literature
converges in this effort to establish it . . converges, indeed, upon Romanticism (Diderot, Rousseau, Stendhal).
In Germany, the same trend passes from Luther to Goethe,
Schopenhauer, Novalis, Nietzsche. The French problem
of creating the personal conscience above the accepted
group marries with the will of northern Europe to break up
the social synthesis of medieval Rome by the creating of
individual souls that shall be *atomic, anarchic,* but once
more creative. The antistrophe is the tragic will of Spain,
and the heroic Jesuit effort, to revive a Body that was
doomed.

In the domain of education, the Society of Jesus does
not swerve far from Spain. And the will of Spain accepts man as he is found. Isabel creates her empire by
use of her countrymen's frailties and lusts. The Jesuit
proceeds in the same spirit. He will work, not from
the departure of an ideal concept of what man should be:
he will work with man, with this miserable, forkèd, naked
son of sin—and build from him the City of his God.
Man in his weakness, man in his vice and blindness, will

face. Acceptance of predestination and of pre-determined grace rests
on acceptance of the inviolable autonomy of the individual soul and
minimizes all objective—i. e., social—effect on it. The Jesuit free will
actually puts the stress on possible change in the individual soul
through social forces, thus minimizing the soul's autonomy. That
this interpretation is correct is borne out by the developments of
Jesuit practice on the one hand and of French-Calvinist-Protestant
cultures on the other.

be a note in the cosmic Song: his muddy heart will be strong as marble. There is a magic to enact this. Its name is Faith. There is a philosophy to enact this. It is the traditional sense, in Spanish thought, of God's immanence and of earth as the immediate pattern of God's will. The Jesuits are not pantheists: but their tolerance and their practical acceptance of *the fact* are the unconscious fruits of five centuries of pantheistic feeling. The Jesuits are not Evangelists. But in their attitude toward Faith as a universal magic, they are close to the Apostles. They take the Christian mystery as a present truth. The age of miracle is eternal. God is here and everywhere: the assertion of a magic Word—as in the Kabbala—transfigures immanence to revelation. The doctrine of Grace, as an inborn personal trait to be achieved (if at all) only by spiritual acts, is too hierarchic. It is the doctrine of peoples tending toward individualism. (In the East, it becomes the doctrine of Caste.) Moreover, in accepting man as he is, the Jesuit cannot place the magic virtue in any of his inherent traits. The divine virtue must be at once impersonal and social. Man is frail and corrupt: his will is frail and corrupt. His life is only in God, even as God's life through Christ is eternally in man. There is no work to be done, beside the assertion that the work *is* done. If grace depended upon man's efforts, we should all be damned. If reason or will or any personal trait had been sufficient, why was Christ crucified? No: the commonest human stone is holy, when it becomes a stone of the House of God. Likewise, man's corruptions, however vile, can be architected by faith into the Church where they are sanctified and transfigured.

The philosophy of the Jesuits explains their methods. Does the builder of a house consult the stones? What can the stone do but put itself into the hands of the builder? The builder must be aggressive, dominant, ruthless. But the Jesuit is more than an architect: he is a soldier. When he sets aside the sword for the word, the cause is strategy. His tactics remain warlike. War is pragmatic. Subtlety, surprise, mobility, deceit are war-like arms.

The world stands at a crisis. The grandiose structure of medieval Rome—the highest spiritual Form ever achieved by Europe—crumbles and sags. Spain strips to save it.

d. The Jurist

At Salamanca a Dominican monk teaches theology. His name is Fray Francisco de Vitoria. Salamanca, fostered by the Catholic King, becomes the leading university of Spain. Spain becomes Austria, Artois, the Netherlands, Franche-Comté, North and South Italy, Sicily, the Balearic and Canary Islands, Africa from Ceuta to Oran, the Moluccas, the Philippines and the Americas from Florida to Tierra del Fuego. Carlos, son of the mad daughter of the Catholic Kings, becomes head of an empire like the dream of Isabel. He, too, is a creature of her will. The vastness of his realm has blotted out his sense of time and space. His religious fervor blurs his vision of mortal values. He will ride Spain as he might ride a horse in battle. He has inherited Spain as a weapon to be wielded. Spain is his, in order that the world be Christ's.

The Dominican monk at Salamanca moves within the will of Carlos and of Spain. The blood of Isabel's empire is justice. Justice nourishes and cleanses. Carlos must be ruthless, but he must not be wrong. He will do what he desires: it must be proven right. The Americas make new challenges of conscience. Vitoria in Salamanca meets the king's need: and modern International Law is ready for the world.

A full century before the Dutchman Grotius (Huig van Groot), Vitoria lays down a rationale of justice for existing Powers, a structure in diapason between their economic needs and their inherited morale. He works for a modern state whose ideal is a theodicy of medieval Rome. The ideal has become more abstractly ethical, more economic. But Woodrow Wilson and the statesmen of the League of Nations are exact heirs of a Dominican monk.

Vitoria studies the problems of America in his *Relectiones de Indis:* the general problems of war in *De Jure Belli.* Both these works, it is significant to note, form part of his *Relectiones theologicæ et morales.* A true creature of the will of Isabel, he has turned international problems into a problem of conscience. He denies independent form to his subject. The law of nations and of peoples is a moral law: it is outside the activities of lawyers. A question rises between the king of Spain and the Indians of Mexico. The "savages" are not subject to the king by human right. Their dealings with him cannot be determined by human law. Only a divine law, moving Spain as a theodicy, has brought about this juncture between the Indians and the king. Only divine law is competent to rule.

Vitoria expands his thesis. There exists this same divine law—*jus inter gentes*—between all States. The States are interdependent. There is a *societas naturalis,* a natural Society of Nations. The link is God. Free to the Spaniard to assume that God's agent in the link be the king of Spain. The world is one society: and between peoples of one society peaceful intercourse may not be forbidden. France may not impede a Spaniard from visiting France, even from settling in France, provided he violate no law and cause no damage. If this is true between Frenchman and Spaniard, it is true between American and European. Through the fact of their civil rights in a society of nations the Indian cannot exclude the Spaniard. There exists therefore *jus communicationis:* the right of immigration. There exists also the freedom of the seas. Spain stands justified in her American penetration.

We are at the mere beginning of Vitoria's subtle structure. *Jus commercii*—the right of commerce—applies not only to the exchange of merchandise between free peoples, but as well to the exchange of ideas. The Spaniard has the right to preach the Gospel to the Indian. The Indian has the right to preach heathenism to the Spaniard. Either may resist conversion (even as either may decline to purchase proffered goods).

Since no State may prevent a stranger from settling on its lands, nor even from becoming a lawful national, here are the Spaniards legally at home in the Americas. But strong Powers must defend by arms the menaced liberties of smaller States. That is a prerogative of a true society of nations. How much more readily therefore shall strong Powers defend the menaced liberties of individuals in every State! All States are "organs of human justice." Spain shall protect the innocent from "religious sacrifice" and "from cannibalism in America." If need be, to protect the innocent, a State may subjugate wholly an unjust nation.

The theologian brings to Spain her "cosmic place" in the Americas as Christ's agent in the society of nations. But this is not enough. That she may be at peace in Zion, she must be alone. So Vitoria evolves in 1500 the modern theory of "spheres of influence." Pope Alexander was *divinely* just in submitting to Spain and Portugal, as God's best tools, the mission of Christianizing the Americas. But the Pope had no *human* right to partition the property of the red man. Vitoria with all the Dominicans behind him stands against Pope and king: declaring that "the Indian has as much right to possess property as the Catholic peasant." The Indians, he holds, are potential equals of the Spaniards. They have the right to plebiscite. A majority of their votes alone can justify America's *annexation* to the empire of Spain. Beyond the divine and human privileges that are general in a society of nations, "Spain must commit no act in the New World, except by treaty."

The Dominican legists part company with the deeds of Spain. Already, Isabel had been misled when her adventurous "tools"—the Conquistadores—instead of saving the Indian, enslaved him. Now the followers of Vitoria raise their voices against the behavior of Cortés and Pizarro. Bartolomé de las Casas in his *Brevissima relación de la destrucción de las Indias* writes pages that are good reading in our own epoch of a "Society of Nations." But the abstract logic of Vitoria was more useful to the State of Spain than the ethical conclusions of Las Casas. That supreme apologia for villainy and greed—International Law —is born and baptized under Christ.

Thus Vitoria: "War is justified when it is forced on a State in the rightful pursuit of commerce, in the rightful propaganda of ideas—and *if the Spaniards have observed all precautions against taking their interests for principles, and their avarice for duty.*" What empire since has not "taken these precautions?" Christianity had been theoretically pacifistic. Jesus was reported to have declared against all violence and the resisting of evil. Being the Son of God, of course, His words were not to be literally construed. Yet such men as Tertullian, the Manichees, Saint Francis, Wyclif, More, Erasmus, had declared unconditionally against warfare. Chiefly, that prophetic Berber, Augustine, took war to be a usable weapon of the just. Vitoria, his neighbor in race and land, leans on Saint Augustine. The anarchic and endemic sin of war is lifted at last from Europe's conscience. Spain invents the Moral War.

"War," says Vitoria, "is justified to right a wrong." But Vitoria is careful:

"Difference of religion is no just cause for war.

"Aggrandizement of empire is no just cause for war.

"*Principis gloria propria, aut aliud commodum, non est causa belli justa.* The Prince may not wage war to further either his glory or his own interests. And the wrong to be righted by war *must be commensurate with the results of war itself* (death, confiscation, rapine) ere a just war can be induced to right it."

The friar seems to be going too far. Hear him:

"The end of war must be, not evil to the foe, but good.

"And victory must be enjoyed in Christian moderation.

"The people shall not suffer through the faults of their princes.

"Finally, a treaty imposed by force—even after victory—is not valid."

Modern International Law is after all no growth from these uncomfortable precepts of a monk: it is a lapse and a decadence. The legal dicta of Vitoria are of an old tradition: they are a birth of the old breaking Synthesis of medieval Europe. International Law is the theoretic shred of what was once a spiritual Body.

e. The Rogue

The Spain of Isabel and Ferdinand, of Carlos and Philip II—wherein is she great? In her idea and Will. These prove the Globe and bind it: these in their own way prove and make her one with God. But Spain, the body of men living in towns and huertas, is indigent and disordered.

At her spiritual climax, under Isabel, Carlos and Philip II, Spain was squalid. By contrast with the state of England, of France, of the German towns and of the cities of Morocco, she was an economic laggard. Her nobles with their retinues cut swathes of gold through the landsides. She was full of heroes and of saints. But the land was arid with neglect. War had razed her forests. Seven centuries of Reconquest, making labor despicable beside the guerdons of battle, had sapped her burghers. What the long wars began, the Inquisition and Expulsions carried on. Jews—a solid class of craftsmen and middlemen—were expelled. The Granadan Moors—ablest of Spain's cultivators—were making homesick songs about their Andalusian farms, in Fez and Marrakech. There were more vagabonds in Spain than farmers, more soldiers than laborers. There were more hidalgos and caballeros than artisans and merchants. There were seven million Spaniards—and nine thousand convents!

Some men are poor because they are weak and dull: some are poor because they are men of genius. Amsterdam and London grow rich, because such is their will. Avila and Toledo remain dingy, because their will is elsewhere. Spain is virile, brilliantly equipped. But Spain has resolved to be a hero and a saint. Spain has no time to pave streets, who paves the way for Christ beyond the sea. Spain has no time for natural science, for agriculture and for the tricks of trade, who is so expert in theology.[1]

In the extremes of her life, none is wider than this between the Spirit of Spain's enterprise and the fact of her condition. The crass and earthly elements of Spain are not destroyed nor repressed by her religious will: they are engaged. They must serve in her armies, even though the fight be a crusade. They must man her ships, even though the mariner's compass be divinely pointed. They are intensified indeed, like all the parts of Spain. And like the other elements of her world, brutality and lust assume in a particular form the wholeness of Spain's will.

Spain is adventuring. Now the sheer impulse of adventure is embodied. The pícaro is born. He has in him the aboriginal Spaniard: that unruly, lusty, atomic man whom Rome encountered, whom the Cid personified. He is an anarch, brutal as the Iberian of the north, shrewd and subtle as the Phœnician of the south. He is this aboriginal, complex man of Spain shaped by the Spanish will. The pícaro is not lawless: he is an outlaw. He reacts from Spain's social purpose, from Spain's social structure, from the mysticism and heroism of this later Spain. Like all reactive bodies, he resembles his opponent. And it is this union in him—the direct issue from the source of Spain and the direct response to Spanish culture—which makes him so true an element in that culture.

The pícaro was long in coming. The Cid promised him in the twelfth century, and the romancero on the eve of the age of Isabel. The genial Juan Ruiz, archpriest of Hita, in 1300 came close to his spirit in the graphic form . . a mingled piety and license . . of his great *Libro de buen amor*. Fernando de Rojas who began *La Celestina* in 1499 did not create the pícaro only because he created something deeper. Like *Don Quixote* at the end of the

[1] "When we lose our dominions, it will be said: You came here to evangelize and to commit outrage. It will not be said: You came here to mine coal." Angel Ganivet.

cycle, *La Celestina* ere its beginning transcends the pícaro and contains him. Now come the Castilian versions of Amadís de Gaul. The spirit of errant adventure waxes so strong that it invades the hagiographa: Spaniards of the age of Carlos read histories of the saints fully as marvelous and picaresque as the profaner tales in the library of Don Quixote. Finally, after these ages of annunciation, the pícaro arrives, full-fleshed. His name is Lazarillo de Tormes: his date is 1554: his author is unknown.

In this pattern of antithesis whose symphony is Spain, the response to Santa Teresa is the procuress of Rojas, the Celestina, that most tender, robustious, scoundrelly, womanly woman. The response to the flame-like San Juan de la Cruz is Lazarillo. San Juan personifies Spain's purpose, which is divine. Lazarillo embodies Spain's methods, which are brutal. San Juan is not abstract: he is an embodiment of purpose. Lazarillo is not mere flesh: in his trickeries and thefts, there is an inverted consciousness of Spain which makes his path through Old and New Castile almost as luminous as the path of the saint.

This consciousness is marked by irony: and irony is in the weave of every picaresque design. For the Spanish rascal is no mere reaction from heroic gesture. He is reversion as well. He is moved by the same energy that has uprisen in the forms of asceticism and crusade. His antiphony is but a subtle swerving back from the life he wars on, to Spain's common base. The pícaro has the resource, the intensity, the method, of conquistador and crusader: he preys on his own land. He has the passionateness of the saint: it is directed toward woman. He is a casuist like the Jesuit: his aim is to filch a purse. He navigates uncharted wastes like Columbus: to fill his belly and to save his skin. This continuous awareness of Spain's noble world, this subtle swerve transforming it into villainy and lust, make the ironic pattern. The low tricks of the pícaro, weaving through the high fabric of his land, once more limn Spain in her fullness.

Lazarillo is but the first of a long line. The book that

tells of him has scarce a hundred pages: yet it seems wide
and deathless as the land from Salamanca to Toledo which
its hero crosses. Lazarillo is a lad born of poor but un-
worthy parents. A blind beggar teaches him how to survive as a rascal in a rascally world. The young virtuoso
outdoes his master. He becomes the servant of a starving,
haughty knight, of a parsimonious churchman, of a shrewd
and lecherous canon with whom he makes a treaty which
includes the sharing of his wife.

Lazarillo encounters Spain; and the land grows alive
at his touch. Disorder, corruption, folly beneath the
façade of splendor. But now, an acute principle syn-
thetizes the chaos: the pícaro like a wistful agent of intelligence, envelops Spain and makes Spain one with pity.
This pity is of a new order, among the emotions of art.
It is neither mystical nor sentimental. It is the child of
a modern autonomy: it is the pity of reason.

The author of Lazarillo does not insist. He has created an engine so revealing that he can afford to rest within his quiet prose. He writes a tiny book: plastic por-
traiture, tender and bitter humor, sweet spirit, dark flesh—
all Spain indeed is in it, as is the tree in the seed. Lazarillo is a seed, from which has sprung a forest. In
Spain, the picaresque merges quickly with profounder
worlds; loses its æsthetic sharpness, and has its share in
the birth of a book which is a Scripture: *Don Quixote.*
The true form shrinks to formula. The symbol of the
rogue, preying on society and so divulging it, is exploited
by minds more analytic than creative. In the hands of
such masters as Quevedo, the pícaro becomes a concept of
pessimism: a chemic force with which to test and to destroy
the world. The pícaro voyages to France. But in Le
Sage and Marivaux (to name but the greatest), the physical and intellectual movements of the rogue are stressed.
France veers backward toward Scapin—toward the scamp
of the classic comedy—whose essential difference is great.
England borrows more deeply. The pícaro's animal joy-
ousness, social revelation, bitterness turned sentimental

come back to life in Smollett, Fielding, Sterne. But they unite in no one work comparable with *Lazarillo*. Even De Foe wants the luminous poetic atmosphere whereby the crass materials of the tale have their dimension.

No master outside Spain can recreate the pícaro entire. For the Spanish rogue is sterile without the aspirational afflatus of his race, in which he adventures, from which he reacts, and which he embodies in ironic contrast. That is why the greatest heirs of the pícaro of Spain are not his direct sons in eighteenth-century France and England. They are his collateral and remote descendants of a modern world in which once again energy has become aspirant and religious. They are the heroes of Stendhal. Above all, they appear in Russia—that other extreme of Europe which touches Spain in the domain of spirit: they are the hero of *Dead Souls* of Gogol, the mystic criminals of Dostoievski. . . . .

f. *Velázquez*

Antithesis even within the personal will of Isabel and her king. Isabel looks to Africa and the west. Mysterious horizons claim her. Africa is the home of Origen and Augustine—Berber Christians and true Spanish minds. America casts a parabola of search alluring to her mystic appetite. But Isabel is wedded to a man who looks toward Europe. The Aragonese king comes from the most assimilated part of Spain. In him, as in his realm, lives the spirit of Catalan, of European Trader. His hungers strain toward Italy and France. And this dichotomy within the will of the monarchs—Europe and the south, politics in Europe and high adventures across the western sea—is stamped upon the classic will of Spain. The concept of the State which Isabel and Ferdinand adapt is Europe. Louis XI and Machiavelli would have hailed it. The purpose of that State would have been better pleasing to Mohammed or Saint Paul. The spirit is Isabel's and is accepted by her husband. But the form is Ferdinand's and here his wife is disciple.

Now, of this division within the will of Spain, that term which is Europe finds a canon. Velázquez, better than the policy of the kings, better than the victories of their captains in Sicily and France, incarnates Spain's desire to be Europe.

But here, too, irony is at work. Velázquez is the favorite painter at the Court of Philip IV. He lives at the Palace; he is sent on diplomatic missions. His career corresponds almost literally with the reign of his king. And this reign marks the rapid ebb of Spain's affairs in Europe. Her will toward Europe has flung her power high into the north and clear across the Latin Sea. Now, while Velázquez molds that will into organic form, his king loses Portugal, loses the Netherlands, loses the Roussillon, half the Pyrenees, and faces insurrection in Barcelona, Spain's European port.

The will of Velázquez' art is objective form. Bodily substance becomes real. Man's moods and passions in themselves suffice. They have their value not in some rapt design beyond man's body or in employing it to mystic ends: the world of appearance *is* the world. Velázquez' traits are traits of modern Europe. Mysticism disappears, both in immanent and transcendental form. The beauty of spiritual strain, so eloquent in Ribera, is replaced by the beauty of physical poise. The hot fluidity of El Greco which recalls the Prophets, the creative incompleteness of the Byzantines, becomes a static peace. In El Greco, as in all mystic art, the moving materials reach the immobility of form only through the focus of a world beyond them. But in Velázquez, there are no colors save those of face and fabric; there are no forms save those of the body. Velázquez is a realist in the restricted modern European sense. He is impressionistic and he is mechanistic. The vast autonomy of the subjective vision is renounced in him. He makes his eye a literal *receiver of impressions:* whereas the mystic eye (and the Spanish eye) has ever been a *creator of expression.*

This type of æsthetic will which, from the Renaissance to Courbet, is to reign in Europe wins perhaps its highest triumph in the alien Velázquez. What tribute to the energy of Spain! For this is not Spain, this is but a fragment. The vision yearning to become complete, the mystic marriage, the parabolic search, the lyric plaint, the ceaseless *cante hondo*, the arabesque which transforms words to body—these, too, are Spain: these are the virtues which create El Greco, Calderón, Lope, Ribera, Cervantes. Velázquez will have none of them. Velázquez will be wholly European. Europe, accepting the world of appearance as the entire world, pours all its energy to the creating of the immense material universe which is our shambles of the machine and applied science. Spain does not follow. But Velázquez leads.[1]

Velázquez was a great lover of El Greco. Manuel Cossío tells us that in his private chambers at the Palace, the court painter had works of the great mystic. His love and study of his antithesis helped to confine him within his own domain. In his religious subjects, Velázquez shows the direct influence—chiefly in composition—of El Greco. And in these works, the graphic might of Velázquez fades: they are the least of his pictures. Where Velázquez is great, El Greco is excluded: the younger man seems willfully to avoid what he must have felt should denature his æsthetic. And in this response, Velázquez achieves once more the miracle of Spain: the infusing of a part with an intensity and essence of the Whole. El Greco is Spain of Africa and of the Semites, Spain the High Priest of Rome, the mystic Spain. And Velázquez is Spain of Europe: the land of analytic grace, of luxuriant elaborations, of immense exclusions.

Spain's craft goes far, when Spain resolves to be "efficient." Study *Las Hilanderas*, *Mercurio y Argos*, the portrait of Margarita de Austria. This grace is the ecstasy of cool and obvious metals. It suggests the modern æsthetic of the Machine. Modeling and texture are composed of immediate masses which are self-sufficient. Neither in part nor in whole are they transmuted into the subjective. Or take the portrait of Mariana de Austria, Philip's second wife. Of the woman there is naught save the weak face and the flat hands. But the black and silver gown is volumnear. Its fringes and its lace hold power that appears almost to be a symbol of this Court—this Court of Spain striving to hold a world within its forces.

The will of Velázquez, at least, does not falter. *Las*

---

[1] It must be added that this realistic art, and this realistic Europe, are doomed today. Cézanne, a disciple of El Greco, marks the turn of the tide, in the domain of painting.

Meninas is forever a shut and earthly room. No glimpse here of the arcana of the soul, of the soul's subtle modeling of arm and face. Think what El Greco would have done with that group: the royal family, the painter, the dwarf, the dog. How they would have flamed; how heaven and hell would have come in and metabolized these bodies!

In the palace of the king of Spain, there were simpletons and dwarfs. They formed part of the Court and Velázquez painted them. He painted them so well because they were part of himself.

The forces which aspire beyond the body, beyond the domain of sense, died not in Velázquez. His æsthetic will allowed them no immediate word. This explains the cramped discomfort of his religious pictures. Here within him were these instincts, these intuitions, unable to speak, unable to die. And here were the twisted courtiers of the king. A good court painter could portray them; for they were of the palace. And since they were pitiful victims of Nature's law, the despised and dispossessed, an artist's soul could use them as a symbol.

In the world there lives a spirit whose name is Christ and his saints. When the world denies, that spirit ceases to be Christ: it becomes a dwarf and a madman. Velázquez has discovered this: he sets down his dark confession after all. Here is a record of the grotesque and the pitiful world, born of his deep denials.

What a page it is! *El Bobo de Coria:* the simplicity of the inane issuing from the breakdown of complex power: sweetness, candor, poetry and grace surviving in the death of idiocy. *El Primo:* a little man beside a gigantic book; pathos, tenderness, pride—the song of frustration. *Don Sebastián de Mora:* a huge body squats, the head empty, the outstretched legs short as a child's—so eloquent, so helpless. And the *Niño de Vallecas,* most poignant of all, for he bespeaks fecundity without intelligence: he is the lush plasm of life, purposeless, spiritually bereft.

This is the confession of Velázquez, enacting Spain's will to be Europe. This is a prophecy of Europe, whose life of mechanical perfection has turned the Christ and saints of its soul into such twisted creatures.

CHAPTER IX

THE WILL OF DON QUIXOTE

 a.   The Birth of the Hero
 b.   The Career of the Hero
 c.   The Book of the Hero

a. The Birth of the Hero

CERVANTES was born in a Europe more than three centuries beyond the noon of chivalry. Knighthood north of Spain begot great books. The *Chanson de Roland* in the form which we possess is earlier than 1100. In the last years of the twelfth century Chrétien de Troies—first master in an unbroken line that perhaps closed with Anatole France—put into gracious and fleet form the Arthurian cycle. A bit later, a profounder German, Wolfram von Eschenbach, composed from French materials the transfiguring masterwork of chivalry, the Poem of Parzival. Joinville's portrait of Saint Louis and of his two Crusades was written about 1290. Thereafter Europe, north of Spain, begins the great decline into the modern era.

The last historic synthesis of western man lies in that Middle Age. It rose from the chaotic impact of the Roman Empire and the Teuton with Alexandria and Judah. Already ere the ancient world had fallen its architects were building. Origen, Tertullian, Jerome, Anthony, Gregory, Charlemagne—such were its foundation-makers. It reaches heights in Abélard, Aquinas, Francis, Dante: in the creators of the Gothic, in the great weavers of polyphonic music, in men of action—Godefroi de Bouillon and Saint Louis. And already, at this heyday, from the disintegrant north come threats of dissolution in such figures as Roger Bacon and Duns Scotus who, positing the primacy of will over the intellect, declare Theology to be not science but revelation and foretell Luther and Kant—creators of the modern chaos.

European thought, after the Cathedrals, Dante, and the great scholastics, is a story of destruction. Men of as high genius as Albertus Magnus or Saint Thomas proceed by vision and by dialectic to take stone from stone in the dismantlement of Christian Europe. Here and there in the vast liquidation a prophet throws up a scheme for a new Synthesis—such a one was Spinoza: the world cannot accept him, neither can it lose him, from cosmic prescience of a future need.

The towers of this great House in which dwelt the soul of Europe touch the year 1300. Dante has devised his vision; Chartres lives upon the Ile-de-France; Saint Bernard in Clairvaux and Saint Francis in Assisi have filled the world with brothers; chivalry has brought war and love into the sacred symphony of Europe; the German foray is Crusade; lust of the flesh bears the Mystery of Tristan and Isolt, of Abélard and Héloïse. Now, the divine Structure nobly curves back to earth. By 1400, Europe dwells once more in the bowels of discord. By 1500, European man is a congeries of atomic wills: the unity of Christ has scattered into exploration, industry and science.

But in this destructive act, Europe is as creative as when the Fathers builded, out of the Prophets, Plato, Paul, the puissant Organism of medieval Europe. To tear down such a body is as divine an act as to build it. Systole and diastole are equal. Schopenhauer and Kant are brothers before God with Aquinas. The long ages of deliquescence from that peak of Rome rightly seem rich to our enlisted eyes since they are as full of saints and heroes consecrate to our work, as were the anchorites of the Thebaid to theirs.

For this is the mysterious law of history: that the divine is present in death even as in life, in the Nay equally with the Yea. God does not build His revelation upon earth and then turn away His face while man tears down. He is there, too, in the destruction. He was there when the Prophets created the Jew: He was there also when the Pharisees and the Essenic Christ destroyed the Jew. He was there when the saints and Fathers builded

Catholic Rome. He was there when Luther, Calvin, Goethe, Blake burned Rome away.

We see Him in the despair of Dostoievski no less than in the joy of Saint Francis. It was while the Jewish world drooped and retched, that the gospels of Jesus flowered. From that nadir was prepared the Dantean zenith. Once more an ebb of the Tide. Spain has become a befuddled chaos. Home from her mad anachronistic dream of establishing on earth what Europe has given up for centuries, she is already rotting. And now, from the bitterness of her awareness rises a new Word. It, too, is entextured of contemporary failure, and is implicit of revelation.

Spain did not conform with the Middle Ages of the north. Roman Iberia received its dominant invasion from the south, whereas in Italy, Gaul and Britain the coefficient of transformation from Rome to Holy Rome was the same Teuton element which held the eastern marches beyond Roman rule. León, Aragon and Castile were medieval in so far as the Visigoth was strong in them. But even here, contact was as great with the Moslem foe of the south as with the brother northward.

Medievalism is an idealism forced upon the world of Appearance. It is a mystical conclusion by the Teuton will, drawn from the logical element of Latin, and the naturalistic element of Semitic, cultures. It is most powerful in the lands where the Teuton is strongest: Germany and England. In France, where the blend was fairest between Frank and Gallo-Roman, it is most balanced and most perfect. In Italy, medievalism is never great. And in a land whose conclusive elements are Semitic or harmonize with the Semitic, it is impossible. Such a land was Spain. The ethnic Iberian base of Spain is more African in nature than European; more aboriginally close to Semite than to German. Arab culture was always naturalistic. Judaism and Mohammedanism are pragmatic systems on different levels, yet both based upon empirical experience and natural law. In medieval Catholicism, the natural laws and the experience of the world are deformed by a mystic idealizing will. In Semitism, the ideal sense is made to converge with natural law: the mystic will is regarded as possessing its true form in the activity of nature.

Semitism in its several shades, or a spirit close to it, impeded Spain from becoming wholly medieval. It was culturally too strong to accept the neo-platonic House of the medieval God. But Semitism is politically weak. Medievalism, repugning the natural body of the world, creates an ideal Organism—a Church—which becomes politically real. Semitism, accepting Nature as God's organic body, has no impulse to erect political substitutes for the wholeness of existence. Politically, it tends toward fragmentation: even as in art it remains lyrical and forms no such organic structures as the Gothic cathedral or the Dantean epic. This political weakness of the Spanish Semite impeded Spain from becoming wholly Semitic. Spain for centuries was in a state of continuous flux and of osmosis between the medieval north and the Semitic south. When at length there came a final issue the north won. Ferdinand and Isabel turned toward Europe. A revised medievalism, equipped with methods of the Renaissance, became the goal of the Spanish will. And at a time when it was already dead in Europe.

This is the year 1500. The Holy Roman Empire is in full liquidation. Luther and Calvin are rising. Copernicus is at work. America has been discovered. Now Spain pours her ideal energy and her blood into the tragic task of becoming medieval. Godefroi, Saint Louis, Parzival, Saint Francis and Aquinas have been dethroned and denied in the countries of their birth. They become the patterns and movers of Castile.

Lest the hostile—the Semitic elements, which in the noon of medieval Europe held Spain from her part in that great Synthesis, hold Spain back now, Isabel drives the Jew and Moslem from her realms. It is too late. The dissident spirit is at work in Spain. And the heroic effort of this land to revive chivalry, to recreate Christ, to re-establish all the world as Christ's Rock and Church becomes a divine farce, a sort of comic Mystery—*Don Quixote*.

.   .   .   .   .

Perhaps Cervantes' family was of gentle blood: but it had come to pitiful fortune when Miguel was born to the poor surgeon in Alcalá de Henares. The year was 1547: and the town upon the *llanura* of Castile was the rival of Salamanca. Naught is more eloquent of the poverty of his people than the fact that Miguel was unable to attend the university round the corner. At twenty-two, however, he was a poet. He went to Italy as the body servant of the Papal Nuncio: later he rose to be a soldier. In 1571, the ships of Philip II defeated the Turk in the waters of Lepanto. A shot crippled the left hand of Cervantes. His officers ordered him below. He refused to leave the deck, and in his blood and pain fought to the close of the engagement. This is a better sign of his unusual nature than his verse. A man of high sensitivity, he exposed himself to physical suffering beyond the duty of a soldier. He was devoted passionately to the Catholic cause. And when in 1575 he took ship from Italy, he had letters to the king from Don Juan of Austria and the Duke of Sessa whom he had served in Naples. He was full of merit: and full of hope he went home for his reward. But the Berber pirates took the vessel and he and his brother, Rodrigo, became slaves in Algiers. Four times in five years Cervantes plotted to escape the stiflement of servitude in the Kasbah of that town which rises within a snow-crowned conch above the hard-blue sea, hiding its reek within the gleam of roofs. Cervantes' sisters and mother bestirred themselves: scraped coin together, borrowed, and at last, ransomed Rodrigo. In 1580, a mendicant monk came to the aid of the sisters, and Cervantes was freed on the eve of his departure eastward. He went to Madrid. He sought protection, and he failed to find it. He had been a hero and a martyr: but such were cheap in Spain. The land swarmed with veterans of the wars which had spread Spain's glory to the Pacific Ocean. Cervantes performed odd diplomatic jobs and tried to be a writer. From thirty-four to forty he wrote thirty plays; he had no financial success. But he wed a landed lady, Doña Catalina de Palacios Salazar y Vozmediano of Esquivias, a town on the fringe of the Manchegan desert which after twenty years was to be transfigured by a hero. At about the time of his marriage, another lady Doña Ana de Rojas bore him a natural daughter, Isabel, whose life was to be fateful in his own. Cervantes' burdens were great as his means were small. He placed all his hopes on a novel in which he believed that he had lavished all his genius. *La Galatea* appeared in 1585, and was an unremunerative *succès d'estime.*

Now come twenty years of Gethsemane to Don Miguel de Cervantes y Saavedra. The silence of oblivion—*el silencio del olvido* whereof he speaks—was their sweetest portion. We follow him hardly, for he had reason to hold to his obscurity. In 1588 he is a commissary in Seville. In 1592 he is in prison for a bungled sale of wheat. Later he is engaged in provisioning the Armada. He tries to get out of Spain: he seeks a post in Guatemala: but he lacks the influence to win it. Once more he sues the stage. Lope de Vega is the master of taste; and once more Cervantes fails. In 1594 he is a tax-collector in Granada: in disgrace: once more in prison. In 1597 we find him released on faith of his word that he will make good a deficit to the Treasury of the King. There is no trace, however, of his payment. For five years, he seems to have touched depths in Andalusia. An obscure actor, Tomás Gutiérrez (blessèd be his name) supports him. In 1603 he is in jail again, the bank in which he had deposited trusted monies having failed. He appears to have been under lock and key at this time, in both Seville and Argamasilla de Alba. This may have been the circumstance in which, judged by his own words, he began to write *Don Quixote*.

In 1604, Part One of the work is written: has even been bruited about Madrid either in manuscript or in an edition prior to the first extant one which bears the date 1605. Lope de Vega is at his height. He is the Stage of Spain. His name outshines the king's: his portrait stands beside a saint's in myriad Spanish homes. Miguel de Cervantes is living in Vallodolid. With him are the two sisters who helped ransom him from slavery, a niece and Isabel; his natural daughter. His wife lives in indifferent ease on her estate in La Mancha. Cervantes is penniless. His labors as tax-farmer have earned him bread in prison and disgrace with the world. He has been forgotten as a writer. And he lives with women who support him. They are good women and he loves them: but they are women, like himself disgraced by fortune. His sisters, Magdalena de Sotomayor and Andrea de Cervantes, have been "kept" women. His niece Constanza is living now with a man to whom she is not married. Cervantes knows this, and eats their bread. His daughter, Isabel, is not of good repute; nor is Cervantes perfectly cleared of implication in her mercenary ways.

He is fifty-seven: he is broken utterly. And his bread is shame. Yet he is still the proud hidalgo who served Don Juan of Austria in Naples, who refused succor and relief at Lepanto: who led gallant sallies in Algiers. He is not Cervantes. He is Miguel de Cervantes y Saavedra.

This man looks out upon his world, with eyes of such a life, and decides, after twenty adverse years, again to write a book. He has read only the decadent offspring of chivalry's literary flower. He does not know the original *chansons de geste* nor the native water-clear *romans d'aventure*. The best he knows is the fifteenth century Romancero; is Ariosto and the ornate Italians; is the Castilian version of Amadís de Gaula which has come to Spain, over-blown, by Portugal out of Brittany and Wales.

These are relatively pure beside their spawn of dull sons performing ridiculous wonders in a world of wooden magic. But the vogue of these knights is past. The books of *caballería,* which tempted the young Santa Teresa to go forth seeking martyrdom and adventure, have already ebbed. On the other hand, *La Celestina* which appeared along with the first Castilian Amadis has thriven and inspired the pícaro who lives still in Spanish and in European letters.

Vivid in Cervantes' mind is the organic music—the first great Castilian prose—in which Fernando de Rojas sang the sordid fate of his Celestina. As with Amadis, this book has medieval roots. But unlike Amadis, it has classic form, and independent greatness. Amadis is a fatty degeneration of Roland, Parzival, Lancelot. La Celestina is a transfigurement of the comedy of Terence and Plautus, as well as of the romance of Aucassin and Nicolette, of Tristan and Isolt, of Romeo and Juliet. It is ironic, realistic, ruthlessly tragic as the romance was never. Chivalry expressed a childlike age which projected its own maturity into a Church and a Heaven. The romance at best was an adolescent form. As the Church dimmed and Heaven grew less sure and man began again to build upon himself, it was transfigured into the modern novel. *La Celestina* is the first towering adult of the childlike race of the fabliaux and romances.

Irony and a profound acceptance of natural justice—such are the transforming elements of *La Celestina.* Love's medieval idyll is rotted and destroyed by the pragmatic world to which it has appealed for fulfillment. Loveliness is killed by lust. The whole infantile fantasy of the Middle Age is confronted with the fate of its own will: a fate of evil and of sordid passion. And Justice is implicit in the nature of events. This meeting of love and lust, of vice and beauty, this hot-and-cold inmixture of vision and of despair gives to the book of Rojas a dimension that relates it to Dostoievski and to Balzac.

The pícaro novels of Spain's sixteenth century continue

the novel of Rojas and announce *Don Quixote*. Counterpoint of irony and naturalistic justice becomes the theme, variantly construed, of *Lazarillo de Tormes*, of Quevedo's *El Buscón*, of Delicado's *Lozana Andaluza*, of the *Guzmán* of Mateo Alemán.

This in the mind of Cervantes looking out upon his world. And with it, a parallel domain of literary expression: one that is not unrelated to the brutal picaresque and to the extravagant tales of chivalry: the mystic. Cervantes knew the renowned *Diálogos de Amor* of León Hebreo. And he knew Santa Teresa, Luis de León, Luis de Granada.

This man whom adversity for twenty years has silenced is a bookish man. But he has been a man of action. He has grown old with his own literary failure. But he has absorbed a century of literary success. He is no primitive. Mature in years and in events, he is the heir of a rich, various heritage of expression.

When he was born, Carlos I was king. His youth spanned the age of Felipe II. While he fought and was exiled, the Escorial rose, a last pinnacle of stone, from the Castilian Guadarrama. Now, in Cervantes' broken age, the grotesque Felipe III leads Spain. Spain has gone on the Crusade Isabel dreamed; and Spain has come to this.

Cervantes looks back over the glorious madness of his land; and he has his earliest vision of the Knight: Quixote wearing a barber's dish, mounted on a nag. For Spain was not like Europe at the dawn of chivalry. Europe then was dawn, itself. Old wines—the wines of the Prophets, of Plato and Saint Augustine—had raged in the young flesh of Teuton hordes. But Spain at this flush of her ambition was already old. Seven centuries of war with Islam, endless ages of conflict with a desert world have parched the skin and turned brittle the bone of this Quixotic hero, abroad in the world to make the world into the House of Christ.

Cervantes looks at Spain. Outward splendor flings

Spain's canopy from Holland to Africa, from Florida to Santa Fe. Paul and the Apostles who voyaged over the world are dead fifteen hundred years; but Columbus charts his way to the Indies from study of the Scriptures. Roland blew his last horn six centuries since: but Cortés and Pizarro raze empires in Peru. The hermits of the Thebaid are buried under millennial dust; but Córdoba has its anchorites. Saint Anthony and Saint Elisabeth are old in Heaven; but here yesterday were Saint John of the Cross and Saint Teresa. Bernard of Clairvaux did not crush the Albigensians with more blood than Torquemada the Jews. Saint Louis of France announces Isabel of Spain. Pope Gregory has his brother—across seven hundred years—in Cisneros, Cardinal of Toledo.[1]

Cervantes looks within Spain. It is a squalid land. Men pray while it lies sterile. Old soldiers are vagabonds on the roads. Farms are waste while the lazy lords watch for gold-filled galleons from the Indies. It is a bloodless land. Women give themselves to Christ, and their wombs shrink. Carlos and Felipe pour the blood of Aragon and Castile into the Flemish sea.

Cervantes looks at himself. He, too, has been a hero. His maimed hand recalls the gesture of Lepanto. He has been a poet—in prison; a servant of the State—who starved. He has helped to provision the Armada whose splendor sank under the modern iron of stripped England. And now, he eats the shame-bread of his women.

Looking within himself or out upon his world, Cervantes sees one thing. Spain and he are home, ashen and sober, from a high Crusade. Spain and he are this single body of his bitterness. Such is the conjunction and dark omen of the birth of a hero.

[1] I hope it will be clear that in these parallels I am suggesting not identity but analogy. Elements of the Renaissance and of the modern world definitely distinguish these Spaniards from the true medievals. The beauty and the irony of the Spanish scene lies precisely in this.

b. *The Career of the Hero*

Don Quixote is but the final name of the ingenious knight of La Mancha. In Chapter One of his book, it is set forth that he was known as Quijada, Quesada or Quejana. Four chapters later a worker in the neighboring fields addresses him as Quijana, and as Quijano he made his will at the end of his last journey. His Christian name was Alonso. Quixote (Quijote in modern Castilian) was the choice of the old man himself. And as Cervantes gives him birth, he is old—old for his fifty years in a frustrate Manchegan village. He is noble but poor. He is an eater of cheap meats. He is a cadaverous, lantern-jawed, brittle-boned, deep-eyed fellow. His house, one room of which is stocked with the chivalric books that have drawn his substance and addled his brains, is cared for by an old Nurse and a niece. There is as well a boy servant who disappears from the tale after the first chapter. Doubtless Cervantes meant to employ him as Don Quixote's squire: but when the independent knight after his first sally made choice of Sancho Panza, there was naught left for the poor *mozo*. Of course, in the stable stands a splay-hoof nag. After four days of meditation on such names as Bucephalus and Babieca (the stallion of the Cid), Quixote christens his jade Rocinante. *Rocín* means hack horse: wherefore Don Quixote meant that his mount was *before* all the other hacks of the world.

This detail, appearing in the first chapter of the Book, might give the canny reader pause. "Why," he might ask, "if the deluded eyes—as we are told—of Don Quixote saw his hack as a mount equal to the steeds of Amadis or Alexander, as he was soon to be equal in renown, did he christen him with a name so comical and so revealing?" The reader will be aware of a curious shift in this Don Quixote's "madness": a note shivering in at once of self-conscious irony.

However, the madman to whom Cervantes introduces us seems on the whole at first to be consistent. A poverty-struck Manchegan, finding his treeless world too empty for his senses, lets them roam in a realm of knight-errants, ogres, fairies, virgins, Magic. Until his senses are strayed. Whereupon, deeming himself a Roland or an Amadis, he buckles on his rusty sword, takes his nag from the stall and sallies forth into a Spain sordidly realistic, sick of heroes, to perform adventures. He cuts a ridiculous figure. And his fate is what a sane man might expect. He is unhorsed, drubbed, pounded. He loses teeth as his molested countrymen lose tempers. The ladies he meets are foul-breathed wenches; the lord of the Castle in which he takes his rest wants his pay, being the keeper of an inn. His battles are with goats, sheep, windmills and Biscayan servants. It is clear that some day his madness will discomfit him entire. At which time he will be forced back to his house where the good Nurse and the niece will staunch his wounds, bathe the dust from his mad eyes and put him to bed. Meantime, there is the tale to tell—with much laughter—of his absurd adventures. Cervantes wishes to laugh at this medieval scarecrow, jousting with the Modern. His fellow Spaniards, sick like himself of gestures and heroics, will roar along—will pay *reales* for the book—will put money in the purse of a scribbler.

Such a Quixote is the child of Cervantes, and is the subject of the early chapters. And now a fundamental difference sets in, marking off this character from others. Most literary creations remain their maker's. As he willed, modeled, developed them, so they live—or die. This is true in great books. The evolution of the hero is explicit in the poet's mind or at least in the action's threshold. But for the analogue to Don Quixote we must go to biology, rather than to art. The mother forms the baby in her womb. It is organically hers, and so for a brief time it will remain. But she has endowed it with a principle which will make her child recede ever more from being her creation. This inner life, seeking substance in the world of sense and of impression, becomes itself. The mother has created a babe—only to lose it. Similar is the fate of Quixote with Cervantes. From the womb of his will and bitter fancy comes the child. But Don Quixote is no sooner set on earth, than he proceeds by an organic evolution, by a series of accretions, assimilations, responses, to change wholly from the intent of his author—to turn indeed against him. He does not lose organic contact with his source, even as the man is child of his own childhood and of his parents in a way deeper than the parents' conscious will or than biologic pattern. But above all, the child becomes himself. He has transcended vastly the amorphous thing lodged in his mother's womb. So Don Quixote is transfigured beyond the sprightly scheme of his maker.

He was conceived and formed, as a broken writer's bitter turning against his heroic soul and his heroic age; he becomes the Body of sublime acceptance—the symbol of what his misfortunes were to mock. Cervantes' conscious will has no firm hold on Don Quixote. And this is plain almost from the outset in the fact that the Manchegan knight, despite his author's assurance, *is not mad*. We had an inkling of this already in the too conscious, too ironic naming of Rocinante. Soon the proofs multiply; for the clown-blows that continue to rain upon Don Quixote in Part One cannot hold him from his organic growth. With Part Two, written ten years later, the blows and buffets are less frequent. Cervantes has had time to catch up with and humbly to accept his son.

In the matter of the selecting of a Lady (that needed spur of every true knight-errant) it is clear that Don Quixote knows the facts about Aldonza Lorenzo, wench daughter of Lorenzo Cochuelo of El Toboso. Quite consciously, he turns her into the divine Dulcinea whom henceforth he will worship. Her he makes his "truth"; there is no evidence that the *fact* of the girl is ever hidden from him. He needs a helmet, indeed he needs Mambrino's magic helmet. A barber comes, riding an ass and on his head (for it is raining) a copper bleeding-dish. This shall be the golden helmet of Mambrino; and as such Don Quixote takes it. But in the parley before and after with Sancho Panza, it is plain that the knight accepts Sancho's *fact* about the dish: he merely turns the fact, for his own purpose, into "truth."

In the Sierra Morena, Don Quixote resolves to follow a tradition. He and Sancho have reached the mountains that bar the smooth plains of La Mancha from the fluid meads of Andalusia southward: mountains of rock flung to sky, titanic gestures of rock, pourings of cosmic might into the waste of rock. The Sierra, sudden beneath La Mancha, suggests delirious excess. So here, Don Quixote will have his knightly spell of madness, in anguish of his absent lady love. How does he set about it? He debates the merits of two schools of madness. There was the furious way of Roland after his Angelica had slept with the Moor Medoro. And there was the quiet melancholy way of Amadis. Don Quixote is fifty: he elects the quieter madness. He takes Sancho to witness of his straits, ere he sends him off to beseech mercy of Dulcinea. Nor is he fooled by Sancho's meeting with the lady. The fact that Sancho has left behind him the very letter which he describes as giving to Dulcinea does not disturb Don Quixote. He is not dwelling with facts, but with truths of his own conscious making. And he tells his squire, speaking in elegiac temper of himself: "That if he did not achieve great matters, he died to achieve them; and if I am indeed not disowned and disdained by Dulcinea del Toboso, it sufficeth me . . to be absent from her." Later he meets the swine girl whom he has transfigured into princess. And since he speaks of the magic making her appear as the facts (and Sancho) would have it—a coarse and silly female with a breath of garlic—it is plain that the facts are in his mind. He is not fooled. Nor is he lying when he speaks of magic. Magic is the deep inner change of attitude. This is the secret of the fakirs of the East. This is *true* magic. Don Quixote's attitude changes the fact of the swine girl into his truth of a princess.

The fooled is Sancho. For Sancho does not understand that fact and truth may be foes. He takes one for the other. He believes that Dulcinea's enchantment, the Cave of Montesino, the Island which he is sent to govern, the Empress whom his master is to wed are facts. As the tale grows, poor Sancho is more and more enmired in confusion. He is in danger of madness, losing his distinction between the world of shapes and this world of ideas in which Don Quixote rides.

The old knight's progress is willful. There is, for instance, the wondrous ride on Clavileño, the wooden horse in the garden of the Duke, upon which the pair are wafted through heaven and hell. Sancho claims to have stolen a glimpse and to have seen them soaring through the firmaments of fire. And Don Quixote answers:

> "If you desire me to believe you in what you have just seen in the sky, I desire that you should believe me in what I saw within the Cave of Montesino. No need for me to say more. . . ."

He is proposing to Sancho what is neither more nor less than a deal; he will accept his squire's lies, if Sancho accepts his own distinction between a glorious truth and a drab world of facts. But Sancho's mind has no such athleticism. He is not Ramón Lull! He has never heard of León Hebreo. He is forever mixing two insoluble realms.

At last Don Quixote meets his fate. In Barcelona, having been acclaimed by crowds with mingled laughter and devotion which they can never understand, he is challenged to combat by the Knight of the White Moon. He is

worsted, of course: and this is his end. For the *caballero
de la luna blanca* is none other than the bachelor Sansón
Carrasco. The goodly Don Antonio cannot understand
this medieval nonsense in his busy modern seaport. Carrasco explains:

"My lord, know that I, the bachelor Sansón
Carrasco, am of the same place as Don Quixote de
la Mancha, whose simplicity and madness have moved
to tears all of us who know him: and among these
none has wept more than I: and believing that there
lay his health and peace, in that he should reside in
his own land and house, I determined to return
him thither; and so three months since I went upon
the road as a knight-errant, calling myself *el caballero
de los espejos,* meaning to fight him, vanquish him
without hurt, and having put as the condition of our
encounter that the vanquished remain in the discre-
tion of the victor: and what I thought to demand of
him (for I judged him beforehand already vanquished) was that he should return to his home, and
sally not forth from it for a whole year; in which
time he might be cured; but fate ordered otherwise,
for I was the defeated. I was hurled from my
horse, and hence my purpose could not take effect;
he went his way, and I returned, beaten, bruised,
mashed by my fall which to be sure was dangerous
enough; but for this I did not give up my meaning
which was to seek him out once more and defeat him,
as you have seen me do this day. And since he is
so punctilious in all that pertains to the knight-
errant, without doubt soever he will obey the order
I have given him, in honor of his word. This, my
lord, is what has passed, without my need to say
another thing; I beseech you, do not discover me
nor say to Don Quixote who I am, in order that these
my good intentions may have effect, and that there
may return to reason a man so excellent in reason,

when he is left alone by the unreasons of
chivalry. . . ."

Carrasco reveals that his deep instinct against Don
Quixote is buttressed by a shallow understanding. When
the old knight saw the familiar face of his friend within
the vizor of the defeated *caballero de los espejos,* he was
not troubled: he knew that magic had turned the truth
of the defeated warrior into the face of his neighbor, the
bachelor Sansón Carrasco. Had he now been told that the
Knight of the White Moon appeared to others as this
same bachelor, he would have found a similar solution—
and obeyed the knight, though his heart broke.

So now, stripped of his harness, Don Quixote makes his
ashen way homeward from Barcelona. He does not yet
know that he is vanquished for good. His word binds him
for a year: thereafter, can he not sally forth again? Meantime, he need not stay idle in a gross world of facts.
"If it seem well to thee," he tells his squire, "I should
like that we turn pastors even for the time I am caught
up." He makes his plans. "I shall buy a few sheep and
all other things needed for the pastoral life." His friends
will share this new transfiguration which has the advantage
of being more sociable than the life of the knight-errant.
He will become the pastor *Quixotiz;* Sancho will become
Pancino. Sancho's wife Teresa will be *Teresona.* The
bachelor Carrasco will be known as *Sansonino* or *Car-
rascón:* being a learned man, he shall take his choice. The
priest *(el cura)* he might call, not knowing his true
name, *el pastor Curiambro.*

These persons, being facts, must change their names ere
they can enter his truthful pastoral Eden. Dulcinea remains Dulcinea: for already *she* is of the world of his
truth. With this last lucid statement of his mind, the old
man comes upon his home where soon he is to die. No
more may he be a knight, dispensing Justice in a real world
inhabited by such true concepts as ogres, virgins, sorcerers.
Even the little interlude of pastor is denied him. He

languishes; and with his strength, his creative will expires.

The child returneth to the mother. Don Alonso Quijano el Bueno lies upon a death-bed and renounces Don Quixote. Again Cervantes' child shrinks to the arms of his parent. He abjures the careers of all knights-errant:

"Ya soy enemigo de Amadís de Gaula y de toda la infinita caterva de su linaje; ya me son odiosas todas las historias profanas de la andante caballería; ya conozco mi necedad y el peligro en que me pusieron harlas leído; ya por misericordia de Díos, escarmentando en cabeza propia, las abomino. . . ."

Don Quixote, as he emerges unscathed from the mind of his author, is a man possessed: not a madman. He is a man possessed as were the Hebrew prophets, or Jesus, or Vardhamana, or Boehme or Plotinus, or any poet. . . . The difference is subtle but is clear beyond the logical distinctions of man's reason. No atheist would call Amos mad, but a man possessed. To Jesus saying: "When ye have lifted up the Son of God, then shall ye know that I am he, and that I do nothing of myself, but as my Father hath taught me" no Jew would ascribe madness, but possession. Quixote is possessed of an Ideal. And since this ideal was mothered of the world struggling toward light, and since now it mothers him entire, becoming his truth and his world, Don Quixote takes his place among the broken and triumphant prophets. Even the alienist durst not call him mad, for in the drama which he enacts he knows his part: and the more fully senses what he calls the truth, knowing its bodily difference from the facts about him.

Reality for the medieval soul was neo-platonic. The conceptual was real: all else was merely fact. The bitter apartness of Jew and Arab from medieval Europe was due to the failure of the Semite, despite Philo and Al Gazali, to assimilate neo-platonism deeply. Plotinus, Porphyry, Augustine, Iamblicus created the psychology of a thousand years of Europe. The real is not this world. We are snared and mired in a viscous web of seeming. All congeries of sense is this. And knowledge tends, not to a translating of this factual film into the real but to the piercing it, the abandoning it altogether. This attitude is far from the naturalistic mysticism of the Hebrew, from the intellectual mysticism of Plato; from the profound nihilism of the Hindu who recognized the unity of the ideal and the factual, interpreting one always in terms of the other. Medievalism is a child—and a childish offshoot—of all these. It declares: There is a real world, and it is not this one. Man can reach the real world, by various means. He must crucify the fact, he must worship the saints, he must lose his body in order to save his soul.

Don Quixote moves through a world neo-platonically real. He is as aware as Sancho of sheep, windmills, inns, country wenches. He chooses to disregard these lies of fact. He erects a systematic symbol whereby his senses vault the phenomena about him, and deliver him the truth. Thereby, the windmill serves him as a giant; the sheep as enchanted armies; the empty cave of Montesino as the scene of Glory, and Maritornes the whore as the virgin lady languishing in love. He has elected to do Justice upon earth. These giants, armies and disasters serve him as means to that end.

By a similar process, the medieval mind made all history into parable and symbol. The medieval mind is subjectivism carried to the intense conclusion made possible by the barbarous Germanic will. Philo's allegories of the Scripture, the Book of Zohar, the way of Egypt and India with all written words, treating them as intricate and recondite symbols, obsessed the mind of medieval Europe. No act is simple, no name is simply a name. The world becomes a dramatic Mystery, with every scene bearing upon the central Plot: the soul's salvation. For a thousand years, literature and art, to be serious, had to be allegory.

The mood of medieval symbolism, while it was fathered

by Plato and the Jews, is neither Greek nor Jewish. With these two adult peoples, symbolism held its place: it remained a relative and ancillary life within the mastering testimony of the world. Already in Plotinus and Saint Augustine, the balance is lost. When we are deep in the Middle Ages, we are deep in an allegoric jungle: the paths of fact are gone; there comes no daylight of reason in this tangle of monster foliage and whelming branches.

Don Quixote's world is medievally real. It is a hypertrophy of such births as Chivalry, Romance and Sainthood. In its character of wholeness, of deliberate disregard for fact, it springs from the fountainhead of neo-platonic thought.

But if this transfiguring of the world to his own will is a medieval act, Don Quixote's impulse is not medieval, is not even Christian. The medieval will, myriad in its flowerings, was childishly simple in its seed: the soul's salvation. Nothing else counted: or rather, everything had its sole significance, indeed its reality, as it bore on this monomaniac problem of each soul: to be saved. That a man's soul might be saved, all acts since Adam had been apportioned. For this, the Hebrews lived, the Prophets preached, Christ died: for this, Peter builded his Church and the Jews remained outside in perpetual testimony of damnation. For this, men went on Crusades, conquered heathens, gave birth to children in holy wedlock. For this there was love and justice: for this there was life and death. But Don Quixote is no more centrally concerned with his soul's salvation than if he had been a Jew. He believes in his soul; he hopes it shall be saved. But his acts are motived by a will far less personal: the enacting of Justice.

Don Quixote looks upon himself as the instrument of Justice. He is the embodied and moving will of Justice. The neo-platonic Christian lived justly, that he might pierce better the Phenomenal Lie and win salvation. The Arab warrior spread justice with his sword because the Prophet was just, and he must serve the Prophet to be saved. The

knight of the Round Table of King Arthur performed
deeds of justice—rescuing the virgin, slaying the bad giant
—because it was good sport and because it was a way
to his salvation. But Don Quixote wills Justice upon earth,
because he hungers after Justice, because there is naught
else true save Justice. If, by the sheer testimony of his
words and deeds, we analyze this passion of Don Quixote,
we learn that for him instinctively Justice meant Unity.
The world must become One: and the means thereto is
Justice.

The symbols with which he works are medieval Christian; his mental mechanism is neo-platonic: his knightly
attitude is more Moorish than Teutonic (as contrasted with
the Germanic tenor of the freebooting Cid). But this
heart of his will is Hebrew. The parabolic line of its
enactment in his life links Don Quixote with the Prophets.

The words God and Christ are surprisingly seldom on
the old knight's lips. He cites Roland and Amadis more
often than the Saints. They, indeed, are his saints. But
his God is Justice. And so impersonal, so monotheistic
is He, that He wants more than a body; almost He lacks
a name. Or rather His body is the world: His name is
Justice.

The eidolon-making Greeks said in wonder of the Jews:
"They are a people who see God everywhere and localize
him nowhere." So Don Quixote created for himself
a world that should consist solely of opportunities for
Justice. To this end he rejects, selects and builds in the
world which meets his eyes. His mind works like the
instinct of an artist. But he is a peculiar sort of artist.
His ethical purpose, the intensity with which he imbues
every action with his vision and turns the social fact into
a spiritual Word, recalls the Prophets. Amos, too, looked
out on a world made wholly the matrix for the vision of
God: and moved in Israel as a flame within the burning
wood. To Hosea, even the wife of his bed was a symbol
of the intention of the Lord. Every detail of the Prophet's
life—even the silence and the dark, even the failure and

the sin—is caught in the unity of his vision and becomes a Word to express it. Thus Don Quixote sets forth to perform Justice. He must perform it constantly. The world must become material—a continuum of material—for his performance. But like every artist and like every prophet Don Quixote must translate his vision into the accepted formulæ of his mind. In his case, these formulæ are the shoddy regalia of decadent knighthood. Justice is to be performed by rescuing virgins, unseating ogres, slaying giants, despiting necromancers. Don Quixote rides through Spain. Along these highways graze sheep, trudge merchants: there are inns but no castles. Don Quixote does not see the enactment of Justice in such terms as these. So he transforms them.

His Justice is an attempt at unity. But it is very simple. The real world of Don Quixote is no intricate entexture of hierarchic values. It is not like the mazed affluence of life which the Hindu fused into One. It has none of the deep involvement of souls and states fused by Hebrew and Hellene into God. It is a simple pyramid. At the base are knights and villains, virgins and married ladies, angels, enchanters, demons, ogres. And at the pyramid's peak is the ideal of all this homogeneous matter: freedom and liberty. This ideal is uncorrupted by any political or sectarian dogma. It is never more clear than in the adventure with the convicts. With clinking chains, this squad of scoundrels is led south by the soldiers of the King, to meet the galley in which they must serve their terms. Here are men in chains: Don Quixote's ideal of Justice demands that chains be stricken off. The soldiers protest that these chains are virtuous and lawful: it avails not. The freed rascals repay their liberator with a shower of stones and make off with Sancho's ass: this avails nothing. Don Quixote will not be swerved from his immaculate conception of Justice.

In such episodes as this, we touch the core of the miracle of Don Quixote. His nature is ridiculously funny, and is Christlike. The freeing of legally judged robbers, the letting of lions out of cages, is farce: and yet illumes a justice above laws whose vision is Christlike and whose enactment brings upon the knight a Christlike fate. In laughing at Don Quixote, we crucify him. Mockery and buffets create the knight of the Sorrowful Figure: our own roars of glee at his well-earned mishaps hail the ridiculous Christ.

And here we come back into the medieval. The Jesus of the Synoptic Gospels is a dominant unbroken man. The Passion on the Cross is a mystic interlude—probably an interpolation—which rends the Temple far more than it does Jesus. His cry, about the ninth hour; "Eli, Eli, lama sabachthani" is a shredding weakness against the serenity and might of the historic Man. Jesus in his true character is almost wholly Hebrew Prophet. With the Lord in his mouth, he is imperious, even overbearing. The Hebrew spirit is as adverse from ill-health—from martyrdom as an end-in-itself—as the Greek. But with the infantilization of the West, with the upshowing of the childish spirit within the iron carapace of Rome, Jesus becomes pitiful. Medieval art makes him lean and ugly; asceticism borrowed from the Hindus and Egyptians mangles his body. Within the splendor of the Gothic church there comes to live a shrunken Christ. And as medievalism stumbled southward, the process gathered. The baroque churches of Seville are fantasmagoria of tropic wealth, writhed like a forest about the Sensitive Plant: Christ, milkpale, blood-spotted.

So at the end, Don Quixote. He is laughter-spotted, blood-spotted. Reason bespatters him and makes him comic. But since in the minds of men this reason is profane, and his mad impulse holy, he is a Christ—a medieval, an unjewish Christ.

His deeds get him into trouble. Part One abounds in buffets that unhorse him, knock out his teeth, bathe him in blood and muddy him all over. Part Two has a less rollicking mood. Cervantes has been affected by Don

Quixote. But there is worse: Don Quixote, enacting Justice, brings trouble to others—and to the best of them. There is the boy whom he frees from a flogging master, and who is flogged the worse, in payment for the humiliation the master has suffered from Don Quixote. There is the freeing of the convicts—a menace to every household in the land. There is the freeing of the lion, to the probable disgrace of the poor keeper. Don Quixote wrecks funerals: he maims an innocent Penitent for life. He unhinges Sancho's peace: brings the anarchy of ambition into the breast of this sweet clod of the earth. He visits destruction upon the unfortunate inns which he takes for castles. He robs a barber of his copper dish. He drubs innocent servants. He smashes the sole fortune of Maese Pedro—his set of puppets. He commits sacrilege even: plunging full-tilt upon a pilgrimage of disciplinants, breaking legs and wresting from the outraged hand of a priest an image of the Virgin.

Though he offends many and amuses more, he convinces no one. That a prophet should inspire jeers and hatred is natural: but that he should have not one disciple? and that at the end of his mission, he should recant, and call his mission folly? How can such win the love of the world?

The strong whom he encounters laugh at him. The weak flee from him. The Nurse and his niece do not laugh: they weep and tear their hair for his unseemly conduct. In the bachelor Carrasco he inspires a nagging irritation. This man is common sense incarnate: he is ill-at-ease before the irreducible vision of the artist. He goes out of his way to down him: dons the armor of folly in order to bring home the fool. This must not be construed as altruism. Carrasco pays tribute to Don Quixote, in despite of himself. It is his own peace he is after. He is aware, albeit far too rational ever to admit it to himself, that this utter idealist stalking La Mancha robs his small reality of ease. Common sense—the sense of approximation and of compromise—is fragile and is nervous. It must sequester the poet-prophet in his home town.

Perhaps the ugliest episode in the book treats of the knight's entertainment in the castle of the Duke and Duchess. They are the worldly-wise, the worldly-cultured, even as Carrasco is the pragmatist. They take Don Quixote in; and make him a show for their own genteel delectation. They are the perpetual patron of the artist. They feed him, flatter him, serve him: everything but believe him. Their minds hold him safe from their hearts. And nowhere does the knight of the Sorrowful Figure appear so pathetic, so ridiculous, so disarmed, as under this ducal roof where he is lionized and where whole pageantries are enacted to pander to his need of enacting Justice.

Quixote survives the sophistical salon of the Duchess and of her lecherous ladies. But while he is among them, he is shrunken. He goes forth at last, aware of the subtle poison of their praise, to seek the adventure of Justice—to be laid low by the bachelor Carrasco.

But there is his squire? are there not moments at least in which the squire is a true disciple? Sancho Panza seems to have come latterly to Cervantes. Indeed, this loamy son of the Manchegan desert is less immediate altogether to the world illumined by Don Quixote. That treeless, sapless plain whose horizons are beyond eye, whose winters are blasts of ice, whose summers are fire, whose indeterminate panorama of details—dust, men, towns, roads— is chaos, is the true mother of Don Quixote. La Mancha is a defeated desert: neither waste nor garden, it imposes the way of gardens upon the mood of the desert. Don Quixote transfigures its inns and sordid villages, its hard-fist peasants and its heavy girls into a ruthless psychic unity; much as the son of the true desert drew its vast horizons and its breastlike slopes into the body of God. But how in this world was Sancho Panza born? For not Falstaff of verdant England is more robustly gay, not Panurge of luxuriant France more subtly sensual.

Sancho is wholly the creation of Cervantes. Don Quixote, born of his author, outgrew him. Sancho, too, grows organically. Contact with his master determines this. But none the less he lies ever full within Cervantes' will: he is the sheer miraculous birth of gayety from the frustrate desert of Cervantes' life.

To Sancho, the "phenomenal" world, the world of facts is everything. Since he conceives no other, and since his master continuously lives within another of his own conceiving, Sancho is held busy translating into factual terms the entire adventure which he rides with Don Quixote.

A vertiginous effort it is, and it ends by making Sancho more nearly mad than his knight. He believes factually in his Island. He believes himself its governor, though he has crossed no water to attain it. The maid who is to wed Don Quixote after he has gone to Africa to slay her foe is factually to him the Princess Micomacoma. This enchantment must be a fact, like the one which befell Dulcinea, turning her into the wench Aldonza. Sancho vacillates forever between the credulity and the skepticism of the literal mind: ignorance is so clearly the matrix of his sanity that the delusions of his master become wise by contrast. There are no dimensions to his thinking. Don Quixote is mad—or he is a true knight-errant: the adventure is wild,—or there will be a veritable island.

His dominant impulse, either way, is greed. Greed makes him doubt: greed makes him trust his master. Yet underneath, there works subtly upon Sancho a sweeter influence: his indefeasible respect for Don Quixote. Howsoever he argue, howsoever clear he see, howsoever he sicken from constant thumpings and sparse earnings, howsoever wry are the pleasures of his Island, Sancho cannot altogether free himself from the dominion of an idealizing will which he can never understand. In a directer way (since he is no intellectual) than that of Sansón Carrasco, he is held and haunted by Don Quixote. When he is absent from his master he is lost. When, in a scene more touching than the pathos of two quarreling lovers,

Don Quixote gives him leave to depart homeward, promising him reward for his past service, Sancho bursts into tears and vows that he cannot forsake him.

He loves his master. Not greed alone, or if so, the greed of devotion to an ungrasped grandeur, holds him astride his dappled ass to follow Don Quixote to the sea. And yet, he despises him; and he betrays him. He judges him, and he exploits him. He makes sure of his reward in Don Quixote's will, and he gives up the comfort of his wife to follow him through ridiculous dangers. He is this sensual, lusty, greedy oaf of the soil. And yet in the love that masters him he is Cervantes, himself: Cervantes who created Don Quixote to laugh and to mock—and who remained to worship.

For this is the crux of the matter. Cervantes needed Sancho to keep Don Quixote in the perspective for laughter. "Common-sense" rides along with the "madman," and constantly shows him up. But here is Sancho, shown up himself! Here is Cervantes, shown up! For Cervantes accepts Don Quixote. And that is why we accept him. Cervantes builds up these countless reasons for rejecting him: the havoc wrought by his acts, the shoddy stuff of his dream, the addled way of his brain. It avails naught. Cervantes ends with love. And we—the more humbly in that we have mocked and roared—avow our veneration.

Of such stuff is made the holiness of Don Quixote: mildewed notions, slapstick downfalls. We laugh at his unfitness to impose his dream upon a stubborn world: we see well enough that Rocinante is a nag and the knight himself, helmeted with a dish, a mangy addled fellow. And we accept, in order that he may live this nonsense, the disruption of inns, the discomfiture of pilgrims, the routing of funerals, the breaking of bones!

Cervantes strives hard to snuff out the aspiring hunger of his soul. For this, Don Quixote is bemuddied and deformed. But Don Quixote lives: and his chief enemy—Cervantes—gives him his blood and his passion, in order that he may triumph.

c. The Book of the Hero

Don Quixote is written in a prose majestical, dense, warm, lucid, still. It is the fulfillment of the Castilian music which Rojas' *La Celestina* promised a century before. The tempo is slow. More correctly, the organic movement of the prose is slow; and the facet movements are swift and nervous. The Cervantine prose is a portrait of the soul of Spain whose cadences of desire and will resolve into an immobile whole.

The accentual music of this prose had already become the innate quality of Castilian. Cervantes heightened his inheritance. The natural genius of the language was already, in the mystics and novelists before him, one that made for a muscular, slow yet sharply surfaced prose. In *Don Quixote*, the music has as its base an almost cosmic beat, within which as in a firmament, the swifter, brighter, more fleeting qualities stand forth. Cervantes makes good use of the agglutinated verb and pronoun, of the syncopations within the general prose rhythm. Above all, he makes use of the loamy expressions of the people, transfiguring them, however, into a tonal design not remotely naturalistic and more akin to the prose of the religious writers than of the pícaro novelists who also helped themselves to the vernacular of the soil.

In the great novel of Rojas there is a like marriage of pungent and ironical stuffs in an exalted orchestration. The difference is one of quality and quantity. Cervantes' instruments are more varied; his themes and the materials that build them are more numerous, even if no one is richer than the central form of *La Celestina*. Indeed, the earlier work is the intenser; its colors are more hot. There is in Cervantes a strain of the north which the Jew Rojas lacked; and which made his æsthetic action longer and slower. The art of the Semite is more lyrical, less architectonic. *La Celestina* is a bomb-like organ; a piston-strong machine driving hard and singly. It is the tale, moreover, of a city where life is vertical and packed. Its form is true to its theme. But *Don Quixote* is the story of a journey—of three journeys rather—over the plains and mountains of La Mancha, Aragon, Catalonia. Its basal movement is panoramic, horizontal. Its loftier dimensions are attained by the associative power of its hero who, riding the roads of Spain, touches incessantly the spiritual realms of a people, of an age, of a soul. The formal values of *La Celestina* are more manifest. Very consciously, an intellectual, nervously coördinated man bound together the counterpoint of his design, so that each element partakes *immediately* of the whole. This is not the case in *Don Quixote*. The materials of the book—persons of the road, interpolated stories, situations—stand end to end, flat for the most part and quite episodic. The knight enters them organically. He transfigures them as a new element in a chemical solution. He enacts a continuous catalysis upon the parts of Spain which he encounters. The result of this is two-fold. There is created for the entire book a *surface of action* and a *line of action*. These hold the attention of the reader: these, indeed, caused the book's popularity when it first appeared. The surface of action in the large is the Spain to which the Spanish people through the picaresque novel had been accustomed for over fifty years. The line of action is the pilgrimage of Quixote and Sancho.

But each of these two actions is complex. In consequence, their organic synthesis is often subtle and hidden. This synthesis gives to the work its unity: and one can enjoy *Don Quixote* without awareness of it. Indeed, the synthesis may take place in the reader's mind, long after he has absorbed its elements and put the book aside.

Consciousness of the organic greatness of *La Celestina*

must come at once; since that greatness is the result of a design preconceived and implicit in the book's several scenes. Consciousness of the greatness of *Don Quixote* came late even to its author and not to Spain until a whole century had passed. For its parts have an immediate life of their own; only after they have become lost and merged in one another does the book's unity, as a synthesis of all these parts, dawn on the reader.

The knight himself is not so much an organ in this ultimate synthesis as a dimension. The synthesis is not articulate in him alone, any more than in the episodes. But it is articulate in the book's language. And the rare individual who understood the æsthetic nature of prose might tell from the first page that *Don Quixote* was a stupendously formal work of art.

This prose is a *becoming* prose. It is heavy and pregnant. It is the antithesis of the immediate prose of Santa Teresa or of the lapidic absoluteness of the verse of Luis de Góngora. It is attuned at every moment to the whole of the book. It lacks swiftness and often sharpness. It is frequently clumsy in the projecting of little scenes. The book abounds in episodes that Quevedo would have fleshed more brightly or the author of Lazarillo pointed to more effect.

Cervantes is forever after deeper game. If, for instance, he describes the cozy dinner at which Quixote and Sancho shared the meat and acorns of six goatherds, the prose is not fundamentally focused upon the *genre:* but upon the tragic implications of Don Quixote's presence and upon the irony of the attitude of the goatherds.

But Cervantes never *states* these deeper implications. His prose *creates* them. And creates them, by the immanent and abstract nature of its music. This immanence runs throughout the work, and thereby Cervantes is permanently saved the unæsthetic makeshift of statement. His direct attention goes unhindered to the presentment of the action. The action's significance, one might say its *soul,* is implicit as is the significance of life implicit and *un-asserted* in material substance and in specific action.

But as in all great art, this deep effect is won at sacrifice of a lesser. Analogously, El Greco maintains the larger anatomy of his vision throughout the details of his paintings, although he loses thereby the grace and accuracy of the anatomy of his subjects.

There are still cavilers at El Greco's drawing; and there have always been depreciators of Cervantes' prose. Lope de Vega whose prosody was an immediate lyric flow of two dimensions, was perhaps sincere in his denigration of Cervantes. And even today Miguel de Unamuno, for all his adoration of Don Quixote, decries the language of Cervantes, for a similar reason: Unamuno's lyric mood can not span the parabolas in which the figure of Don Quixote is limned.

These parabolas are the *lines* of the prose: and they are not, like simpler curves, to be plotted in the segment of any specific action in the book. But they are to be *felt* in every page. That is why the first chapter of *Don Quixote* announces the inscrutable tragi-comedy, although Cervantes when he wrote it had no knowledge of his undertaking. The music of his prose is the mother of his book. It is the beginning of the book's significance, and it is the conclusion. Nor can it be translated.

.   .   .   .   .   .

A work of art in whose making significant forces have not played is inconceivable. The veriest trash, the most incompetent effort must in some wise have issued from a man's life, from a people's will, from an epoch's spirit. What lies between such work and work significant in itself is not difference of material, but form. The poor work is one in which the elements of life are inchoate and, failing to achieve a unity of form, cannot be said to achieve life itself. The real work of art is that in which these elements achieve a body: is that of which these elements *are* the body. But the bodies of men and age whence its elements of life have sprung will rot away.

Other men and other ages will succeed; and these in their will to know essential union with all men and all ages preserve the true work of art. For in it only, do those moldered lives of other men and ages touch them. The real work of art, builded of the substances of time, therefore alone does not exist in time. And a consideration of the work of art, whose basis is not equally beyond time—is not metaphysical or religious—is inadequate to art's function in the world of time.

Before all else, *Don Quixote* is in form the life of Cervantes.

Toward the end of his last adventure, on the way to Barcelona, Don Quixote with Sancho attempts to hold the road against a herd of bulls. But they are overturned, trampled, bemudded. They find a limpid spring garlanded with trees and wash the blood and mire from their sore bodies. Sancho brings food from the saddlebags. But his master is too disconsolate to eat. Sancho waits patiently: seeing no end to Don Quixote's sorrow nor to his own hunger, he falls to.

"Eat, friend Sancho," says Don Quixote. "Sustain the life which means more to you than to me, and leave me to die in the embrace of my thoughts and in the power of my disgraces. I, Sancho, was born to live dying; you, to die eating. And that you may see how I speak truth in this, behold me printed in history, celebrated in arms, commended in all my acts, respected in principles, desired by damsels; from end to end, whilst I awaited the palms, triumphs and crowns merited by my valorous deeds, you have seen me as this morning laid low, outraged and ground down, under the hoofs of obscene and filthy brutes. . ."

The roars and blows that greet the Sorrowful Knight might, in the jargon of our day, be termed Cervantes' masochistic satisfaction. Cervantes ridicules himself for the dreaming fool he has been. But the strain is too deep. This figure that he sets going to make mock of is after all his soul. He grows away from his embittered pose. He can still laugh at his creature; still gather him at the end back into the logic of his story. But in Part Two, he is seen defending him against the laughter of others. He is seen regarding his knight, for all his folly, as purer than the sensible world: and at the last, more real.

But the times were out of joint. Spain and Don Quixote were pitted against Reasons: the logic of their ideal against the reasons of a world breaking from the unity of God which once had been the Roman Church, into a multiverse of fragmentary facts which is our modern crisis.

Frustrate brilliance, seeking to be healed, is the one unity of the modern story. Since Columbus voyaged, we have voyaged and bruised ourselves in spiritual chaos: seeking the salvation of wholeness and seeking it in vain.

From our search has come the national concept of the State, for instance: a degenerate medievalism, this—a wistful effort to achieve the wholeness of Rome without the holiness that informed it. Has come the Marxian International—an inverted idealism which put up the economic process in place of the Hegelian Spirit. Has come the faith in science as Revelation. Has come with Rousseau, the seeking of salvation through the return to the unity of man's primordial needs: with Nietzsche, the same seeking in the but seeming opposite direction of the superman. And finally, Darwin inspired us to hope that God might be inserted as the principle of flux in biologic process. All these prophecies and dogmatic actions strove alike to enlist mankind once more in a full unity of life and impulse. All who believed in them, to the extent of their devotion, have been Quixotes.

Don Quixote gave himself to make the world One, through the application of measures that strike us as shoddy and unreal. His were the old "magics" of chivalry—of a Europe peopled by Germanic children and schooled by adolescents from Athens, Alexandria and Rome. The magics no longer *worked*: had indeed not worked to build a universal House, since Dante. But we, laughing betimes at Quixote, patronizing Dante, have for five hundred years been struggling to construct our house with materials equally inadequate. The primacy of reason or of subjective intuition, the autonomy of science or of economic purpose, the ideal of the State or social interstate, the dream of communism or the return to nature—one and all are magics as impotent and as unreal as those of the old knight who rode La Mancha on a bony nag, with a barber's dish on his brow, and in his head a neo-platonic vision.

. . . . . .

Don Quixote and Faust are the great antistrophes to the Commedia of Dante. The body of Dante's poem had the same elements as the body of Dante's world. They were the Judæo-Christian revelation, Aristotelian logic, Euclidean Nature, the Ptolemaic cosmos. They cracked, and with them Catholic Europe passed. Only in Dante and in certain other art forms, like the Gothic churches, has that body lived.

Don Quixote and Faust are bodies of Europe's dissolution—forms of our modern formlessness and of our need to be whole. They are perhaps the most vital æsthetic organs of the activity into which modern man was thrown by the deliquescence of his medieval world. As a poem, the Spanish work is the greater. Faust is the child of personal lyrism and speculative will. His sources, like the Knight's, are medieval. He seeks knowledge and through knowledge personal redemption. He knows that he cannot be redeemed, save by a cosmic understanding; and his sense of understanding is in this, the mystic's: that it implies possession of what is understood, and a dynamic act. But Faust remains the atom, the unfertile seed of human will. His way to unify the world is to dominate and absorb it within the complex of personal volition. This is heroic, but it is savage. It ignores the fundamental wisdom of the Jews and Hindus which taught that the health of the personal will lies through the threshold of its death. Faust seeks knowledge through its extended acquisition. Mefisto is the symbol of his faith in the reality of extension. If he can garner the right catchwords, he can swallow the world; and the world will become one within him. This bluntly is the means toward a new synthesis adapted by all the centuries of Europe that intervene between the Renaissance and us: and it is Kabbalistic! The personal will, in its endeavor to achieve fusion with the world, has concocted formulæ that were to act directly on the world, and by magic to control it. These formulæ of course became external organisms: they became a machine, an empire or empiric law. Instead of lending themselves to a solution, they spawned a multitude of problems. They could not fecundate the personal will, from which they issued. For it is the Law that from personal will, alone when it is rendered fertile by its own disaster (like a rotted seed) can cosmic will and a cosmic synthesis arise.

The legend of Christ was deeper: deeper the blundering way of Quixote. For he sought the grace of union not by absorbing the world into himself, but by transmuting himself into an impersonal symbol of the world.

He failed; but his book lives; for with the failure is the triumphant impulse that led up to it. The effect of the crusade was death; the cause was life.

The magics of Don Quixote are as absurd as our own. But his impulse was as true as the Prophets'. The Old and the New Testaments also are a tale of sins and follies. But these are visible, because the light of God shines on them. In the effect that passes, all the prophets and all the Christs have failed. None of them has failed, in the cause that remains. The cause of Don Quixote's life strikes us as truer than the realities which brought about his death. This is the pitiful best that we can say for him—or for any of the prophets.

One and all, they encountered *reasons* which put their *truth* to flight. And the world was able to live whole within their truth only in ages which willfully made reason servile. In the violence of his divorce from the world which he aspired to unite, in the ridiculousness of his discord from it, Don Quixote stands the last prophet of our historic Order. He bespeaks our need: a dynamic understanding which shall enlist ideal and reason, thought and act, knowledge and experience; which shall preserve the personal within the mystical will; which shall unite the world of fact in which we suffer all together, with the world of dream in which we are alone. . . .

CHAPTER X

THE WILL OF GOD

a. The Bull Fight
b. Man and Woman
c. Madrid

VANDALIA
PM
1965
ILL.

Vi Provinzano
311 Lincoln
Vandalia, Ill.

VANDALIA COUNTRY AND GOLF CLUB

WILLIAM R. SIMMONS
817 W. Johnson St.
VANDALIA, ILL.   62471

a. The Bull Fight

THE bull fight is older than Spain; the art of the bull fight has little more than a hundred years of history. Perhaps Crete, which gave El Greco to Toledo, gave the bull worship to Tartessos. Perhaps the Romans turned the bull rite into spectacle. The Visigoths assuredly had bull fights: and the medieval lords of Spain jousted with bulls as Amadis with dragons. The *toreo* was held in the public squares of towns, alternating possibly with *autos de fe*. In the one sport, the actors were nobles and the victims were bulls. In the other, officiated captains of the Church and the victims were Jews. In both, the religious norm was more or less lost sight of, as the spectacular appeal grew greater. But no æsthetic norm had been evolved to take its place. The bull fight was a daredevil game to which the young bloods of the Court—in their lack of Moors to fight—became addicted after the Reconquest. It was a dangerous sport, and it cost the kings of Spain many good horses and not a few good soldiers. Still, it throve until in 1700 a puritan, Philip V, ascended to the throne. He disliked the bull fight. It lost caste among the nobles. But its usage was too deeply, too immemorially engrained. The gentleman *toreador* went out: the professional *torero* and *banderillero* came in.

Francisco Goya has recorded in genial sketches and engravings the nature of this bull fight. It was still chiefly a game of prowess. If an art, it was more allied to the art of the clown and acrobat than to the dance or the drama. The professional torero was a gymnast. He had to risk his skin in elaborate ways: and skill was primarily confined to his grace in going off unhurt. He fought the bull, hobbled on a table, or lashed to a chair, or riding a forerunner in a coach, or saddled to another bull.

Only after the War of Independence against the French and after the lapse caused by Napoleon, whose generals disapproved of so barbarous an art, did Spain's popular tragedy arise: the modern, profound *corrida*. Its birthday was the same as that of the jota of Aragon which sprang directly from the incitement against the French. Like the jota, the bull fight was new only as an integration of old elements. And like the ancient bull-rite of Tartessos it reached its climax in Andalusia: more particularly in the Province of Seville.

The *plaza de toros* is of course the Roman circus. Rome created no more powerful form for an æsthetic action than this rounded, human mass concentered on sand and blood. With its arena, the bull fight wins a vantage over such western spectacles as cricket, baseball, the theater. In all of these, the audience is a partial unit: it is not above the action, but beside it. The arena of the bull fight is a pith of passion, wholly fleshed by the passionate human wills around it.

The *plaza* is too sure of its essential virtue to expend energy in architectural display. Here it scores another point over the modern theater whose plush and murals and tapestries and candelabras so often overbear the paleness of the play. The plaza has tiers of backless seats terracing up to balcony and boxes. The seats are of stone: the upper reaches are a series of plain arcades. The plaza is grim and silent. It is stripped for action. It is prepared to receive intensity. The human mass that fills it takes from the sand of the arena, glowing in the sun, a color of rapt anticipation. These thousands of men and women, since the moment when they have bought their tickets, have lived in a sweet excitement. Hours before the bugle, they are on their way. They examine the great brutes whose deaths they are to witness. They march up and down the sand which will soon rise with blood.

Bright shawls are flung on the palcos. Women's voices paint the murmur of the men. A bugle sounds, and there is silence. The crimson and gold *mantones* stand like fixed fires in this firmament of attention. The multitudinous eyes are rods holding in diapason the sky and the arena. Two horsemen (*alguaciles*) prance forward through the gates. Black velvet capes fold above their doublets. From their black hats wave red and yellow plumes.

They salute the royal or presidential box; circle the ring in opposite directions and return to the gate. The music flares. They proceed once more on their proud stallions, and behind them file the actors in the drama. The toreros are first: four of them: they wear gold-laid jackets, gold-fronted breeches backed in blue, rose-colored stockings. The banderilleros in silver drape their pied *capas* across their arms. The *picadores* follow. They are heavy brutish men, with chamois leggings and trousers drawn like gloves over their wooden armor. They are astride pitiful nags, each of which is Rocinante. The shoes are encased in stirrups of steel; the spurs are savage against the pitiful flanks. Behind the picadores are the red-bloused grooms, costumed like villains. It is their task to clean up entrails and gore. And the procession closes with two trios of mules, festooned and belled, who draw the drag to which the bodies of slaughtered bulls and horses will be attached.

The cavalcade crosses and salutes. Toreros, banderilleros, picadores on nervous nags, scatter along the barriers. Again, the bugle sounds. Doors open on the interior passage which two high barriers hold as a protective cordon between the audience and the arena. A bull leaps into the glare.

His massive body is a form for the emotion of rage and for the act of plunging. The forelegs are slight beneath the heft of his shoulders whence he tapers down, so that the shoulders and head are like a swinging turret. The brute is all infuriated flesh pivoting the exquisite ferocity of horns. They are slender and curved, needle-sharp, lance-long. The bull is aware of the strange ten-thousand-headed creature that shouts at him and drives its will upon him. He understands that the mob is his foe. He bellows, circles, plunges at last to reach it. The barrier jerks him up, splintering with his onslaught. He is bewildered and stopped, pawing the sand, while the mob prepares to send its single emissaries to engage him.

The first act of the drama is formless and ends in farce. Toreros and banderilleros toy with the bull. They fling capes, side-step, dawdle with him. But gradually they withdraw the brute's first fury from the indeterminate mob ringing him round to the accessible lives in the arena. The bull sees a horse. It capers before him in a blind presentiment of death. Its ears are tied, its eye is bandaged. Upon it a picador levels an enormous pike, steel-pointed. The bull charges and a horn sinks in the belly. Horse and rider rise and are flung in a clatter of bone, in a drench of flesh, against the barrier. The bull draws out his ensanguined horn and charges a banderillero whose cape is there protecting the picador. The crowd roars. The horse is whipped to its feet by grooms. The picador is hoisted back. The old nag's entrails hang in a coiled horror within a foot of the ground.

The horse is the comedian of the drama. The bull tosses him. He lies on his back and his four anguished legs beat like drumsticks on the barrier. Or, losing his saddle, he plunges mad and blind around the ring, kicking his own intestines, until death takes him. Or the bull mangles him at once, and he disappears in a swirl of flesh. This is farce; and also this is the sense of the immanence of danger. The bull is drunken with his victory. The crowd, beholding the fate of a horse, laughs with a tinge of terror. For what has happened there, may happen to a man.

Enough horses have been slaughtered: their poor flesh shredded into the gleaming unconquerable sands. A bugle summons the second act of the drama.

This is the scene of the banderilleros. They are the

critics, the epigrammatists, the *graciosos*, the chorus of the accelerant play. They bespeak the bull. They test him. They show off his subtle points—and their own. If he has faults—clumsiness, cowardice, lethargy—they correct him. They call forth his finest rage; and as he plunges on them they leave gay ribboned darts within his flesh. If he is slow to anger, they will employ darts that explode beneath the skin of their victim. They enrage him. But all the while, they sober him as well, making him realize that the holiday of the horses is no more: a harder enemy is on the field.

Often the bull is put into a meditative mood. He stands, panting in the center of the arena. Blood drips from his mouth. His horns are carmine and the laced *banderillas* dance on the scruff of his shoulder, biting, nagging. He wants to understand what his life has become. The fields of Andalusia—the good grass, the warm care —have been wiped out in this blare of terror. That background of pleasaunce merely serves to sharp the tense present—this delirium of men and sun. A banderillero dances up. The bull faces him, asking a question. But the man will not tell. His smile is false; that swing of his cape is treachery. There is nothing to do but plunge— whatever it means. The cape of red and blue folds over the eyes of the bull and vanishes like a cloud: a dart bites his flesh. The crowd roars. The good life behind and the peace beyond are mist: life is this glare and this roar and this goad of steel.

The second act is over: the bull is chastened. He has been cleansed for the tragedy, after his brief triumph. Once again the bugle: the torero to whose lot this bull has fallen, selects his slender sword and his red *capa*. He steps forward for the ultimate tragic scene.

Toreros are of many kinds. This one is called Belmonte and he is one of two great *espadas* of recent years in Spain. He is a small man, smaller than the average and more swarthy. His body moves rhythmic and slight into the hard glitter of the sand.

The elemental glare of Spanish sunlight makes that body, striding so quiet toward the bull, frail and helpless. Could this man run away, as do so many? could he, if need be, vault the high barrier to safety just as the bull splintered the wood beneath him? The head is heavy. The nose is large and sharp; the mouth is wide; the lower jaw thrust out. But the brow is sensitive and smooth. Close by, this is the face of a neurotic. The arena's flame bakes it into a brooding gloom above the body so ironically decked in gold and silk.

Belmonte in this instant has already awakened in the crowd the troubling emotion of pity mixed with fear. He salutes the bull and spreads his red mantle (the capa) across the fragile sword. He steps in close; and while the arena hardens into silence, he lifts the mantle toward the eyes of the brute.

Within an instant, breathless save for the breath of the bull, something goes forth from Belmonte to the beast and marries them. The bull is the enemy, and they are joined more close, more terribly than love. He plunges. Belmonte, motionless, swings the mantle to his side and the bull, as if attached to it, grazes the frail body. The mantle lifts. The bull lifts and turns, as if ligated by the mantle to Belmonte's will. The cloth thrusts to the other side. The bull along. Back and forth they go, in rigorous dance. The torero's body does not break from its repose. He is as cool as sculpture; he is as fluid as music. The bloody beast is attuned by a will, hard and subtle as Belmonte's sword. His clumsy movements are molded into grace: his rage is refined into these exquisite feints. He, too, like the torero, leaves the plane of nature, and becomes a symbol.

As the torero stepped out to the sand, his rôle was godlike. His minions had played with the great innocent victim: fed him victory and blood: taunted him: taught him. Now he, to enact the ultimate rite of life . . the ultimate gift of the gods . . the only gift which they give unstintingly . . death.

But this dance has transfigured the torero. Meeting the brute upon the plane of danger, he becomes a man. Those hypnotized horns graze human flesh: where they touch they rend. That gold-lined body is a sheath, holding the blood of a man. The bull could plunge through it . . plunging so near, so rhythmically near . . as if it were indeed the mist and dream of mortal life.

And now another change in the beauty of their locked encounter. The man becomes the woman. This dance of human will and brutish power is the dance of death no longer. It is the dance of life. It is a searching symbol of the sexual act. The bull is male; the exquisite torero, stirring and unstirred, with hidden ecstasy controlling the plunges of the bull, is female.

The crowd acts its part. The little man is but a gleam of fire, the bull but a tongue of dionysian act within this dark flame of ten thousand souls. From them come dream and desire and memory of sense: concentrate upon this spot of drama: merge with it and marry it to themselves. At every pass of the bull from side to side of Belmonte, the crowd is released in a terrific roar. So silent the dance of the two coupled dancers: so vast the response of the crowd. Now, Belmonte kneels and his mantle rhythmically wipes the furious bloody head, making the plunge of horns diagonal athwart the torero's breast. *Verónica* is the name of this classic gesture. And the allusion is to the handkerchief of the Saint, which smoothed the sweat from the forehead of the Christ. The ancient orgy of Dionysius and Priapus is tinged with Christian pity. The commingled symbolisms of many Spains meet in the dance: become abstracted and restrained. The whole is the silent balance of the wills of Spain.

The bugle signals for the final action. Belmonte has risen; has exchanged the capa for the small *muleta* with which he covers his steel. Now he withdraws the muleta from the slender sword. It is a flexible two-edged steel, dipped at the end. He stands still before the brute whose

sweat rolls red from the heaving rugose flanks. He stands
with heels clicked together, holding the brute with his
eye, and raises the blade deliberately forward. The steel
points not at the head, but slightly above it. In that mountain of flesh beyond the deadly horns there is an unmarked
spot which the sword must find. It is the tiny crutch
formed by the bones of the shoulder. Within its aperture
the blade can strike, unimpeded, to the heart. Anywhere
else, the blade will not bring death but a mere ugly plunging rage.

Belmonte has chosen to stand and make the bull plunge
on him. He is frail and erect. His shoulders are flexed;
his head is slightly forward. Grace becomes subtly rigor.
The bull obeys. He leaps. The blade sinks to the
gemmed hilt. A wave of blood gushes to the sand, as
the dead bull sinks.

This is the archetype of the Spanish bull fight. It describes a masterpiece. And in an art so profound and
dangerous, the masterwork is rare, even as in other æsthetic
fields. But if great toreros are rare, one actor in the
play is constant and is always masterful. The crowds of
Spain, against the agitation of intellectuals and of Church,
hold to their dear drama. In the *corrida,* all the desires
which history has bred and then denied an issue, find
an issue. Conflict is the stratified peace of the Spanish
soul. For too many ages has the Spaniard lived on war
to be able to do without it. In war, the lusts of the
world and the lust for God became one. Christ and
Priapus were joined in its full ecstasy. And in this dumb
show of a man and a bull, they are conjoined again.

Gross comedy of blood; sex, dionysian and sadistic; the
ancient rites of the brute and of the Christ meet here in
the final image of stability. Spain's warring elements reach
their locked fusion—Spain's ultimate form. For although
everything is in the bull ring, and although anything may

happen, *nothing happens*. Circus, blood, dance, death equate to nullity:[1] Like life in Spain, this spectacle is self-sufficient, issueless. . . .

[1] The elements which go to the making of a great *corrida* in Madrid, Seville, Barcelona, Zaragoza, San Sebastián, are intricate and varied. If any of them fails, the consummation fails. The rearing of perfect bulls is a science in Spain. Only a few preëminent ranches—*ganaderías de toros bravos*—are equipped to supply them. They are either in the province of Salamanca or in Andalusia. The *toreros* study the bulls in the field, coöperating in their upbring. Experts breed and train them, and prepare them for their supreme moment in the sun of the arena. And before the conflict, they are examined by veterinary surgeons. If they are one jot less than perfect, they may not enter the ring of a true *corrida*. They are then consigned to the *corridas de novilleros*: the innumerable encounters of the apprentice fighters—who must go through several seasons and win the applause of the most exacting critics ere they are admitted to the rank of *espada*.

Yet despite this care, imperfect bulls (bulls who refuse to fight, who fight erratically, who flinch at crucial moments) do enter the best *corrida* and blot out the artistry of the most expert *matador*. Indeed, the skill of the *torero* lies in great measure in his ability to control the bull. The genuine artist must possess hypnotic power. He must compel him in the instant of confrontation to forget the multitude, the flashing *capas*, the *banderillas* that bite his flesh: to concentrate upon his own frail grace all the bull's hate and all the bull's vigor. He must compel a brute to be the partner of an exquisite dancer.

He must control his own body as perfectly as any artist on a stage. Utter purity of form, of pace, of measure must be preserved within this threat of death. There is no virtuosity like this in all the world. Beyond is the crowd, not at all loth to seeing him undone: before him, *his colleague,* is a maddened bull whose horns are more terrible than swords. He must control the crowd; he must model the lunges of the brute into the design of an essential dance. And all this he must do in coolness.

The *torero* who can achieve this, not one time in a career but with reasonable frequency, and before the most savagely critical—and the most savage—audience in the world, comes not often in a decade's passing. Most *toreros* are at the mercy of the bull. If he behaves they acquit themselves with credit. If he baulks, they must trust to luck—to the saving *capas* of the *banderilleros*—even to their heels. Hisses are more frequent in the *plaza* than cheers.

All artists must labor against the inclement will of their materials. The temper of the bull, the action of the *cuadro de banderilleros,* the mood of the crowd present the common problem of technique. What distinguishes the art of the *torero* is the immediacy of death. If the dancer slips, he fails and that is all: if the acrobat misses, he lands in a net: if the actor forgets his line, he hears the prompter. If the *torero* makes a false step, he is dead.

And the *corrida* will go on without him! for he is never alone. But he is alone with his skill and with his nerve. The slightest trace of haste or sign of fear will spoil the pure line of his style. If for an instant he breaks from the perfection of his pose to save his life, he loses his art. And if in that moment he elects rather to hold to his art, he may not live to reap its glory.

In recent years, two *toreros* of genius have arisen in Spain. One, Joselito, died on the horns of the bull: and the *corrida* went on despite the mourning of the nation. Joselito shared with Belmonte the summit of his art. He was an Apollonian classicist. Chance and inspiration were reduced to a minimum. He had control over the brute: but it appeared to be less of hypnosis than of reason. He operated on the bull with so cool an accuracy that the infuriated beast was soothed into an obedient opposition to the *torero*. Joselito was exact, unostentatious. But when he had coupled with his enemy, his art became ornate. He moved facilely, he gave delicate steps. When he was killed in Valencia, Spain lost the most exquisite if not the profoundest of her tragic dancers.

Nature has aided Belmonte with its abstruse law of compensation for inferiorities. In this abnormally frail body live courage, rhythmic articulation, dionysian gesture. When Belmonte steps out to meet his bull the mind falls into heroic channels. For the head is brooding. And when, as once when I saw him, there is a white bandage across the brow with a touch of blood upon it, the effect is magic.

Belmonte at his worst is an ugly boy vaguely at odds with an unwieldy task. At his best, he is the propounder of rapture. He does not abstract the individuality of the bull like Joselito, and then perform his cold objective art. He measures the foe. He accepts him as he is. He plunges into the bull's fury. And thence, he rises to his high victory. There is always a moment in Belmonte's act when he is lost. The crowd gasps. Gone altogether beneath the fury of the brute, he emerges. His body sways in the prepossessive grace of one who has come through death. His art is perhaps greater than that of Joselito because its content is greater. Joselito excluded from his victory the reality of defeat. Psychologically, he crushed his foe first, and then worked on him at ease. Belmonte begins by submitting to the bull's might. And then, from this submission of the man, from this faltering of the god, he creates a form sculpturally superb.

b. Man and Woman

Queen Isabel may rest in peace. She is having her will although she would not recognize its way. Her conscious will was to make Spain one: it has become the unconscious will of every Spaniard. Her concept of the State of Spain has become a universal state of mind. Here was Spain, this sea of elements tossing and titanic. Here was the Spaniard, pressed by the amorphous world in which he lived to establish unity within himself: to become a person, in defense from the chaos that was Spain. In his will to create Spain, he could not change the theater of his action. He must create Spain *within himself*. The first stage of his endeavor was that of the intense crystallizations which made Spain's *siglos de oro*. These saints and sinners are not fragments: they are entire forms of Spanish energy. And the elements which they personify exist in every Spanish soul. If, therefore, Spain was to be unified within each Spaniard, La Celestina must be equated with Saint Teresa, Quixote and Amadis with Lazarillo and the Cid. . . Although the energic sum of all these forces might in each individual soul add up to zero!

To the intensely individual Spaniard, Spain became more and more subjective: until at last the boundary to the outer world was lost. Politics, war and church became subjective. The Spaniard saw the world only in terms of himself. This is why he strove to make the State the mentor of conscience: this is why he strove to make the domains of the State a sort of spiritual body. To inculcate faith by Inquisition; to establish truth by the sword; to drive dissenters in spirit from the soil—these were the mad and logical acts of a man who beheld the world in his own image. Willing to create a Spain, each Spaniard remained the anarchic personal creature whose separatism Strabo had noted and Rome endured.

The tragedy of Spain—her reaching of success! First her energy broke up into dominant forms of will: then she equated these forms into the equilibrium she desired. And no energy was left! All of her opponent tensions merge to rest in every Spanish soul. The titanic efforts toward conquest, toward art, toward God which have made Spain great balance each other at the end. The energy is not gone, not weakened: it is equated. And the result is sleep.

The energy of a people is the sum of its personal propulsions. The dynamic race is that in which the individual *as an individual* is incomplete. Consider the United States. The immigrant in losing his old land loses the completion which he achieved in his own share of its life. As an American he espouses America's incompletion. He injects his restlessness into America; and conversely America's lack of final form becomes his lack and his need. The result is a social body moving toward completion, and energetic in so far as it is barred from completion save in the act of moving. In Russia, the incompleteness of the individual soul is a paradoxical result of its consonance with the land. Russia is vast, uncharted, indefinite. The Russian spirit, identified with the soil, becomes imbued with a symbolic sense of vastitude and longing. Spirit is therefore national in Russia: and spiritual energy floods the land, precisely because the land is an incomplete experience in each Russian mind.

There are indeed permanent forms of spiritual incompleteness, and one of these exists in every energetic people. The Frenchman's soul is part of a social soul. The Frenchman is organically incomplete, in so far as his mind and sense know themselves integral components of the nation. From this knowledge comes the automatic flow of individual energy into social channels: this is balanced by the impersonal character of the French nation which receives the energy it requires and discharges back into the individual life a transformed power: the protection and unity of the enveloping organism. This perpetual interplay between the Frenchman and his group is an equilibrium in incompleteness: it makes permanent the impermanent achievement of individual and nation, the need of each for the other, the flow of energy between them. The Jew possesses another form of permanized incompleteness. The Jewish soul yearns for Zion and for God. The Jew's intelligence successfully places both Zion and God beyond his reach. His incompleteness is hence perpetual: and the Jewish energy has not ebbed.

But the Spaniard elected a form of achievement and a form of truth which he could reach: and as he reached it, he stopped moving. Truth became the Church of Rome: he attained that truth and rejected every other. His ideal of unity was homogeneity: the simple fusion in every Spaniard of thought and faith, according to a fixed ideal. To this end he impoverished the elements of his psychic world into sharp antitheses: these he balanced against each other: the result was indeed simplicity, homogeneity, a neutralization of energy summing to zero.

The Spaniard is not decadent: neither is he weak. There is as great force in him as in the days when his still unfused power conquered half Europe, discovered America and poured the vision of Cervantes, Rojas, Calderón and Velázquez upon the world. But now, all this energy is *locked* in its own willed equation. Its original dualisms are not dead; they are controlled and neutralized. The equilibrium is complete: and what energy is left from it the Spaniard must expend in holding the equation. There is no energy unemployed: and it is precisely the excess energy of man, the energy that is unable to find its goal within the organism, which creates intellect and which creates creation.

Had he been less heroic in his will, or more objective in his way to it, the Spaniard would not be this cripple: this giant shattered by his success, this giant imprisoned in the reality of his ideal.

The most willful of men, he appears will-less. For his power of will goes to dominate himself—and to hold his dominion. So that no power is left wherewith to dominate the world. The unity of Spain exists, subjectively and multiplied by millions. In consequence the Spaniard is not adhesive: he is too complete: the motive toward adhesiveness is the sense of incompletion. The most secret impulse of the Frenchman or the Jew has its social dimension. No Jew can people Zion in solitude. No French mystic or philosopher is an anchorite. Pascal and Descartes are Catholic: Paul Cézanne strives to create a new museum art. The rebel in France is a rebel against monarchs. But the Spaniard is an empire and a god unto himself. The perfected Spanish person makes permanent the social Spanish chaos.

The most intellectual of men, he appears unintelligent. He lives so wholly within his Idea, that no energy is left for further ideation. Creative intelligence is the birth of conflict between the personal will and life: it is born of the pause between impulse and response and of the excess energy which remains after the instinctive action. In the Spaniard, this excess energy is small: he is too self-sufficient to know richly the pauses between will and deed; and in the relativity of values which springs from a chaotic or incompleted conscience he is poor. Having achieved his Idea, he is weak in intellect: having created his imagined world, he is weak in imagination.

Therefore he understands vaguely the causes of his incompetence, and struggles weakly against them. His contemporary literature is strong in plaint: it is wanting in self-knowledge and constructiveness. It is weak, also, in creative imagination: even as it is strong in fantasy. The Spanish mind has become like the mind of a child. The child's intellect is not inferior to the man's: it is merely too preoccupied within itself to have achieved the power of association and of objective experience which comes with maturity and which begets analysis and imagination. The child is credulous, because its belief is subjective fantasy

and finds no opponent in the real world. Also, the child
is cruel because it cannot imagine pain in others, it is
anti-social because it has not associated its life with the
life around it. The Spaniard is still the victim of the
infantile beliefs of medieval Europe. He accepts the
literal Heaven and Hell, having no imagination strong
enough to make them real, and in consequence to reject
them. He is cruel. And his separatism, his want of the
adhesive impulse make him a ready victim to tyranny in
government. Unable to organize a social body, he accepts
the simple body of the King or the alien body of the Church
of Rome.

He has the virtues of his state. His personal develop-
ment brings him a personal integrity, a true personal pride
unknown in Europe. He has natural dignity. Whatever
his rank, he is a *caballero:* a true microcosm of the Spanish
nation. There is no artifice in him. He is clean, self-
controlled and independent. In his veins lives the impulse of heroism; in his mind is the knowledge and the
acceptance of heroism's price. Cowardice, compromise,
hypocrisy are traits more common in more social races.
And cant requires no word in *castellano.* Even the Spanish
thief is sincere: the tradition of the pícaro has not died.
And the power of endurance, of sacrifice, of devotion is
developed in the average Spaniard beyond the dream of the
romantic north.

The once furious and unleashed elements of the Spanish
soul have been woven into this counterpoint of rest: they
make a quiet music. It is natural that the Spaniard's love
of music and gift for music should be supreme. This art
of vigorous abstracted balance, so subjective, so ruthlessly
legal, is the symbol of the Spanish nature. And as with
his classic *canto hondo,* the effect in counterpoise and control is almost that of silence. By the same token he is a
great dancer: his dance is a synthesis of movements equated
to rest. And he loves the drama: where the torrential
forces of mankind are fused into a unitary form.

The world nurses two myths concerning Spain. The first, that she is decadent, Spain believes herself, and thereby proves, if other proof were lacking, her failure in self-knowledge. The other myth is that Spain is romantic.

The first myth rests upon ignorance of psychological mechanics. The second is a confusion of words. The philology of the term *romance* is clear. In the formative eras of modern Europe, the Latin dialects which were to become French, Italian, Castilian, Portuguese, Galician, Provençal, etc., were lumped as the *romance* to distinguish them from the pure tongue of Latin. They were popular vernaculars and despite the early instance of such men as Dante and Petrarca, or the Arcipreste de Hita, they were not deemed worthy vehicles of exalted thought. The writer whose ideas were holy or philosophic was supposed to clothe them in Latin. Only if he treated of such vulgar subjects as earthly love, might he employ the vulgar language. By association, *romance* was transferred from the tongue to the subject for which it was disposed: a story of profane love or profane adventure became *romance;* and becoming so, remained trivial and vulgar. The essential attitude of the Spaniard toward the subjects of romance was, however, the very contrary of what we mean by romantic.

Now came the hour of confusion. The knights of Portugal and Spain fought for God, for Mohammed, for the King: for anything but what we call *romantic* reasons. The Iberian north is Celt and is contiguous with the Celtic cultures of Britain and of France. The Iberian knight went northward out of Spain; and when he returned he had become what today we call a "nordic." He was sentimental, tender, monogamous, and chaste. He was the very converse of the old Spanish knight, Arab or pagan-Christian whose canny materialism speaks so clear in the *Poema del Cid*. He was, indeed, Tristan, Arthur, Lancelot, or Amadís of Gaul. The books that were written about him were published in romance: so that the qualities of passionate devotion which in Spain has been confined to the religious—to subjects too high for romance—became romantic.

The romance, therefore, is of the south: the romantic is of the north; and they negate each other. It is the German metaphysicians who invented the romanticism of Calderón; it is Byron and the French æsthetes who created romantic Spain. But the best efforts of Schlegel, Goethe, Mérimée, Gautier, Byron have failed to make the Spanish man or woman in the least romantic.

She is serene and she is incurious. Her Anglo-Saxon sister would call her inactive, even as the *Parisienne* would find her dull. Since sexual adventurousness is normally the result of intellectual curiosity—sensual stimulation by ideas—she is chaste and dispassionate. But if her lack of amorousness is due to her lack of thinking, her serenity and her external inactivity are due to her tremendous power. Women are most clamorous for "rights" in lands where culturally they have counted least. Witness England or the United States where for all her liberties woman is spiritually sterile. In contrast witness France whose women are the subtle partners of all deep events; or matriarchal Spain in which suffragists are as rare as they would be superfluous.[1]

The Spanish woman is a pragmatist in love. Love to her is the means of raising children in the grace of Christ. No less sensual, no less amorous woman exists in Europe. As a girl she is lovely: a crisp expectancy makes her flesh sweet and rounds her darkling eyes. She looks to marriage as the highest and most powerful career. Once she is mated, the natural coquetry of Spring falls from her like a season: she is instantly sedate, full-fleshed,

---

[1] In the winter of 1924 the Dictator of Spain, Primo de Rivera, on his own initiative conferred the municipal suffrage upon women. They did not agitate for it; and it seems clear that if they exercise this new privilege it will be in the same spirit of compliance with which they accede to all the demands of men.

maternal. She has no instinct for the game of love. Sexual virtuosity in woman is a slow process nurtured at the expense of the maternal passion. This diversion is rare in Spain. The French or American woman's sexual science is an undeciphered, an irrelevant perversion to the woman of Spain who wears upon her head an invisible crown of matriarchal power.

For she is powerful: this discreet female in a land of furiously dreaming males! Events have sobered her and made her worldly-wise. Her man is the theater of opponent passions, ideals, hungers equating into nothing. She is the compensatory act. She is steady, unemotional, unmystical, canny. She distrusts excess—even of maternal service. Her man has made magic of such words as State, God, Honor. Hers the task to materialize these words which in his mouth bespeak inaction. The family, the garden, the morrow; these become her Word.

The woman of Spain leans on the Church of Rome. No small part this of her dominance in a land incapable of social institutions. Spain with her separatist nature, her inadhesiveness, could never have created Rome: but Rome has gone far toward giving Spain that minimum of organic body which the millions of individual "Spains"— her men—required. The Spanish woman by her massed support makes the Church Spanish.

If the Church belongs to the woman, ruling Spain through her, she has remained outside the exhaustive activities of her husband. The Spanish woman has been untouched by metaphysics: her heroine, Santa Teresa de Jesús, is an ennobled *house-cleaner*, a glorified matron of Christ. The Spaniard's wife has not, like him, been split into intricate traits of will and of expression: nor in the sequel need she spend herself to win back unity from an inner chaos. She is naturally whole: she is the foe of even the fairest anarchies of the spirit. There is in her an heroic amplitude that recalls the poised women of the Hebrews. She is the savior of Spain, for she is the Responder to Spain's excesses of action and inaction.

The land has become a matriarchy—by default. The Spaniard has been too busy establishing theodicy on earth to rule Spain well: at last too involved in the equating of his embattled impulse to rule Spain at all. Imperceptibly, unofficially, woman has taken hold. She allows man many liberties—trivial liberties of the sort she would call romantic, if she knew the word. He may "govern," vote, own; he may fight; he may drink, gamble, whore. He may act indeed the perfect child thinking himself the center of the world because of his exultant vices (of which politics and journalism are the most absurd). Meantime, she with her compass Christ, and her wheel, the priest, steers the slow ship of Spain. In her disposal are the education of her children, intellectual and moral, the molding of those customs which go deeper than statute. In her hands is the family, and the family is Spain. She is the true controller of finance. It is a common thing in Spain for the man to own the money of his wife, and for the wife to distribute the money of her husband. In the peasant classes, she is arbiter of culture and thought: in the middle classes she is economic judge: in the noble classes the lineage descends through her in equality with her husband.

The nature of Spain calls imperatively for the dominance of woman. Woman's mind is individualistic, and Spain is a congeries of consonant parts rather than an organism. Woman builds her familial molecule from the Spanish atoms: she erects a great simplicity in which her man can dwell.

In Spain there are two kinds of women: the mother and the prostitute. And both are mothers. The land is sensuous in its air, its flowers. The Spaniard is not sensuous at all. In the nineteenth century, a group of romantic Spanish poets endeavored to sing of Spain as had the Germans and the English. No more frustrate coldness exists in all the literature of failure. "*Kennst du das Land wo die Citronen bluehen*" could never have been written by a Spaniard about Spain. For the Spaniard is as abstract in his bodily lusts as he is concrete in his ideals. Of his wife, he seeks the haven of morale: of his prostitute, he seeks the peace of respite. The Spanish prostitute with her Cross lying within her breasts is the least mercenary, the most womanly of her class. She is mellow and maternal. She bears with her a great sense of sin: and the man who touches her lips touches pity. From man she receives two treasures, bread and shame: she is eager to give, in return, her humility and comfort. She has no delights of subtle sense to barter: but he who comes to her, weary and broken, will find her arms mysteriously soothing, as if her acceptance of sin were a Christian solace, as if her acceptance of shame were heartening to his pride.

And the Spanish wife knows of the prostitute and suffers her. She brings for the husband an escape from the chaste rigors of family and church into the anarchy of unorganized affection and of Christian pity. She makes the work of the wife less arduous.

.   .   .   .   .   .

Human happiness is the full deep flow of human energy. It has many ways, nor is it rare. The madman is happy since all of his thought and sense falls into the pattern of his will. The lover is happy. Children are happy, eating or at play. Soldiers are happy in battle. And everyone is happy in dream.

There are happy nations: nations at war, nations in the madness of any enterprise, whether it be of growth or dissolution. But Spain is not happy. Her energy does not flow. It stands locked in a diapason of pause.

Nor is Spain unhappy. Unhappiness is the thwarted need of energy to flow. Spain's energy is not thwarted. It does not flow: it does not need to flow. It is absorbed in its own perpetual balance.

Spain is a dark soul. Sun is a flame in her land, and her land is a storm of color. But the soul of Spain is neither sun nor storm. It is neither gayety nor grief. It is a dark contentment, midway held between ecstasy and sleep.

Outside the tremor and traffic of spiritual movement, Spain moves like a somnambulant. Her body moves: but within her shut eyes there is a vision truer than her stirring: a vision stirless and composed.

Her mood is dark and stagnant. Yet it is pleasant, for it is not pain. Her soul is caressed passively by this rhythmic swing between the extremes of action: as if the long ages of Spain's agitation had bred this sensuous delight in their denial.

Within her heroic memory, within her heroic land, Spain wanders unobtrusively and scatheless. She does not forget nor remember. Upon the surface of her life, intellect pricks, passion stirs, action clamors. But her depths are limpid in a dark and dreamless slumber. . . . .

c. Madrid

In the eighteenth century one Spaniard out of three is
an ecclesiastic, a noble or a servant. (This takes no toll
of rogues and beggars.) The special rights of Aragon,
Valencia, Catalonia are annulled. Those of the Basques
are a dead letter, although they linger on the books until
the Carlist wars. Spain has become a receding unity,
under a single monarch. Her American possessions wait
only the full tide of growth in order to set loose. Castile's
will has leveled Spain. Her huertas give wine and fruit
just in the amount to balance the desert dearth about them.
Her high towns are fossils of recalcitrance, or backfires
smoldering against each other. Although the diapason of
will has its home in every Spanish soul, no one city is its
symbol. Toledo, Avila, Seville, Barcelona, Jaca, Murcia,
Mérida, Oviedo . . they bespeak their pasts, their individual dynamisms, whose sum is zero. To be the symbol of
this sum—Spain's tragic consummation—there must be a
modern city.

Madrid stands for the ultimate achievement—and for
none of its factors. It is the capital of Spain—and of
no old Spanish region. It is a pleasing town. Its populous
quarters bespeak the eighteenth century. The cabs blotched
under gas-lamps, the shuttered stores, the sumptuous theaters, the cobbled streets and alleys holding a bar, a flower-
stand, a beggar, recall old prints of Paris. The reminiscent
age of Balzac and of Daumier has taken refuge here. In
Paris, the twentieth century has jostled out the last; it seems
to keep better terms with the Paris of Louis XIV, of
Henri IV, even of François Villon than it does with the
Paris of Voltaire. But in Madrid, the eighteenth century
has mellowed to the next; they strike together a plaintive

reminiscence against the modern city: the Madrid of broad
Avenidas, of the Gran Via, of dapper taxicabs and monu-
mental banks.   This Madrid is pleasant also: it might be
almost any provincial capital of central Europe.

Madrid is noisy.   In the modern streets, the chauffeurs
toot as if they had just discovered horns and were intent,
like children, to break the new toy ere bedtime.   In the
older, more populous streets there is a texture of ancient
voices.   Shut your eyes and the windowed walls of Europe
fade away: the breath of the desert and the steeps of the
mountain north, the watery chatter of the Catalan, the
grunt of the Aragonese, the gracious Andalusian palaver
merge into a music of the air and make Madrid a maze of
memory.

Yet for all the noise and all the business, there is upon
the town a subtle and a gentle quiet.   This assertiveness
is only for itself: it is a heightened murmur of assent to
Spain's rich past.   Beneath the bruit, Madrid is silent,
like Spain's history.   Beneath its animal turbulence it
broods.   And for all its mingled moods, its final one is
a dream.

On Sundays, the *rastro*—the great city fair—boils down
hill, a human torrent through a canyon of tattered houses
to the dry *Manzanares*.   On feast days in spring or
summer, the town roars at the bull-ring.   And when the
last death is written in the sands, it swarms in lorries,
motors, tally-hos, back to the Plaza de la Cíbeles; it spreads
in numberless café tables on the broad sidewalks of the
Alcalá.   The Puerta del Sol—theater of revolutions—is
a somber well whose sides are gray soiled houses and whose
crowds are a thick condiment.   Trolleys, lottery vendors,
beggars, loafers, make a bright shuttle through the sluggish
maze.   At the Carnival of Spring, the gutters of the
barrios de Toledo and de Manzanares pour their lives into
the Castellana.   Rogues, prostitutes, shopgirls, mothers with
babes at the breast flow back and forth under the statue
of Columbus and the austere walls of the Biblioteca
Nacional: queer costumes grimace through confetti clouds;

a murmur of sexual release agglutinates the swarms; a glow as of rich earth breaking to grass rises beneath the sere March sky. . . And yet, there is a silence, there is a stillness on Madrid. The songs of the turbulent streets are songs of silence. This parade of pleasures and of passions, of crimes and revolutions, is somnambular.

Populous Madrid falls from the Plaza Mayor fan-wise to the arid curve of river upon whose treeless banks are stuck the shanties of the breadless. And above the river and the shanties is the Palace of the King, a cold and granite jewel set upon misery. If you would see it well, go down to where the starving *madrileños* stack their huts and air their tattered shirts—ironic flags under the flag of Spain.

Through populous Madrid—a massive flesh—runs the artery of the calle de Toledo. The cobbled streets are moist with sweat of lives. The high walls rise, blind in a mood of siesta under the blazing sun. Winter presses like icy steel upon the open wound of Madrid's poverty. But even in winter, the fever is there. It is damp in summer, in winter it is frozen. These streets have a cellar mood. Their stones seem porous with a fungus warmth or with a fungus odor. They are straight and steep—not gyring Moorish streets; they funnel the dark song of life, or let it escape like fume into the dry air of the meseta. Some of them are short: the leisurely streets of the old inns— posadas—of the stagecoach, of the itinerant milker with his flock of goats. Through a huge oak door, one passes into a patio. A fig tree, old as a satyr, thrusts its branches through the ancient iron balcony. Below is another patio with a pump, a rose-bush, a pile of manure, a flock of hens and a woman kneeling before a basin. Her hair and her gown are black, her lips are scarlet. Vice and compassion rise from the old close like perfumes; for this aged posada was once a convent, and bright fleshed maidens told their rosaries where now this woman looks into her mirror.

All the people are emanations of the past. Girls in the street are lovely and rank, roses overblown. Women walk like wafts of a hot night through the day. Men are lean, high-tensioned, and isolate as lusts. But though they tide the streets, though their deeds are a storm, this agitance and lushness of Madrid fades to mirage. . .

It has become a very modern city. Its boulevards are superb; it is full of smart shops and theaters; it has restaurants as expensive as the best of Paris. Its traffic is dense and efficiently controlled; its wealthy sections have the empty glitter of similar districts of Paris or New York. Madrid cannot overcome the spirit of its being, which is a spirit of stillness. Other towns in Spain grew from the needs of conquest, of commerce, of defense. God—or profit—gave them energy. But Madrid is of no such beginning: Madrid is of the *end*. It is a consummation. It stands for the Spain that has annulled its motions.

Its greatness is but the stubborn Castilian will to remain and to hold all Spain in perfect equilibrium of forces. Madrid is the town of politicians, of social servants, of soldiers. It is a *conservative* town. It wants things as they are. From here goes forth the will to repress Barcelona, to exploit the Basques, to muzzle Unamuno, to tax Andalusia, to play at empire in Morocco. A town of government—a parasite town, it is the converse of such towns as London or Paris. For in these, greatness came first, and made them govern.

There is this subtle melancholy in Madrid, this silence under all its voices—of a life come to dark pause. And yet this same dark element is fecund. Like a culture-bed, it nurtures even with its rot.

Beside the parasite, here is the thinker; beside the exploiter, here is the creator. Along the Gran Via, the calle de Alcalà or near the Puerta del Sol are the *tertulias*. They are cafés in which the men of the town congregate each night. You will find each of them in his appointed place, from close of work until nine, when the householder returns to dinner. The café is dark and the smoke fumes are thick. The muscular integument of the Castilian language is darker and thicker. It fills the air with a heavy yet swift texture. It is fluent, agile, potent. The plastic rigor of the Spanish world is in this tongue of Spain. The men sip coffee or vermouth. They are small drinkers. One can live in Spain a year and see no drunkard. They are too busy in talk, to think of alcohol. They are talkers, neither brilliant nor dull. Their speech has weight, acuity, vigor. It is too solid to be bright: it is like the pigment of a Velázquez.

Most of these men in the tertulias are of the intricate army of bureaucratic Spain. Postman or Minister, clerk, alguacil or General—all attend their tertulia with a ritual devotion. They think that they are "running Spain"— directing a State more or less modern and which, since the choice of Ferdinand and Carlos, has willed to be European. But like all Spaniards, they are unselfconscious and are actors in a drama deeply beyond them. They are the tools of the Spanish will to remain in equilibrium—to remain in sleep. All their conservative energy goes to this end, whose symbol is Madrid.

But beside them, at other tables, in the tertulias of other cafés, are other men who form the antiphony of their neighbors. These are the intellectuals. They too are largely unselfconscious. They believe, perhaps, that they are artists creating in word or color things of intrinsic beauty, like their Parisian models. So they also put their heads close together over smoky tables and drink coffee and talk "shop." But in truth, they are the inevitable response —the stir against and within the sleep of Spain. They are the germs of dissolution. The bureaucrats hold Spain together—in sleep. The intellectuals plot and dream to burst Spain asunder—in a new waking.

END OF PART TWO

PART THREE
Beyond Spain

CHAPTER XI
THE RIFT IN BARCELONA

THE cathedrals of Spain are splendors heaped by the hand of chaos. Well they sing the discord of a world too full of life to find perfection save in the dream of death. Most of them rise from stones that formed a mosque; the mosque ofttimes was a converted citadel of Visigoth or Roman. And here Spain brought her will to unity. Where could these rank lusts of a hundred factions, these voices of continents and peoples meet, save in death? The simple romanesque is buried under the aspiring jungle of baroque, plateresque, Gothic, *churriguera*. Window, *reja*, *retablo*, altar flourish like fevers and sum up to silence.

If this is Spain, Barcelona is of another land. The cathedral of the great town of the Catalans is luminous and graceful. Although it could be lost in the vastitudes of the cathedrals of Seville or Salamanca its voice is clear and carries farther: it bespeaks the living.

Yet here, too, the church is dark. The brown-black stones are lifted by the day of the deep windows into a rosy flush. The Choir is so low that the line from *cimborio* to *capilla mayor* is free. Toward the Altar, the Choir is open. Its sides are exquisite spires that rise in tremulous shadow. The windows are small. They hold light in their stained glass like eyes. The church is a reticent life gazing within itself. And what it sees is an inset of twenty columns making a sort of inner body, a dark and mystic body in the gaze of the glowing outward walls.

The loveliest monument of the Catalans, their church bespeaks them. It is a thing of beauty: but unlike the beauty that resides in Spain, it is not tragic. Beauty is consummation: in Castile the goal is immobility or death. Here the perfected mood is wakefulness. The grace is gentle and assured: it is not tortured, neither is it prophetic. Close is the ease of the fields of France, of

France's churches. Close is the balance of Attica. . . . . .

Islam had short shrift in the Catalan Province which rests upon the Pyrenees and faces east across the sea toward Italy and Greece. When the Moslem came, the Catalan retreated into France. And in less than a hundred years (in 797) the great town of Gerona (you can still see its walls and its fortress-church) fell to the Frankish Christians. In 801, the vassals of Charlemagne drove out the Crescent forever. Barcelona became Frankish: Catalonia was apportioned to Frankish nobles. This strain of alien blood is a symbol of the wavering dissonance that has endured in Catalonia forever. For the yearning of Spain was to be Spain: and the will of the Catalans was to be part of Europe.

The Teuton element in Spain is Visigothic. With the Franks there came across the dwindling spurs of the Pyrenees the Gallo-Romans of Provincia, a different intensity of the Idea of Rome from that of the Ibero-Romans. Catalonia straddled the mountains, mingling in spirit and in affairs with France. Almost at once after the Reconquest, it took the lead in the Mediterranean trade of the Provincian littoral. Feudalism flourished here, as it never did in Spain—a true French feudalism, heritage of Charlemagne who indeed had held Spain clear to the Ebro. The domains of the great Counts of Barcelona were as wide north of the Pyrenees as south. And already, sharing this participance of France, in the eleventh century there are Italians (Pisans) fighting under the pennants of Barcelona against the Valencian Moor. Even today, the spirit and the tongue of the Catalans bestrides the Eastern Pyrenees from Lérida to the French Roussillon, from Tarragona to the French Port Vendres.

The Catalan of Spain is an outsider within the gates. Ere Spain stratified her chaos into locked unity, Catalonia was free to be exploited by the hardier will of Aragon. But as Aragon was set within the grip of Isabel of Castile, Catalonia became an irrepressible motion—needing to be repressed. Its flow of energy in an immobile

State meant anarchy: its lyrism was discord within Spain whose counterpoint of themes summed into silence. Spain achieved her union. Madrid on the roof of Castile became the symbol of union: Barcelona, at the half open gate which led to Italy and France, to Greece and Africa, became the symbol of disruption.

Castile tried to woo this province, as it wooed Valencia, Galicia, Extremadura, Andalusia. But the Catalan blood could not respond to the immobile ecstasy of Castile: nor could the winds and the songs which blew in at the door of Barcelona be shut out. The Catalan remained light, moving, gay. When the unity of Spain was strong, the Catalan was a tonic discord. Now that Spain's unity is flaccid, the Catalan is a menace.

But if Barcelona is not Spain, neither is it France. The Catalan is a unique organic compound of the Mediterranean, of the Mountain and of Spain. His cathedral is set in a town that beats with a rich fervor. The *Ramblas*—wide, gay avenues—descend to the sea and the town faces with them from the wooded hills. It is an old ripe city: a labyrinth of streets that are fresh with the salt, dark with the feudal yoke, yet glamorously flowing as if in cognizance of the genius of this people to outlast all yokes. This is no strong race, as the Aragonese or even the Basques are strong. It is a subtle and a gracious people. Its secret of survival is manifest in the women: delicate daughters of Eve, perhaps the fairest of all Europe, hued like April orchards, and with eyes like twilight. They have the permanence not of the eternal, but of the evanescent which returns. The flower that was Greece has been cast here upon a coast of Spain and has grown afresh. This life does not resist: it returns. France mastered the Catalans: and they returned. Aragon used them ruthlessly in war: they returned. Castile stifles and racks them: they are returning. For they are like the Spring, the evanescent Spring—which returns. . . . .

Their rising song begins to be heard over the shut land.

It is not heroic song: it is after all the assertion of a race of traders. It is not thunderous. What thunders is the Castilian silence. And the heroic is the Spanish sleep. And the enduring is the Spanish drama of which the Catalans, even in their apartness, must be part. Spain has a dawning will to break from the unity which its will created: her atoms, anarchic but pregnant, stir to be loosed and to begin again. Despite its denial, Catalonia shares in this unborn Spain. Once the resistance of the Catalans helped to rouse Aragon and Castile with greater energy and clearer mind: helped to create Spain. Now this same resistance of the Catalans, even if it disrupts, may serve to create Spain again.

CHAPTER XII

THE COMEDY OF THE BASQUE

In the north where the Cantabrian ranges and the Pyrenees rim the Bay of Biscay, lives a peculiar people. Even its land is different from Spain's. The air is temperate, moist. Mountains are clad in forest. Fields of high grass bring honeyed redolence. The green plateaux come down above the sea, like masses of the Alps brought to the Spanish coast. These lands, so like Europe, so unlike Spain, are studded with stone towns. Houses are gabled, narrow streets are cobbled: there is a note of canniness and of seclusion in the towns of the Basque.

When the Romans made a province of Iberia, the Basque lived unconcerned. When the Moslem swept north, the Basque withdrew into the mountains and withstood him. When the Visigoth came through the passes of the Pyrenees, the Basque stood aside and let him go. When Catholic Roland with the troops of Charlemagne followed the Visigoth, it was the Basque not the "Saracen," who beat them at Roncesvalles. When, finally, the kings of Castile, having cleared Spain of Moor and Jew, turned to subdue the Basque, he submitted only as a vassal bowing the head to a more powerful alien. By decree, Fernando VI ennobled all the Basques in the Province of Vizcaya: already in 1200, the entire population of the Province of Guipúzcoa had been declared hidalgos.

An indelible, an archaic people! They seem to be a race in an archaic fashion: a race *by blood!* Spaniards, Chinese, Frenchmen, Jews are a race *by culture.* But the Basques appear to have had no culture. Their language was unwritten. They possessed no history, no social records, no underlying base of ethic, or religion. If they possessed a culture, it was almost biologic. It persisted in blood, in instinct, rather than in concept. A certain haleness of self-sufficiency, a certain gusto for aloofness kept them intact and unique in a land which for three thousand years boiled with invasion.

In their survival they became neither tragic nor heroic. Naught could be farther from the Basque than such other peculiar peoples as the Armenian or Jew. The Basques had no separate Book, no separate God. Very early, they accepted Christ. He did not make them merge with their Catholic neighbors, because their instincts were differently attuned. Spain is a world of Tragedy, of mystic ideals, of devotion to unseen spirits. The Basque is concrete, light, canny. The Spaniard faces all that he encounters: this confrontation is the genius of Tragedy. But the Basque *evades:* and this evasion is the genius of Comedy.

Who the Basques were is not clear: doubtless early dwellers in the Peninsula—part of the peoples whom the Phœnicians found when they first skirted Spain. Their music suggests kinship with the Celt; but this may well be due to the neighborhood of the Celts who named the Spanish province of Galicia. Their music as well suggests kinship with the Berbers—the Rifians of Morocco. Their language is inscrutably alone: it bears no relation with any of the tongues of Babel. But whoever they were they remain. Their blood in the small towns is little mixed; and their heads unmixed also. While through the ages, Spain drank a torrent of Ideas—Greek, Roman, Moslem, Christian, Jew—and bent to the tragic fusing of Africa, Asia, Europe, America into a single Spain, the Basque quite simply kept on being himself.

His virtues, like those of his mountains, are conservatism and power of non-absorption. The Basque language paints this well. It contains no word for *God*, no word for *spirit*. This is a people rooted to the earth and which kept to its pastures and farmyards.[1] Not alone had the

[1] This statement is not literally correct. The Basques became eminent navigators in the sixteenth century; their American settlements ranged from Canada to the Argentine. Yet, intellectually and spiritually, they remained, as a people, rooted.

Basque mind not reached metaphysics and religion when his tongue was formed: even common concepts were beyond it. There is a Basque word for dog, pig, cow, lizard: there is none for *animal*. There is a Basque word for oak, pine, chestnut: there is none for *tree*. A most excellently defended, anti-platonic people! Their mountains and their mountain-courage warded them free of many floods of races. And their heads kept them clear of metaphysics. Concepts of God, time, substance are drains upon the business of life. For the interims of business, there is the singing of songs, there is the gathering in eights to dance the bland *aurrescu*.

The towns of the Basques express them. The little Guipúzcoan village lies between the mountains and the sea. The mountains slope into a level field with cattle and kine growing fat in the lush grasses. The field rolls to a precipitous edge of rock which falls a thousand feet into the Bay of Biscay. The beach is a conch with sand as smooth and white as the heart of a sea-shell. Through the town, a road girding the villages runs on the sea-wall. On the one side of the road, the Bay of Biscay —blue as a bluebell: on the other, the precipice with stone-hewn steps that lead to an Alpine verdance of pasture and of dingle.

The streets of the town are massive. The houses look as if builded for siege. But they are not forbidding: they are too sure of themselves. They are smiling even; though they are dense and strong. Through the narrow streets moves a mellow race in gesture of traffic and trade. Like the houses, these men and women face the world in sober colors. But their eyes are large, and here one reads peace: the lips have the fret of a smile, and there is laughter tingling the cadence of their talk. At night they gather in the Plaza, lined with cafés: and while the old ones drink, the young ones dance. Their dance is a pleasant casual exercise—not far from the usual way of walk and word. It is a hopping and bobbing of couples, a weaving of bodily life and bodily sense into the already existent pattern of their social ease. That is why they dance in the public Square, while the old ones gossip. . . .

Every Sunday morning, as the sun tips over the town, three men—one with a drum, two with *dulsinya* or *chistu* (a shrill metallic pipe which bears much resemblance to the pipe of the African Berber)—march through the silent streets, through every street and alley of the town, incessantly playing: so that no Vasco, good or bad, shall oversleep the Mass. This music trills through the morning like the cool sun-filaments through dawn. It has the dogged filigree of a Scottish bagpipe. It is more resolved, however, shriller, less fluid: and its notations are wider. The tune of the *chistu* interweaves with the plang of drum, and makes the houses smile and dance a bit ere they are quite awake.

The dance, the smile, the song are never absent. Afternoons, when work is done in shop or field, the girls will sing till the late hour of *cena*. Rosa is not pretty. Her face is a little long and has a tilt which is not of Europe. The nose droops, the mouth is large, the eyes are resilient and black under the strangely curving brow. But Rosa is charming. A white kerchief lies on her shoulders, pointed to the throat. The naked arms are bright against the marron velvet of the bodice; the breasts are caught by a diagonal sash something like the straps of a grenadier. Rosa's hips are wide; her legs, stockinged in gray wool, have a full firmness—like her breasts—that bespeaks valiance in emotion.

The room is cool and bare: through the high windows comes the mellow murmur of the folk walking the rigid street, between the sea and the mountain. The girls are a warm fragrance in the room. They sing. The songs warm them: they dance. Their heads sway, their throats pulse, their arms rise and fall.

These songs are older than the tambour and the pipe: the girls sing them without accompaniment. Many have sad themes. But even as tragedy invades the brightest *fado* of Portugal, so here a tripping flexible gait overbears the pathos. The music bespeaks a clever, winning people. It has mobility, but it is not plastic. It has the nature of sun splintered on cloud or running upon water, of the patter of rain on house-tops, of waves pelting the hull of a sail-boat. It is a music of light, of surface-patterns of light. On all the earth, there is no music stranger to that of Spain—to the plastic, sculptural, soul-deep song of Spain.

It is good music: its mobile patterns are abstracted into grace and hardness: its swiftness never blurs, its poignance does not become sentimental. It is not deep music. It remains of the periphery, and its moods are varieties of reflection, rather than of creation. The Basque remains *one*. What varies is the circumstance of life; so he wards it off, he holds it well outside him. Through a hundred ages, Spain has moved in a processional whose faiths and passions the Spaniard has absorbed. But the Basque shuts out. So his song—trilling, skipping, flashing in color and light—is a music of intimations, rather than of experience.

Was this pagan people first enticed to become Catholic, because of the occasions offered by a Calendar of Saints for singing and for dancing? Every church festival is a *fiesta*, a *romería* for the Basque. The fiesta of San Iñigo de Loyola is one of the great days of the land, for Iñigo Lopez de Recalde, founder of the Society of Jesus, was a Basque. The day of the author of the ruthless Exercises, of the chronicler of Hell, becomes a day of merriment: foot races, water races, trials of strength lead up to the climax—the contests in the arts of song and dance. The Spaniard is no sportsman. His bull fight is an ordeal and an art. His games are pretexts for gambling. His Carnival is a means of fierce release for the instincts repressed by morality, caste and honor. But the Basque is a sportsman. He is incapable of the true carnival spirit. He turns his feast-days into sport-days.

An altar has been decked out on the façade of a house

in the Plaza. Under a bower of gilt, the priest harangues in *vascuence*.[1] His theme is the curse of Modernism and Socialism, the hellish lust which hides in the laborer's appetite for better wages. (The Basques are the industrialists of Spain: the ore and factories of Bilbao are not far off.) On one side of the Square is the summer palace of an Andalusian Duke. His balconies are hung with great mantones; gorgeous splotches of gold and green and crimson in the sun. The altar faces an esplanade which steps down to the sea. But the Basque throng is aloof from the priest in his garish altar, from the flash of Spain on the walls of the Duke's palace, aloof even from the sea. It is a packed, resilient body. It is waiting to play. Its mood is very like the mood of a sporting crowd in England. Here is none of the hot dark fervor which Spain brings even to the bull fight.

The races are over, and the last Mass. The crowds circle the platform for the dance contest. There is a piper and a drummer. The cadences of the *chistu* are thin and cool. The drummer weaves a tattoo that becomes the matted background for the imponderous figures of the pipe. When the dancer and piper cease, the drum goes on in an incantation which is moving precisely because it is so unemphatic, so subhumanly cool, so pale. It reminds one, indeed, of the nixies of the Celt, the blond green creatures of the northern marshes. It seems as far from Spain as are the braes of Scotland. The designs of the dance are brief. Here is grace in line and point: daintiness; above all spiritual aloofness. In the pauses of dance and music, ever unceasing the weave of the drum. The elves also of the Atlas are around the corner: but Spain is miles away.

Agura, contrapas, anarxuma, zaspi, trititzka, soka, aguruku, taladera—numberless Basque dance-figures. What distinguishes them is that they are all social: that they are stylized from details of the common life. The dance of Andalusia is a plastic form for the soul. These dances

[1] The Basque language.

are scenes of bodily acts. Their stuff is not spirit, nor essence of emotion. It is a synthesis of homely gestures taken from farm or field. Here is an *apple dance*, an intricate elaboration of the bestowal of apples. Here is a *chair dance*, a design of men and women in easy social converse. The *Siete Saltos* is a stylization of the walk— of men walking together. The music is major; the dance is comedic. Indeed, it holds the trait of social comedy which in France produced Molière. But also, it has a purity of abstract line which recalls the classic dance of the Pueblo Indians or of the Pacific Negroes. With, again, a difference of tone and subject: the dances of the "savage" are elemental, they call rain, they invoke harvest, they enact sexual passion.

In another part of town there is a match of *pelota*. This game is originally Basque; its pure form of sport lives still in the Basque village where boys play on a dirt court against a plaster wall, or against the wall of the church if the hamlet is very modest. The Spaniards, however, have taken to pelota. It has become a game for professionals; and although all the crack players are Basque, the spirit of the sport has been transformed. It is played in the *frontón:* a court, three sides of which are high walls of cement. The fourth side (the long one, to the right of the players who all face one way) is for the public whose tiers of seats are placed in a sort of open building. A pair of players make a team, and two teams make a match. To the right hand of each athlete is strapped a thin short wooden bat called *pala*, or else, in a variant of the game, a basket, known as *cesta*, or *remonte*, shaped a little like the curved beak of some bird, scooped and long and narrow. The principle of pelota is like our handball which may indeed be a derivation. But the Basque game with its great distance of service and return, its complexity of movement due to the use of three walls for the rebounds of the fast ball, achieves an extraordinary brilliance. Volleys last for minutes: the ball flashes back and forth from the front wall to the side

and rear ones. There is something of the delicacy of
billiards, the grace of tennis: and there is a spill of sheer
physical prowess which tennis does not approach. It is a
beautiful game: the game of a sane, healthily outward
people. But in the hands of the Spaniard, all this becomes
minor.

Between the public and the court is a railing which
until the game starts is empty. With the first volley,
however, a large group of men in red *boinas* line up here,
facing the public, with their backs to the players. They
are the *cobradores*, the bookies: the true principals in what
Spain has made of pelota. With the first service, they
gather their first odds and cry their bets. And until the
last of the game, the shifting of odds, the placing of bets
continue: the players themselves serving as a mere pretext for the gambling, like the *petits chevaux* of wood at
a gaming table.[1]

These are invasions of Spain upon the Basque land.
There are whole towns in Guipúzcoa, Vizcaya, Alava,
where Castile has rooted and worked havoc. Such a town
is San Sebastián, summer capital of the king and of the
intellectuals of Madrid. There are even towns which
Castile has destroyed. . .

The *carrera* runs along the breasting cliffs from San
Sebastián to Santander beside a sea blue as the summer
sky. It crosses the tip of a little city resting on land

---

[1] The bookies serve as middlemen between the individual bettors.
Each bookie has a little rubber ball with a hole. In this hole, he
places a slip of paper declaring the odds of the moment, and by tossing the ball to the man who has laid odds and to the man who has
taken him on, the bet is established. The true pelota fan does not
wager once: he wagers a dozen times as the game progresses: he
concocts an intricate system of varying odds: his mind is on the
betting and his balance: he is aware of the game only as the machine
that automatically shifts the chances. Indeed, to go to a pelota
match and observe the game, and refrain from betting, is so anom-
alous as to attract attention. The sport is still there: the Basque
players enact it: but the Spanish public does not participate.

that tongues from the mountain far into the Bay. The land is high and steep: the streets twine. And in their midst, coiled all about by alleys, stands a smothered church. It is blackened by the salt of seven hundred years. It stands low: there is a street at its door, and there are other streets at rising levels on its four façades, so that it is plunged and buried in the town. And the windows are rare, or are blanked by pavements and by the cellars of adjoining houses. Only the steeple is sheer to the open heaven.

It is an ignoble church, foul like a ship's bottom after a voyage round the seven seas. Its nave is foul with shadows; its windows have a yellow blear like the eyes of the beggar at the gate.

The town is stifled and somber: it is like an apple rotted by this old church at its core. The Basque here has forgotten how to dance. He has not turned his saints' days into merry making. The church has conquered: the Empiry of Castile.

But more significant than such invasions of the end of old Spain upon the Basque, are the invasions of the modern Basque into the life of Spain. While the Spaniard gave himself to crusades and conquest, the Basque held aloof with his energy untapped. To resist invasion of body and of spirit took courage. But the effort was as naught beside the effort of the Spaniard to fuse Moslem, Jew, German, Roman, Celt, into one Spanish soul. The Spanish soul was achieved: but Spanish spirit locked in the exertion. This was the moment of the Basque with his reserve of virgin power. He had no culture but the most primitive; no world for the expanding of his might save a strip of rocky soil. Spain offered a profound culture and the sea, and worlds beyond the sea. Now the Basque passes from his spiritual sleep—passes into Spain, through the door which Spain herself had battered open. . . . .

CHAPTER XIII

TWO ANDALUSIANS

a. The Sleepers
b. The Awakeners
c. The Sleepless Spirit

a. *The Sleepers*

SPAIN is not a failure; Spain is not decadent; Spain is complete. By the too literal achievement of kings and mystics, the vital forces of a vital land lock as in sleep. This sleep is one of the two moods of art and letters in contemporary Spain. It has been long upon the land and the land loves it. Poets have found in it all the delight of cradled balance, all the delight of dream. They have made of this sleep of Spain a passionate Nirvana in which the actions of Spain's waking life return in pageantry. The ghosts of fire and blood are here: and a pleasant hopelessness which saves from the scourge of ambition. Spain becomes a mirrored play of faces and of scenes, for her own self-adoring. First of all despair. This perennially ironic race has distilled the love of failure from its too great success. Spain in the nineteenth century knew an ecstatic impotence which only Russia equaled. It was about 1835 that Larra wrote: *"Escribir en Madrid es llorar*—to write in Madrid is to weep." "Do not attempt to create," he told his fellows. "Ye are Spaniards; the task is hopeless. Must ye wield a pen? Then translate from the French." Larra's last logical act was to blow out his brains. But the spirit of Larra is still upon the tables of the cafés of Madrid. Sleep here is a wine of Spain's historic act. Despair is voluptuous. Incompetence is a cult. And votaries of this narcistic trance are among Spain's finest writers.

Chief of them all perhaps is Don Ramón María del Valle-Inclán.[1] Cervantes had a crippled hand; Don Ramón lacks an arm. Rojas who wrote *La Celestina* four centuries ago split his novel into dialogue and acts. Don

[1] Born 1870.

Ramón does likewise—and interweaves with his Castilian words and forms that even Rojas would have found archaic. Don Ramón's books sell not for current pesetas, but for obsolete *reales*. His typography is studiously ancient. Upon his works is printed *opera omnia:* and they are illumined with medieval wood-cuts. His texts reveal a virtuosity in the use of old Castilian with a mingling of the pure vocables of Galician, once the poetic tongue of Spain, so imaginative as to be an art. It is an art of tone and verbal plastic. Don Ramón is an hidalgo of Galicia, that rocky northwest province which the Arabs scarce pierced: and he boasts of his Celtic blood. There is a strong and curious kinship between the dialogue of his books and that of Synge. But the kinship goes no deeper than an echo. The volumnear body of Valle-Inclán's prose serves to mass a death: his drama is one of furious rhetoric. All the more glorious ghosts of Spain stalk in his books. The Church with its "charity of the sword," chivalry mildewed and broken from its long passage southward, clan warfare, mystic fealty and love are personified in the were-wolf bombast of his scenes. But though these shapes be ghosts, they have no charnel odor: the salt of modern irony—the perennial Spanish irony— is on them. Their puissance is not to be challenged. The dark firm candor of this prose is so enchanting that one accepts the nightmarish or sentimental dumb-show: this gesturing pageantry of Dream which is the Dream of Spain.

A pendant to Don Ramón is José Martínez Ruiz, known as Azorín.[1] Valle-Inclán is dramatic and dionysian: his mood is perpendicular like the mountain steeps of his Galicia. Azorín's elegiac tone is smooth as the subtle huertas of Valencia where he was born. His books are haunting, climaxless: they spread the nostalgia which inspires them. In them lives the small *pueblo* of high Spain. He loves the village for the pure success of its equilibrium in sleep. He loves to follow Don Quixote

[1]Born 1874.

over the *llanura* of La Mancha. He loves to doze in the manure-soaked inns of the Castilian desert. For this world is full of ghosts. And Azorín casts the wide net of wistfulness to snare them all. His prose, unlike the mighty, archaic organ of Valle-Inclán, has been tinged with the perfumed winds of France which mingle oddly enough, across the Pyrenees, with the rank heat of the posadas of Toledo or with the ciceronian rhetoric of a peasant from Medina. Azorín's passive, apollonian state has left him open to invading foreign accents. Yet his central impulse is authentic, and his form is Spanish. Here is the pleasant pain of dream—against the nightmare mood of Don Ramón: a minor note within Spain's sleep. After the battalions of Moor and Catholic have trampled on, here is the plaint in which the fields and towns sink back upon themselves. . . .

Spain's most popular poet, Antonio Machado [1] is an Andalusian: but he sings of Castile. His theme is the robust and brutal world in which the pícaro careered. Unlike Valle-Inclán, Machado does not recreate this world of four centuries past with archaic language or atavistic mood. His means is more subtle. That world lives on, evaporate and refined, in the subconscious tone of Spain. Machado captures the old splendor by imaging its reverberations. His prosody is a canon of echoes. The echo is the shell of the shout. So the rounded and mellow music of Machado suggests the hollow form of an heroic life. The graphic density of life in heroic Spain has left this pattern. If the hard bodies of the Spanish soil were bubbles holding a void as hollow as the Spanish sky, they would be the poems of Machado. He harks back to Velázquez: the supreme graphic master reappears in words, diminished, lyrical, plaintive. The voice of the stark past of Spain comes muffled in this sleep.

The ecstatic revery is rich in changes. Against Machado who sings the larger currents of the Dream is set the ex-

[1] Born 1875.

quisite, scholarly Ramón Pérez de Ayala.[1] Ayala, who is an Asturian, is his epoch's most cultivated novelist and most fanciful poet. This man who in *Política y Toros* has written the profoundest apologia of the bull fight and the subtlest satire on Spain's political abulia, beneath his disguise of timeliness is an archaicizer also: one who dwells as deep as his neighbor Valle-Inclán within Spain's narcistic adoration. But it is the schools and cloisters which haunt Ayala: his way to the past is that of meditation and of learning. Like Azorín, Ayala has not been proof against French literary currents. The note of Anatole France is a bit too clear in his novels. But perhaps there is an organic kinship between the Spaniard and the last master of the French contemplative tradition. Like Anatole France, Ayala is a musing man: a man of satiric, wistful fancy rather than of imagination. His style progenitors are those amazing mystics of sixteenth century Spain who managed to endow ecstasy with Horatian polish. The sedulous, synthetic texts of Ayala are a panoply of dream: Spain dreaming of her cathedrals and her schools, Spain blowing lovely and seductive patterns—two volumes upon the Names of Christ—from the effluvia of medieval culture. The modern in Ayala is the ironic salt of intellectual awareness.[2]

There is a moment between sleep and waking, when the mind spans the abyss between eternity and time. Consciousness turns inward on the realm of sleep; the materials and meanings of the dream form to the measure of thought, live an instant the spatial, temporal life ere they dissolve. In this encounter the worlds of sleep and waking are both broken up. Their fragments make a

[1] Born 1881.

[2] Another remarkable expression of this state is the Valencian Gabriel Miró (born 1879). Miró makes gorgeous word-tapestries of legendary life, such as the Mystery of Christ. In his prose are lurid and elementary colors that suggest some medieval canvas protected for ages from the sun, together with pale modern water-tints of psychological introspection.

counterpoint of exquisite discord; but the relation between them brings a subtle vision. The minute and the
infinite merge. Essence of dream takes the conforming
shape of the categories of the intellect; and the objective
sense for once is applied to what is real. This mysterious
hinterland Ramón Gómez de la Serna has made his realm.
He has mastered it. He has been mastered by it.[1]

Spain stands at this transition, between sleep and waking. Ramón is the elegist of its dissolving colors, of its
shattered and luminous shapes. Valery Larbaud has com-
pared Ramón with Arthur Rimbaud. The æsthetic object of Ramón is indeed the atom; but whereas in Rimbaud
the atom is explosive, bursting the cerements of cultured
France, the atom in Ramón merges forever with the intricate flow of waking sense and thought. His true fellow is not Rimbaud but Marcel Proust. Proust made a
portrait of a society in deliquescence: of its break-up into
the essences, atoms, maggots of dissolution. Ramón also
weaves the filmy spell of a dissolving world, although in
him the dissolution is not social but subjective. Spain stirs
in this limbo: her eye peers back into the fleeting images of
dream. Ramón is her eye.

Wherefore the contradictions in his work. Rich in
color, it is evanescent. Affluent in intimations of form, it
is formless. His books are collections of uncollectible
items. His true form is chaos. He is indeed the runner
of a rainbow; and should he stop one moment, he would
fall through mist. His one subject is the instant of palpable
inarticulation. But his world is still the dreamed Body
of Spain. However dissolute her state, Spain yet looks
inward on her slumber. Ramón is no prophet; save unconsciously. In him, Spain says to herself: "I am asleep"
—the sign of waking. . .

---

[1] Ramón, as he calls himself, was born in 1891. His works already
fill sixty volumes. And yet his true artistic unit is the paragraph—
when it is not the sentence or the phrase.

b. The Awakeners

The entire nineteenth century of Spain was the stormy and dark threshold of this waking. In 1898, Spain suffered more from the loss of the Isle of Cuba than she had suffered from the previous loss of the worlds from Mexico to Tierra del Fuego. So the "generation of 1898" became the symbol, when it was but the sequel, of Spain's stir. Spain suffered more in 1898 because she was nearer waking.

The earliest signs were perhaps political. The extraordinary Constitution of 1812—more radical than the present one of England—gave way to absolutism. Quixotism tremored on, in the sleep of Spain. Carlism, the extreme of reaction, swung back into a republic. But the republic [1] was a mere parade of presidents. High-minded, eloquent men, they had no contact with organic Spain. The face twitched; the mind slept.

More prophetic of spiritual action was the work of a professor and scholar, Francisco Giner de los Ríos.[2] Don Francisco was the friend of the makers of the brief republic. But instead of holding office, he founded a school. (His *Institución libre de Enseñanza* stands still in Madrid, environed by convents.) And instead of delivering orations, he gathered about him the intelligent discontent of Spain. He was a leader and nourisher of men. And the sons of his spirit have written the dynamic books of the age. Giner's weapon for awakening Spain was Europe. He sent his followers to France, Italy, Germany and England—to bring home seed and leaven. He saw the problem of his land as a simple one of retardation. Spain for organic reasons had lagged. Let her catch up.

[1] 1873-1874.　　　　　　　　　　　　　　　[2] 1839-1915.

While his school flourished—a little hearth of Europe at which the Spanish intellectual might warm his hand—a young diplomat, Angel Ganivet,[1] published a work that was the antiphony of this Modern hymn. The *Idearium Español* looms large in the tale of Spain's renascence. Ganivet was a poor historian and a weak logician. His little book bristles with arguments, æsthetic and ethnic, which no one can accept. Yet it holds a deep philosophy of Spain's career. To Ganivet, Spain is not of Europe: the trend of her growth must be toward Africa as it has been from Africa. All of the adventure in America and Europe was a false step. The "Age of Gold" was an age of madness. The effort to adopt the pragmatic materialist culture of the West was doomed to failure. Spain is Christian, not Roman; Christian in the way of the Spanish Stoic, Seneca, of the African patrists, Origen and Augustine, of the Semitic spirit of Don Quixote. Ganivet scorns the standards and success of modern Europe. He senses the heroism—the need of heroism—in the Spanish soul: its peculiar way of sudden climaxes followed by periods of sleep. The down leveling of Europe is as alien and abhorrent to him as it was to Nietzsche. He fears the *aurea mediocritas* of England as a poison to the Spanish blood. He looks with equanimity on Spain's colonial disasters since Spain colonized "not for coal but for souls"; and on the nadir of Spain's culture, since from it shall rise again such sudden giants as were Cervantes, Velázquez, Góngora, Lope. He pleads for the acceptance, in the spirit of a religious sacrifice, of Spain's difference from the brilliant capabilities of France and England. His book, appearing in 1896, urged the relinquishment of the last Colonies. Two years later, Cuba and the Philippines were gone. But though his book was a Jeremiah's prophecy, Ganivet lacked the strength to face the apathy of his people. In that same year, he died by his own hand.

Not, however, before he had met the opposing, clamor-

[1] 1865-1898.

ous word of the man who, gradually, was to veer to his own vision. Miguel de Unamuno [1] had corresponded with Ganivet while they were young in Madrid. The result of their exchange was *El Porvenir de España,* a volume in which they estimate the opposing doctrines: that Spain must be awakened by letting in "ultra-pyrenean currents," and that Spain has been ruined precisely by these currents. To Ganivet, the history of Spain reveals no "Spanish period." Let there be one! he cries. Unamuno counters that eclecticism is the unity of Spain. "Spain is still to be discovered," he thunders, "and will be discovered only by European Spaniards." In the volume which defines this attitude of his youth, *En Torno al Casticizmo,* he diagnoses the abulia of Spain. The Inquisition was bad because it shut out the four winds of Europe: Spain was forced to feed upon herself. Spain's historical tradition was bad, because it was anti-European. He declares for the *corrientes ultrapirenáicas.* Ganivet was dead. Even had he lived, this mystic afield in history must have lacked the power to answer Unamuno. Unamuno is the strongest moralist of our day. Wells and Shaw have thin voices beside his well-aimed uproar. There was no one, then, in Spain to answer Unamuno. Unamuno answered himself.

His answer is not analytic. This radical mystic scorns the fuss of argument. The Inquisition, shutting out the "four winds" from Spain was indeed "bad." Its purpose —unity—was good. Its confusing homogeneity for unity and its means of action were not Spanish at all: were of Rome, of France, of Europe. Spain had been the most tolerant land of all the West: even Islam grew tolerant in Spain: Rome alone, making the Visigoth into crusader and winning Isabel to its own waning theoditic dream, made Spain intolerant. The historical tradition which won in Spain was also European: it was a mixture of the state policy of France and the church policy of Rome. (France was never guilty of such nonsense: France the

[1] Born, 1864.

ᐊ 282 ᐅ

State was consistently anti-Roman.) Finally, whence came these "ultrapyrenean currents" that were to flush Spain once more with fecund air? They were ideas that reached Western Europe by the very ethnic worlds of which Spain is the organic integer. Ideas from the Greek and Alexandrian, from the Jew and Egyptian and Arab: many entered Europe directly by the door of Spain; none came to Spain by way of western Europe. They came by the sea and the south—in that long germinal embrace whereby Phœnician, Carthaginian, Greek, Roman, Jew, Copt, Arab, Moor were poured into Spain's womb. What Western Europe did was to transform and finally to betray these living thoughts. The Visigoth minority represented Spain's medievalism: and its action was a retarded and arbitrary form of what in Germanic Europe produced the noble synthesis of Catholic culture. In Spain, the naturalistic Semites were too dominant for a culture based on transcendental values. Medievalism in Spain became a maniacal gesture. Modernism? It is the breakdown of the medieval culture: its intellectualism, its systematization is a vast Machine proficient at destroying, and creating nothing. Is this what Spain must come to, to be saved? Unamuno reconsiders; and by 1905 he has his answer—which is indeed a conversion.

Unamuno is an expression of dynamic egoism. This atom has got loose from the locked coil of Spain; and what a surge it has! Yet all his doctrine comes rather simply down to the assertion of an immense personal will emerging from the stratified social trammels of his land. The intrinsic substance of Unamuno's thought will strike the Western mind as meager; but the drama of its formulation is a new act in Spain, the flesh of its assertion is a fresh embodiment of the Spanish spirit.

This announcement of a personal will recalls at once earlier apocalypses of the north: Blake, Whitman, Dostoievski, Nietzsche. Unamuno's assertion is important, because it is made up of the conflicting substances of Spain. The voice of this man declaring that he will never die, and that he will never live according to the herd-patterns of modern Europe, becomes palpable and true, because it is so deeply Spanish. Perhaps the æsthetic value of the utterances of Whitman, Dostoievski, Nietzsche, Blake is similarly grounded in racial substance. The case is evident in Unamuno. Freeing himself from the still equipoise of Spain he frees himself from nothing that is Spanish.

In Unamuno, the same Spanish spirit heretofore held in tragic unison—in the actless unison of its will—swings once more into motion. Instead of equating each other, the elements of the Spanish soul line up *behind* the soul of Unamuno and serve to project him, parabola-wise, into his personal heaven. Here is Spain's neo-medieval sense of the futility of life; here is Christ; here is Spain's narcistic love of the extremes within her, whence arose the pícaro and the saint. Here above all is Spain, enemy of pragmatism and of rational progress, worshiper of the Absolute—Spain that will be heaven or hell, and never merely earth; and yet will not loose her hold on earth, in all her visions of heaven.

Unamuno transfigures the despised and comic person of Don Quixote. This symbol of his land's wrong-headed action becomes for Unamuno the god of a new Order, the prophet of a new national revelation. Don Miguel de Unamuno of the Basques identifies his cause of pure and personal effort with the crusade of the old hidalgo of La Mancha. Like that knight, he will construct his world platonically from the ideals of his inheritance and go forth *really* that it may prevail. As Quixote fought common sense, Unamuno fights "business." The old windmills are now factories, the old inns are industrial cities, the old King's police are the votaries of Demos. Where all that is glorious has become so sterile, all that is serious so low, let Don Quixote be savior. The final jest of the bitter, broken Cervantes becomes our Man of Sorrows. Does not the mockery of modern Europe call for a ridiculous Messiah? The sterile and impotent meseta of Castile

—that butt of Europe—shall be the mount of the new Zion, for the new Sermon.

So with inimitable verve and wit, Unamuno identifies his will with the old body of Spain: and hobbles forth, like Quixote, to enact justice. He wants it for himself. But since Spain is in him, since Spain is his Rocinante, Spain must go along. Spain must wake, if only for his sake.

Unamuno's philosophy is a tissue of compensations: which by no means proves it to be false. He feels inferior in Europe as a Spaniard? he will assert his immortal soul against all Germany and England. He feels his people's cultural impotence before the sure voice of France? he will turn this anguish into the travail of birth. The method is persuasive. Our modern world is so very shoddy, that any honest light can show it up. The prose fabric of our civilization is so thin, that any song can tear it. And Unamuno is essentially a poet, even though his best vehicle is the short personal essay which, indeed, his pen has made a powerful æsthetic organ.

The atomic individualism of Unamuno is strictly modern: it springs from Rousseau and the German romantics. It is the inevitable impulse to "return to a beginning" which has overwhelmed the modern soul since the breakdown of the Medieval House. But if this atomic will is modern, the values it propels in Unamuno remain medieval.

.   .   .   .

The intrinsic value of such work either as thought or as æsthetic form is very slight. Interest in Unamuno hinges on interest in Spain. The power of this soul, one feels, approaches that of Whitman or Dostoievski. But the substance in which it has clothed itself is less negotiable. Like Don Quixote, Unamuno fails to realize that the modern world can be defeated only with modern weapons. Our multiverse, our chaos of sterile facts, is the result of an abuse of analytic methods. The true savior will have to understand and accept this analytic world, ere he can transform it. Unamuno, believing that he preaches to the world a new Salvation, is merely rousing Spain from her old ordered sleep.[1]

[1] To go beyond Unamuno—into the present constructive period of Spain's waking, into the transition from her "old ordered sleep" to the new ordered consciousness now dawning, would be to turn this chapter into a discussion of writers and young literary movements: and this would be to digress from the formal province of my book. Since Unamuno answered Ganivet, there have arisen leaders in æsthetic and social criticism, in the novel, in the drama, in the field of creative erudition, whose aggregate work makes the contemporary literature of Spain perhaps the most pregnant of the West. I regret that this is not the place to analyze these younger men. The modern writers whom I have mentioned at all I have chosen arbitrarily for the distinct formal purpose of my portrait of Spain. It must be understood that whereas I consider them important, I have been silent about others equally important. Throughout, I have felt called on, no more to discuss all of Spain's great men, than to describe all her cities.

c. The Sleepless Spirit

In this new stir of Spain, it is not wonderful that the land which created Córdoba, Cádiz, Seville, which perfected the Dance and the cante hondo, which gave birth to Gabírol, to Góngora, should lead in the fresh emergence of Spain's perennial spirit. For Andalús achieved the Spanish Balance without the Castilian rigor; obeyed like every part of Spain the will of Castile to make Spain's chaos into One and yet contrived to keep that Oneness green. A painter and a poet of modern Andalusia voice so clearly the spirit of the land, that they speak again for the world. They are Pablo Picasso and Juan Ramón Jiménez.[1]

Picasso is a man of Málaga who came to Paris, and by the strategy of time and place conquered the plastic world. To the French, he appeared the Heaven-sent inheritor of Cézanne. Cézanne, naturalistic mystic and lover of El Greco, made of each stroke of his brush a preachment of the sanctity of form. Pure form, in his work, had its ritual of sacrament in its intrinsic stuffs. The Body and the Blood of life were to Cézanne the volumes and the movements palpable to the eye. El Greco, in a devout Catholic Age, was able to retain the legendary forms of Christianity as at least subsidiary means to express his vision. Cézanne was driven back on what seemed to him

---

[1] A third name might be added: that of Manuel de Falla, Spain's leading composer and a pure Andalusian, also. Falla in tonal structures hard, fluid, irreducible, conveys into æsthetic form elements of life that are very close to those which we shall consider in Picasso and Jiménez. He may be said to recreate the *body* of Andalusian folk-song, as Picasso recreates physical shapes and Jiménez physical sensations, into a new arabesque.

"primary" matter: the hills and the haystacks and the human body. His work implicitly rejects the concepts of European culture by its refusal of them all, as aids to revelation. Not religion, not ethics, not "beauty" shall be syllables for Cézanne, as for his predecessors, in the spelling of his Word. In this sense, Cézanne aspires to the primitivism which accepts the essences of previous culture and rejects its forms. Ideationally, he created and bequeathed a void: but an expectant and a fertile one. The successor of Cézanne was bound to be a man with concepts to fill in his abstract wording.

Concepts come to Europe from the east. It appears that Western Europe can create no concepts of the Real, although she creates the greatest Forms for concepts.[1] Like Cézanne, Schopenhauer, Nietzsche, Dostoievski, Blake, Whitman, Wagner were in this sense inviters of the east; the line of nineteenth century masters was long, who in their rejection of the conceptual forms of their inheritance, filled the world once more with a clamorous hunger for fresh Ideas to make incarnate. It is this hunger that explains, in art, the vogue of El Greco, of African sculpture, of Picasso.

The Idea in Picasso is the *arabesque*. The Moslem needed to harmonize his love of beauty and his fear of idols. He required a plastic form which would not, like the forms of physical nature, recall the old idolatries of the desert. The letters of his holy Arabic language served him, even as the Hebrew letters served, in the Kabbala, to make a Temple for the medieval Jews. These letters of the Arab held Allah and all the world of Islam, and yet were freed of natural associations. In Picasso, there is a similar impulse. His need also, as an artist, is to make designs; but his fear was an idolatry of another sort. The asso-

---

[1] I—at least—know of no Forms, in the east, so great as (to choose haphazard) the Medieval Church of Rome, the Gothic Cathedral, Dante's Poem, the music of Palestrina and of Bach, the Ethic of Spinoza. Yet the concepts in these Forms are invariably of the east.

ciations attached to physical forms—religion, sentiment, moral value—were already so unconvincing in the nineteenth century that Cézanne refused them, as Moses the Golden Calf. Now, even the sensory organisms formed by the eye must be rejected. To the hand of a Raphael, a woman's body is amenable to art through its motherhood, its sanctity, its sexual appeal. These are cogent means for his æsthetic work. To Cézanne a woman's body is still a woman's body. Picasso rejects even the associative concept of *woman:* her body becomes a configuration of planes, densities, colors.

This formal use of transfigured substances is old in Spain. Spain's wildest excess of sculpture and ornament in the *plateresque* holds an element of transformed abstraction that recalls Egypt. The Spanish dance resolves dramatic gesture into a formal end. And now, Picasso makes an *arabesque* of the letters and signs of nature.

Paris has worked perhaps too much upon Picasso. It has made him a "court" painter. This is intrinsically no ill thing: Ronsard and Racine were poets of the Court. The essential dynamism of Picasso has been urbanized; his intellectual stuffs have been turned at times into theory, into impulse. From creation, he has been deflected into analysis which is the antithesis of creation.[1] All this, because Paris is a Court of painters, with the tendency to cultivate the statement which clarifies at the expense of the creation; to address only itself; to polish surfaces rather than plumb new depths. Or, perhaps, the trouble is that this Court of Paris is not Picasso's. It has needed him, more than he Paris. Too often has Picasso fragmented his invention into sharp annunciations of the theory others builded from his work. Yet for all that, he has brought light to the west: it came with him from Má-

---

[1] Æsthetic creation is an act from the unitary self upon the objective world. It is the contrary of analysis which breaks up that world—*unreally.* But analysis may precede creation, if the elements broken up by it are reabsorbed and fused into a new subjective unity.

laga: it rises from Andalusian depths older than Spain and yet forever Spanish.

Juan Ramón Jiménez [1] has come far indeed since the early poems and the sweet idyll, *Platero y Yo,* which appeared in 1907. That book was written in a prose crisp as young leaves. Yet it was the conveyancer of old emotions. The poet's spirit was already old; only his senses urged him to the gait of youth. Such delicacy promised rather to crack than to reveal in later years what is perhaps the profoundest poetic intelligence today in Europe.

Jiménez has lost the audience which his earlier work won him. He is very little read. He has sloughed off cleverness and minor sentiment. His work has become stark and stripped. He has gone from exquisite grace to a virtuosic clumsiness and uncouthness, which brings astoundingly close the face of truth, and turns it into a strange, impersonal thing. He has become a recluse. Yet his seclusion has not divorced him from contact on his own terms with his generation. No poet serves youth more sedulously than he. He is the master and the friend of the young poets of Castilian, not alone in Spain but in the greater Spain across the sea. He is in touch with Paris, with Germany and Austria. And he has read the work of Whitman, of Emily Dickinson, of Frost, of Robinson and Sandburg. . . . .

Jiménez, indeed, is a mystic of the naturalistic order of Walt Whitman. He traces the constant divine in life; he ignores the transcendental. He finds God in the sea, in the subtle sense-play of love, in the landscapes of Spain; or in the gyring thoughts of his own meditation. Yet no poet's accent could more radically differ from that of the Bible, of Spinoza or of Whitman. Not the least magic of Jiménez' work is its perpetual counterpoint of meaning and substance. The meaning is cosmic, the stuff is light and casual. Often a seeming haphazard of expres-

[1] Born in 1881.

sion fringes the ineffable; a drop of water miraculously turns into a universe. No tinge of cosmic rhetoric mars the body of his words. The universe is implicit. The ultimate gift of Jiménez is a song of life, liquid and gemmed, within whose moment silence is an inner flame. This flame is simple and constant. The variation in the poems is the outturning into surfaces of mood and color. The flame is One. Life's mystery is its becoming form, its creating for itself out of a single depth numberless facets, out of whiteness many tints, out of silence, song. This is the process of life: and this is the process of Jiménez' writing. When he speaks of *La Obra* he means his record of these inscrutable *becomings*, of which he is a rapt and consecrated witness. If his poems are many, so are the shapes of life: if they are fleet, fragmentary, snatches of a Form whose symmetry lies in dimensions beyond the fragments, so is our visible world a phantasm of shreds, thrusts, flashes. And to see it whole, the eye must be beyond as well as within it.

Jiménez' work is a sort of *comédie mystique*. Singly, the poems have variety of notes. Yet there is a cryptic quality in them, and a subtle allusiveness to something not explicit, which must repugn the shallow sense, even as it entrances the mind hungry for great vistas. His poems have prosodic value. Yet their chiefest value is that they *create æsthetically* a sense of incompleteness. Æsthetically, they are whole because they contain this *lack*—this positive surge toward an apocalyptic sense which lives in them only by the imprint of its absence. Each of his poems is at once a sensory form, and a spiritual inchoation. Like the atom, it is complete, yet holds in the whirlwind of electrons an infinitude and a contingency with infinitude: it is appearance forever tending to disappear into the Real. One might say that a poem of Jiménez is like an instant in a human life: full-limned, full-equipped with thought, emotion, will; and yet this fullness is but the passing function of an implicit unity which transcends and subscends it.

No Castilian poet since Luis de Góngora has equaled Jiménez in craft and virtuosic power. Jiménez makes of the language an instrument subtle and intricately ranged, whose farthest flexes yet lie within the natural genius of Castilian. This is his superiority as a craftsman over his master, Góngora. Góngora worked as if in minerals. His arabesques were cut and carved, like the original arabesques, in stone. In Jiménez, the arabesque is of organic substance: it is traced in flesh, blood, breath. This makes his work less assured, less sheer than the verse of Góngora which, after three centuries of misprizal, comes at last, with the work of his friend El Greco, into its kingdom of appreciation. At first glance, one doubts that the poetry of Jiménez can live as long: so fine are its lineaments, so exquisite its reliefs from the organic atmosphere on which it stands. Flowers of spirit, will they fade like flowers? The answer is, that such flowers do not fade. To examine this frail prosody, is to find it made of certainties. Jiménez has lifted from life his overtones into a form that is life's natural emergence into consciousness from the eternal infraconscious flow. His arabesques are therefore as organic as their base. Jiménez belongs to the race of Góngora and San Juan de la Cruz —a race of poets who are immortal, and hermetic.

. . . . . .

Again Spain is speaking for the world. This painter and this lyrist, in the true sense, are *poets*. Their word is a creation, immediate as life and as eternal: and this conjunction of time and of eternity is birth.

CHAPTER XIV

THE PORT OF COLUMBUS

The Scene is a bare height over a little town, white huddled with shard roofs. Coppery, the río Tinto widens and swirls through sands into the Gulf of Cádiz. Upon the height, stand two old men, bareheaded. They are clad in the gentility of their days. But the cloth is thread, the brocade is dim, the velvet shines and yellow is the lace. The one is tall. He holds behind his back, martially, an arm with a crippled hand. He is erect. His features are hard and large: only his mouth, too delicate and his eyes, tender and dark as a womb, belie the warrior. The second man is short. Beaked is his nose, and the eyes have a watery gleam. His hair is silken white above the swarthy skin. The tall man speaks:

CERVANTES—Why did you ask that I should meet you here?

COLUMBUS—This is Palos de la Frontera. [*There is a pause in which with a hard hand he wipes his watery eyes.*] From here the first time we sailed. Here, seven months later, we returned. Bringing back——

CERVANTES—A world.

COLUMBUS—Nay. Bringing back a Grave.

CERVANTES—[*Regarding the town and not* COLUMBUS' *words.*]—Here, now, is nothing.

COLUMBUS—Look beyond the fat sands of the Gulf. Look beyond the sea.

[*They stand in silence toward the west. The low sun swims above the brooding water, vaults the hard roofs, and lights the shabbiness of the watchers.*]

COLUMBUS—[*Nervously.*] Well? Are you looking? Tell me what you see.

CERVANTES—I see America.

COLUMBUS—[*Rubbing his hands in ironic satisfaction.*]
They robbed it of my name, because they thought I did
not know what I had found. They robbed me of my kingdom, because they thought I aspired to be a king. Because
my eyes kept watch, they are dim.

CERVANTES—I shall tell you, friend, what I see.

COLUMBUS—Be careful of your eyes!

CERVANTES—A City of White Towers! The men
who live in it are little motes. Yet they uphold these
Towers! And in their hand, they wield a golden weapon
making them the world's master.

COLUMBUS—Look sharp.

CERVANTES—They are not masters of themselves. They
are full of chaos——

COLUMBUS—Spain?

CERVANTES—Within this serried, glittering Order—
Chaos! Chaos of races, traditions, dreams. They are un-
easy. They build the Towers higher. The Towers are
high, in order to enclose them safely from their chaos.
Towers of stone, machines of subtle iron—to shut out
bloods, dreams, words, making this Confusion which they
hate.

COLUMBUS—[*Smiling shrewdly.*] Are you looking at
America, or Spain?

CERVANTES—They have lost sight of the True God.
Yet they are full of God-hunger, of God-search. To their
own works they turn—and worship God in these.

COLUMBUS—Look beyond: beyond the Towers.

CERVANTES—[*Heeding only what he sees.*] They ban
new pioneers! Lusting for Unity they crush what is not
One. They shut out thoughts which might rise loftier
than the highest Towers.

COLUMBUS—[*Chuckling.*] Leap from your Spain, I
tell you. Beyond the Towers——?

CERVANTES—Continents!

COLUMBUS—Now you hold me!

CERVANTES—What childish peoples, there! Beyond the
Towers one can see them clearer, although they are the

same as those beneath the Towers. Savages, who can not even speak, who can not even think—who spin about in quaint machines.

COLUMBUS—Where do you see them?

CERVANTES—Everywhere. Upon two Continents I see them, like an Itch on the rugose World. Yet within them, there is a world of Desire. I can hear their clamor; though they use words English, Spanish, Portuguese, I cannot read their reason. They are dumb as children.

COLUMBUS—They have their Inquisition, I suppose? They drive out the Infidel? They go to their Cathedrals, and would bind all men in Christ?

CERVANTES—Their names for these are different. And unlike Spain, I see that they have not succeeded.

COLUMBUS—[*Quickened.*] There is my hope! If I could go and tell them: therein is *their* hope! They shall not, like Spain, succeed.

CERVANTES—[*Not turning.*] Your voice rings glad?

COLUMBUS—Why should I not be glad? The New World is in them, underneath the Towers. When they have learned that they can not succeed: that all the Towers and all the machines and all the gold on earth can not crush down this unborn need in them for a true New World—then it will arise.

CERVANTES—[*turns and looks at* COLUMBUS.] You speak in Parables.

COLUMBUS—I am a practical man.

CERVANTES—I am sick of parables and stories.

COLUMBUS—Good. You want history? The Book of Moses—is that history enough for your hard sense? Well, do you recall how the Lord led the children of Israel out of Egypt? They too crossed a Sea. But did they come into their promised land, their new world flowing with milk and honey, when they had crossed the sea?

CERVANTES—Yes. After forty years.

COLUMBUS—You are a shallow reader. Not one came into the Promised Land—not even Moses! They went into the wilderness, and they died. From Marah to the wilderness of Sin, from Horeb to the wilderness of Moab—they roamed, and rotted, and were dead forever! Not Aaron the Priest, not Miriam the mother, not Moses the Prophet came to the Promised Land. For it is written that the Seed shall die, ere Life may be reborn.

CERVANTES—[*Incredulous.*] If that is Death yonder across the sea, it is a death most stable and most splendid.

COLUMBUS—Death *is* the most sumptuous song. This golden-towered America is but the Grave of Europe.

CERVANTES—I do not understand.

COLUMBUS—What do you find there?

CERVANTES—Mighty stones——

COLUMBUS—Are not stones of Europe?

CERVANTES—Gold——

COLUMBUS—Is not gold a lust of the old world?

CERVANTES—Marvelous machines——

COLUMBUS—Did you, then, not know England, that you should think them new?

CERVANTES—Never with us were gold and stone and iron of so high a glory.

COLUMBUS—Does not Europe merit a high Sepulcher?

CERVANTES—Still you speak in parables, my friend.

COLUMBUS—[*Testily.*] What would you have me say? Teach me the words for the New World, if you have them! Since its gold and its stones and its machines are unknown to the Old, what words can the old tongues give us?

[CERVANTES *looks in silence to the west, while the weak eyes of* COLUMBUS *watch him. Suddenly,* CERVANTES *clutches at the short man's arm.*]

CERVANTES—Look! Can't you see? . . . No! . . . God, the Towers are falling!

COLUMBUS—Glory to Jehovah!

CERVANTES—They veer, they twist. They have sunk in this mire of men.

COLUMBUS—The Seed shall rot.

CERVANTES—They are a turmoil of blind maggots.

Their world is become as were their souls—a quicksand.
The gleaming Towers are gone!

COLUMBUS—Now shall be the birth of the World
which I discovered.

CERVANTES—[*Sternly gazes west in a deep silence.
Then he turns to his friend.*] Gone is the city. Continents of chaos. What shall rise?

COLUMBUS—The Dream of the Old World, at last—
a New World!

CERVANTES—Spain?

COLUMBUS—Nay. Spain's Grave is over there, with
Europe's.

CERVANTES—I shall believe your dim eyes. Tell me,
mariner, what your dim eyes see.

COLUMBUS—[*With a laugh.*] Then keep your sharp
eyes westward.

CERVANTES—[*He turns again, complying, to the west.*]
It is easy to look away from Spain, when one has loved
Spain.

COLUMBUS—You shall not be alone, in loving Spain.

CERVANTES—Prophetic Spain.

COLUMBUS—Spain which, creating life, has never lived.

CERVANTES—Her fields are shrunken and her eyes are
hot.

COLUMBUS—God has begotten on her, and He has
passed her by.

CERVANTES—She is a mother.

COLUMBUS—A mother of beginnings.

CERVANTES—Always the Seed in her—never the life
itself?

COLUMBUS—It was ever so. When Rome lived, Spain
did not live in Rome: she bore her Stoics and her Saints
for Holy Rome. When Holy Rome was hale, Spain was
not holy. She bore, with her Jews and Arabs, the death
of Christ. When Holy Rome was dead and Modern
Europe flourished, Spain was not modern and Spain was
not Europe. She bore America.

CERVANTES—Europe has used my mother! Even you, landless mariner, have used her.

COLUMBUS—God has used her.

CERVANTES—Why then are her fields hungry?

COLUMBUS—All worlds have come in, unto her: of all worlds, she has begotten worlds. And she has lain untouched.

CERVANTES—My tragic mother.

COLUMBUS—[*Suddenly remembering and exalted.*] But the White Towers have toppled. Ready, Spain! You must stir again. You must give again. Europe has rotted at last into the Grave they called America. Your work is not quite done. You, most broken mother of all Europe, you have preserved a Seed.

. . [CERVANTES *has turned from the west, and facing inland, kneels.* COLUMBUS *does not heed him.*]

COLUMBUS—Your spirit, Spain. They above all will need it, in the north: they whose speech is English and who have led in the building of the Towers which are the Grave of Europe. For it is written that these shall also lead in the birth of the true New World—the true America which I discovered. Let them see you, Spain; let them take from you, O mother. For their spirit is weak and childish. They are cowards, not masters, before life. But you, Spain, dared to be what you believed: you knew the wisdom of what small men call "madness." You dared to make of life itself the Body of your Vision, the Word of your Prayer. You did not flinch, proud Spain, from being laughed at—from being wrong—from being right! Give to the New World now your spirit, that it may surpass you.

[*There is a silence, Columbus still facing west, while his comrade kneels toward Spain.*]

CERVANTES—[*Still kneeling and praying.*] I understand, my mother, why we have always loved Our Lady. What this man says is true. Unpossessed, you have borne a Word. And the Word, even as Christ unto His mother, has turned and has denied you.

COLUMBUS—[*Lifting* CERVANTES *up.*]   Look again.
You are sure?   The White Towers—?
  CERVANTES—[*Rises and looks again westward, stand-
ing beside* COLUMBUS.]   The City of Towers is gone.

As they gaze in silence, CERVANTES *seeing,* COLUMBUS
  *understanding, the sun goes down in the sea.   And
    over their shoulders to the east, the sky is
      suddenly aflame with sunrise.*

FINIS

1921-1925